THE OAKWOOD LIBRARY OF RAILWAY HISTORY

THE LEADBURN, LINTON AND DOLPHINTON RAILWAY

By Train to West Linton

by
Donald Cattanach

Leadburn station in the late 19th century, looking towards Edinburgh. Dolphinton trains used the far side of the main platform. The new signal box and up platform with siding are in use; the goods shed at the north end of the main platform has not yet been built.
Oakwood collection

THE OAKWOOD PRESS

© Donald Cattanach, 2019.

ISBN 978-0-85361-571-2

Printed by
Claro Print Ltd, Office 26/27, 1 Spiersbridge Way, Glasgow, G46 8NG

Rail, road and river – 'the Splash': the ford at Bogsbank Bridge, half a mile south-west of Broomlee, on 5th July, 1930 with a motor car crossing the West Water. This was the scene of the accident on 27th November, 1921. *Rae Montgomery collection*

Published by
The Oakwood Press, 54-58 Mill Square, Catrine, KA5 6RD
Telephone: 01290 551122   Website: www.stenlake.co.uk

Contents

Foreword		5
Acknowledgements and Sources		7
Prologue: A Railway is Promoted		9
One	Previous Schemes and Early Communications	11
Two	Obtaining an Act	27
Three	Building the Railway	39
Four	Along the Line	65
Five	Train Services	131
Six	Special Workings	147
Seven	Locomotives and Carriages	159
Eight	Signalling and other Operational Matters	177
Nine	The Caledonian Railway's Dolphinton Branch, and the proposed Douglas & Dolphinton Railway	185
Ten	The LNER Era, and Closure	193
Eleven	Wartime Renaissance and Final Closure	213

Appendices

One	Inspections	227
Two	Passenger and Goods Statistics	229

Index ... 232

4   THE LEADBURN, LINTON AND DOLPHINTON RAILWAY

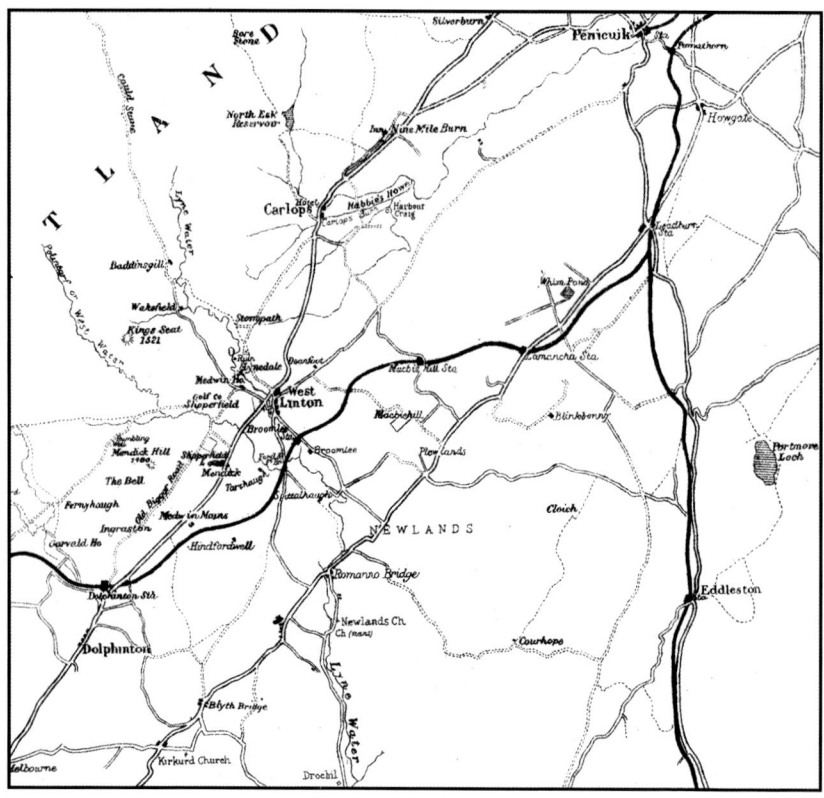

Extract from Map published by Geo Wood, Stationer, West Linton.

Rae Montgomery collection

Front cover: A group photo from around 1920. Standing at the back are porter Archie Finlayson *(left)* and signalman Jock Wilson. Seated are John Dickson, clerk; John Lawson, station master, Robert Brown, junior clerk at Dolphinton, and John Fleming signalman. Jock Wilson and John Dickson had both returned safely from the First World War. The lettering on the station sign looks the worse for wear and is perhaps being prepared for repainting.

Rae Montgomery collection

Back cover:The seal of the LL&DR.

From the collection of Scottish Borders Council administered by Live Borders (Tweeddale Museum & Gallery).

Foreword

At first glance, the Leadburn, Linton and Dolphinton Railway (LL&DR) may not seem to have had much going for it! It served the public for only 69 years and closed in 1933; its independent existence was short, and it failed to fulfil the ambitions of its promoters. The principal station, serving the main centre of population, West Linton, was half a mile from the village, and the only two wayside stations were in sparsely populated agricultural countryside. The village of Dolphinton proper lay across the Lanarkshire county boundary, over half a mile away from the terminus of the line in Peeblesshire. When the Caledonian Railway arrived at Dolphinton from the west a few years later, it made a grudging end-on connection with the LL&DR, and there were then two stations, two station masters, two engine sheds, two turntables, in fact two of everything – but no through passenger service. Between 1851 and 1861, the population of the Lanarkshire parish of Dolphington [sic] had actually declined from 305 to 260.

The story might have been very different. Dolphinton and West Linton almost found themselves on the Caledonian Railway's main line from Carlisle to Edinburgh; three subsequent schemes to connect the villages to the national railway network also failed to come to fruition. A third railway line to Dolphinton – backed by the North British Railway and the Glasgow and South Western Railway in order to thwart their common enemy, the Caledonian – was promoted in 1864 as the Douglas and Dolphinton Railway, but never built; it would have seen West Linton on a through route from Ayr to Edinburgh. In 1864, however, West Linton and Dolphinton did at last gain a railway connection from the Peebles Railway at Leadburn, only for the branch to close in 1933 as a result of road competition. The track at the northern end of the line had not been lifted and, during the Second World War, the line gained a new lease of life in serving the strategic armaments depot strung out alongside it.

While it existed, the railway – 'our railway' to the local community, even after it had closed – was very much part of the life of the area that it served in its modest, unpretentious way (although it did have its moments!), and its closure was met with more than a little regret. Even today, almost 90 years after its closure to passengers, it is still remembered, thanks to those who, over the years, have recorded, and researched, and kept its memory alive through articles, talks and exhibitions.

The bulk of the research for this book was undertaken by three individuals over several decades. Alex Aitken MA (1905-1981), was born near Eddleston, and became a History master in Edinburgh. He was also instrumental in the revival of the West Linton Whipman Play in 1931. Edward Jefferies (1917-1987) was an Inspector with the London & North Eastern Railway Company (LNER) and left British Railways to work on Malay Railways, becoming Port Superintendent for Malay States; on his return home, he became Postmaster at West Linton. Rae Montgomery is a retired railway professional with a lifelong interest in the area, where he now resides. My job has been to add to the material and to bring it all together, with the aim of keeping alive the memory of the LL&DR for future generations.

Edinburgh
2019

Note on Currency

Pre-decimal currency was in pounds, shillings and pence (£ s. d.); there were 20 shillings in a pound and 12 pennies in a shilling. Decimal coinage was introduced on 15th February, 1971. Until 1914, the value of money had remained fairly stable. Thereafter the purchasing power of the pound sterling declined, and wages rose. For a rough indication of today's value, the website www.measuringworth.com is recommended.

Acknowledgments and Sources

This book resulted from an exhibition held in West Linton in October 2013 to mark the 80th anniversary of the closure of the Leadburn to Dolphinton railway. It was organized by Rae Montgomery and Chris Atkinson, fellow members of the North British Railway Study Group, on behalf of West Linton and District Historical Association (WLDHA), and a small booklet was produced in conjunction with the excellent exhibition. Having suggested to Rae and Chris that the booklet should be expanded into a fuller history of the railway, I somehow found myself undertaking that task. The large amount of material to which Rae had fallen heir from Alex Aitken and Eddie Jefferies, together with Rae's own substantial contribution of photographs and other material, and the archives of the WLDHA, got me off to a flying start.

I am particularly grateful to Rae for his encouragement, information and advice and to Chris for contributing his considerable knowledge of the history of West Linton and area; both read the manuscript in draft and suggested corrections and improvements. Marion Moore, granddaughter of the last Broomlee station master, George Greig, generously made available many of the photographs included in the book as well as her grandfather's official LNER notebook and other material, and added her reminiscences of him and of her 'Uncle' Alex Aitken. Fellow Study Group members were generous with their time and information: Allan Rodgers provided much of the information and identified many of the photographs on which Chapter Seven (Locomotives and Carriages) is based, and David Stirling corrected my misconceptions on signalling systems (Chapter Eight) as well as supplying helpful documentation. Any remaining mistakes are, of course, mine. Bill Lynn was his usual ever-obliging source of information and photographs, including some from the Hennigan archive. Alistair Nisbet, Russell Wear and John McGregor provided detailed information from their own researches and Christine McGregor contributed her reminiscences of living in the former Broomlee station/station house, initially in its spartan, unconverted state. Alison MacDonald and Colin Whittemore from the Howgate Village Historical Society provided useful information about Leadburn, and Alison allowed me to quote from her book *Stories from the History of Howgate: Leadburn*. Andrew Harper provided photographs and information about his family's motor bus services in the 1920s.

I am grateful to the staff of the National Records of Scotland (NRS), the National Library of Scotland, The National Archives, Kew, the British Library, the Parliamentary Records Office, the National Railway Museum, Hampshire County Council Records Office, Scottish Water, and to the WLDHA and Christine Sawers of the Tweeddale Museum and Gallery, Peebles (Live Borders), for access to records.

I am most grateful to all those who provided photographs, as individually attributed. Michael Stewart and David Geldard provided images of railway tickets from their collections. Ian Brown pointed me to the photographs of Royal Navy Armaments Depot (RNAD) Leadburn held by Hampshire County Council Records Office. The West Linton and Newlands Curling Clubs kindly allowed me to photograph the Waddell Medal for which they compete annually (with thanks to Mairi McDonald). Alan Young drew the maps.

Thanks, too, to Jimmy Brown, Jean Gilchrist, Ron Glendinning, Penny Jackson, Ray Nolton and Eric Stevenson for their contributions.

Anyone interested in the history of the North British Railway (NBR) and its constituents and successors can find more information about the NBR Study Group on its website at www.nbrstudygroup.co.uk. The Study Group is a registered Scottish charity No. SC044351.

Images

Wherever possible, the current holder of the copyright in an image has been duly acknowledged, but in some cases attempts to trace the rights holder have proved unsuccessful. Such images are usually credited to the 'collection' of a contributor. If photographs or images have been used without due credit or acknowledgement, apologies are offered. If anyone believes this to be the case, then please let the publishers know and the necessary credit will be added to any future edition.

NBR standard milepost indicating the 6-mile point from the junction with the Peebles line at Leadburn. It was originally located on the approach to Broomlee station.
Rae Montgomery

Prologue

A Railway is Promoted

At Edinburgh the first day of August Eighteen hundred and sixty one years, and within the Chambers of Messrs Mackenzie & Kermack W.S. At a meeting of Gentlemen friendly to the promotion of a Line of Railway through the Upper District of Peeblesshire.

So begins the Minute Book of the Leadburn, Linton and Dolphinton Railway Company. Present at that meeting in the solicitors' office at 9 Hill Street were John Ord Mackenzie WS* of Dolphinton House, a partner in the firm, William Allan Woddrop of Garvald, Alexander McNeill of Bordland, John White of Drummelzier, William Brand of Broomlee, James Murray of Callands, Archibald Suter for Mr Webster,** John Bathgate, Writer***, Peebles (and Secretary of the Peebles Railway Company), Rev Dr Aiton, Dolphinton, William Forbes of Medwyn, and Richard Gordon of Halmyre. Most of the principal landowners in the parishes of Linton, Newlands and Kirkurd, within the County of Peebles, were represented.

> Mr Bathgate reported that as the endeavour to promote a Line of Railway from Leadburn to Carstairs could not at present be carried successfully through, it was very desirable that another session should not be lost in trying to accomplish as much of the undertaking as might be found practicable; that he had seen Mr Hodgson the Chairman of the North British Railway Company who was willing to guarantee four per cent on the Capital necessary to execute a Line from Leadburn to Dolphinton.

The meeting resolved:

> That it is highly expedient in order to secure the benefit of Railway communication to the Upper District of Peeblesshire and neighbourhood, and develop its dormant resources by affording a more rapid conveyance to the numerous passengers at present obliged to travel in Stage Coaches and private vehicles, and a ready means of transport to its abundant limestone, freestone and other minerals as well as its wood, and agricultural produce, and enabling also its Water power to be profitably employed, that a branch Line of Railway be formed from a point of [sic] the Peebles Railway near to Leadburn Station or other convenient place to Dolphinton; ...

> To take the project forward, the gentlemen present formed themselves

---

* Writer to the Signet, or solicitor
** Presumably Andrew Webster of Rutherford
*** Solicitors

into a Provisional Committee, which proprietors and tenants along the route and in the vicinity would be invited to join.* The detailed arrangements were delegated to a sub-committee, of which John Ord Mackenzie would be Convener. John Bathgate was appointed the Committee's Agent, and Thomas Bouch CE, Edinburgh, its Engineer.

As can be gathered from Bathgate's remarks, this was not the first attempt to introduce the railway to the Upper District of Peeblesshire. West Linton and Dolphinton had featured in a number of earlier railway proposals.

9-year-old Patrick Angus, son of signalman Sandy Angus, on platform duty c.1933.
Marion Moore collection

---

* Alexander McNeill and James Murray subsequently withdrew their names.

Chapter One

Previous Schemes and Early Communications

Previous Schemes

Thomas Telford's Proposed Iron Railway between Glasgow and Berwick

First in the field was Thomas Telford, with a proposed horse-drawn railway connecting the River Clyde and the Forth and Clyde Canal in industrial Glasgow with the town of Berwick and the fertile agricultural district of the Tweed, to the advantage of both. Telford's detailed survey, reproduced in the *Scots Magazine* of 1st May, 1810 and shown on James Kirkwood's 1810 map of Scotland, describes the railway on its west to east route via Carnwath and Peebles as 'crossing the road from Edinburgh to Biggar at Dolphingstoun [sic]'. Future schemes would be for south to north routes to connect Peeblesshire with the capital.

The Caledonian Railway's Edinburgh Branch

In the late 1830s, there were several schemes in prospect for railways between Scotland and England – by east coast or west coast, by Annandale or by Nithsdale – and the accepted wisdom was that there was insufficient traffic to justify the capital expenditure on more than one line. In November 1839, the government appointed Lt-Col Sir Frederic Smith RE, the first Inspector General of Railways, and Professor Peter Barlow FRS of the Royal Military Academy, Woolwich, as Commissioners to conduct an inquiry 'respecting railway communication between London, [Dublin], Edinburgh and Glasgow'. In their final report of 15th March, 1841, the Commissioners felt 'under the necessity of recommending, at present, the construction of one line only; and after a careful review … we give the preference to the Line from Carlisle by Lockerby [sic], Beattock, Lanark and Hamilton to Glasgow, with a branch from Thankerton or Symington to Edinburgh, as being the general route which would fulfil the greater number of requisites …'. In the event, the first railway across the Border was the North British Railway's east coast route from Edinburgh to Berwick-upon-Tweed, opened on 18th June, 1846, although through traffic beyond that point was not possible without a change of train until 2nd September, 1848, when a temporary bridge across the Tweed was opened for traffic, uniting the North British with the York, Newcastle & Berwick Railway.

(The permanent structure – the Royal Border Bridge – was opened by Queen Victoria on 29th August, 1850.)

From Thankerton, the west coast route from Carlisle to Edinburgh would have run north-west of the Pentland Hills; the Symington route would have run to the south-east. In the submission to the Commissioners by engineers McCallum and Dundas, they described the latter route, journeying south from Edinburgh:

> From Glencorse we keep along a valley parallel with the turnpike road, leaving Pennycuick [sic] about a quarter of a mile on our left; the Line enters Sir George Clerk's grounds near the tower, keeping within a few chains of the Carlops road, until it emerges from the park beyond the north-west porter's lodge; it then crosses Eight Mile Burn at a sudden bend below the present road, stretching along the bank of the Esk to near Marfield, where it curves to the right, crossing successively Monk's Burn, North Esk and Carlops Burn … From Carlops Burn the moss to the west of Harbour Craig is crossed, and after passing Back Burn proceeds along the face of the hill towards Linton, crossing the turnpike road about a quarter mile north of the village, and the Lyne Water by a bridge of two 55 feet arches above the present Linton Bridge …

The proposed line then ran west of the turnpike road and along the lower slopes of Mendick Hill to near Ingraston, where the turnpike was crossed, and along the east side of Kippit Hill at Dolphinton to cross the Garvald Burn. From there it was on to the outskirts of Biggar and the village of Symington, where it would connect with the proposed line to Glasgow.

The Caledonian Railway (CR) was incorporated on 31st July, 1845 to construct the line from Carlisle to Edinburgh and Glasgow, and appointed as its Engineers Joseph Locke and John Errington. The talented and eminent engineer Locke had first undertaken the surveys for a Carlisle to Glasgow line in 1835 at the behest of the merchants and business men of Liverpool, at that time the centre of investment in the major trunk railway routes, and it was his assistants, Messrs McCallum and Dundas, who had surveyed the Symington route to Edinburgh. For the Glasgow branch, the route taken up was broadly that recommended by the Commissioners, but the route of the Edinburgh branch – north-west or south-east of the Pentlands – had yet to be decided; this was a matter of no small importance to Peebles, which wanted to be on the railway network. In compliance with a requisition by a number of prominent County gentlemen, the 8th Earl of Wemyss and March, Lord Lieutenant of the County of Peeblesshire, called a meeting in the Tontine Inn on 18th June, 1844 to consider the formation of a branch railway to Peebles from the Caledonian Railway, in the event of that line taking the south-east route. On 5th August, 1844, however, Locke recommended to the Caledonian Board that the north-west route should be adopted, to leave the Glasgow branch at Carstairs and reach Edinburgh via Carnwath and Midcalder. Although the south-eastern route via Linton was slightly shorter, the gradients were more difficult and a large number of earthworks would be required, particularly for the descent into Edinburgh. The Caledonian Railway opened from Carlisle to Beattock on 10th September, 1847 and from Beattock to Glasgow and Edinburgh on 15th February, 1848.

Perhaps West Linton had a lucky escape. Had it found itself on the west coast main line from Carlisle to Edinburgh it is doubtful whether the charming village of today would still exist.

The Carnwath and West Linton Railway

1845 saw the peak of the 'Railway Mania' – a speculative frenzy of massive over-investment in a huge, unaffordable number of railway schemes. Every town of any significance wanted a railway and the number of schemes mushroomed. Money was cheap, the value of railway shares was increasing and dividends were strong, and a shareholding could be obtained with borrowed money on payment of a deposit only – to be sold at a profit as the value rose. It was against this unstable background that the Edinburgh & Peebles Railway was promoted for a line between the County town and 'the most eligible point in the outskirts of Edinburgh'. An invitation to apply for the 10,000 shares of £25 each appeared in the Press in the second week of June 1845; when the Provisional Committee met in Edinburgh on 23rd June it was told that there had been applications for almost 30,000 shares. A Prospectus appeared in the *Peeblesshire Monthly Advertiser and Tweedside Journal* (which had been founded by John Bathgate in February of that year) on 1st July. The line was to join the North British Railway's Dalkeith branch near Cairnie, the latter company agreeing to lease the line and to guarantee four per cent on the capital. In October, the capital was increased to £350,000, the Promoters having agreed to build the line as double track, rather than single, and taken power to build branches to Lasswade, Roslin and West Linton. An 1845 map shows the 'Proposed Linton Branch' from the Wellington Inn, just north of Leadburn, to West Linton.

Meanwhile, the *Peeblesshire* had reported that a 'numerous and respectable meeting' had taken place in Mr Alexander's Inn at Linton on

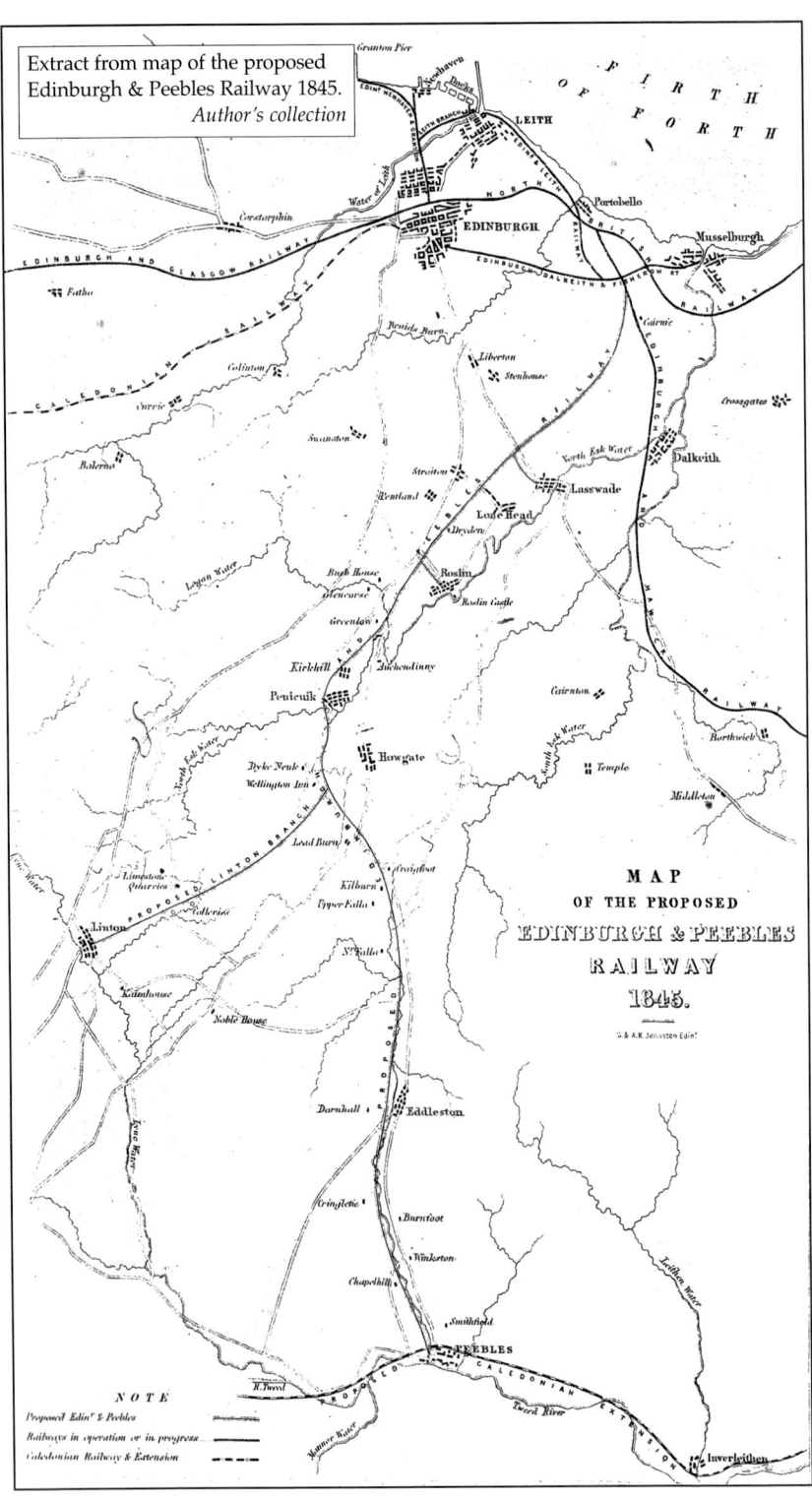

26th August 'for the purpose of considering the propriety of a branch line of railway, to join the projected Edinburgh and Peebles Railway at any convenient point betwixt Leadburn and Penicuik'. Many of those attending were proprietors and tenants in the neighbourhood and they pledged themselves to support such an extension 'by every means in their power'. A committee was appointed. If only a line could be built, the 'inexhaustible stores of freestone, coal, limestone and brick-clay' could be sent to market, both in the southern parts of the County and in Edinburgh, and agriculture developed. The original proposal was for a single line northwards from Linton, but the Prospectus that appeared in the *Scotsman* on 15th October, 1845 was for a more ambitious scheme – a Carnwath and West Linton Railway – commencing at the proposed Carnwath station of the Caledonian Railway (on which construction had just begun), thus 'forming a junction between the Caledonian, the [proposed] Caledonian Extension, and North British Railways'. The members of the Provisional Committee included a number of local proprietors, including Richard Mackenzie of Dolphinton House, Deputy Keeper of Her Majesty's Signet and father of John Ord Mackenzie in whose office the meeting of 1st August, 1861 took place (he had also been on the Provisional Committee for the Caledonian Railway Bill in 1844), as well as a number of prominent individuals including the great ironmasters, the Bairds of Gartsherrie, and John Learmonth, then Chairman of both the Edinburgh & Glasgow, and North British, railway companies. The line would be 12 miles long and the capital was to be £160,000 in £20 shares. Five days later, a notice was issued by the Committee intimating its intention to extend the line for a further six or seven miles to Wellington Farm, replacing the proposed Edinburgh & Peebles Railway's branch to Linton, and to increase the authorized capital to £200,000. The plans lodged in Parliament at the end of November 1845 settled the proposed junction of the two lines immediately north of Leadburn; at Carstairs, there would be a connection both to the north- and south-bound Caledonian main line. The Engineer was James Leslie.

Leaving nothing to chance, West Linton submitted a Petition in favour of the Bill to the House of Commons:

> Unto the Honourable the Commons of Great Britain and Ireland in Parliament assembled. The petition of the inhabitants of West Linton in Peeblesshire and its vicinity, sheweth, that the district in which your petitioners reside, though in a state of superior cultivation, and capable of much further improvement, abounding in produce and possessed of valuable

minerals, the seat of well-known markets for cattle and sheep, and the route by which passengers and traffic from the south-west of Scotland reach the Lothians, the ports on the east coast, and the east of Scotland generally, is, notwithstanding these advantages, retarded in the march of improvement in consequence of its distance from great centres of trade, and its want of the means of cheap and ready conveyance; that the proposed Carnwath and West Linton Railway, if carried into execution, will remove all those difficulties as to means of communication which have pressed so long and heavily upon the resources of the district, and connecting as it does with Caledonian lines on the west, and the North British on the east, will open up an access to all the great markets in Lanarkshire, Ayrshire, and the Lothians, and thus both the exports and the imports of the district will be indefinitely increased and a considerable addition be made to the general trade of the country; that the proposed railway, not only as regards this district but the whole tract with which it is connected, is an excellent and praiseworthy undertaking and would be productive of the most beneficial results. May it therefore please your Honourable House to take the premises into your consideration, and to give your sanction to this bill for the Carnwath and West Linton Railway now depending before your Honourable House.

Being unopposed, the Carnwath Bill quickly passed the House of Commons, but soon foundered in the wreckage of the Railway Mania as the speculative bubble burst in January 1846. Railway shares collapsed in value, money became dearer, and the cost of construction increased. With many speculators finding themselves unable to pay the calls for the balance of the price of their shares, the prospects of raising the necessary capital – even for the many worthwhile schemes – vanished. Parliament hurriedly legislated to allow a meeting of shareholders to decide to abandon their application for a Bill, and to be reimbursed with what was left of their deposits, and that was the fate of both the Peebles and Carnwath schemes. In the case of the latter, £166,300 of the authorized capital of £200,000 had been subscribed by 378 individuals, but only 20 of these could be said to have a local interest, and their contributions amounted only to £16,900. Of the £2 deposit paid per share, 18 shillings had been swallowed up in expenses. A reincarnated 'Peebles Railway Company' got its Act on 8th July, 1853 for a line from Eskbank (Hardengreen Junction), on the Edinburgh and Hawick line, via Leadburn, to the County town and opened on 4th July, 1855. West Linton would have to wait a while longer for a railway. The North British Railway took over the working of the line for the Peebles Company on 1st February, 1861, leased it on 11th July of the same year and finally absorbed it on 1st August, 1876.

PREVIOUS SCHEMES AND EARLY COMMUNICATIONS 17

The Lyne Valley Railway

On Thursday 1st December, 1853, under the heading 'Lyne Valley Railway', the *Peeblesshire Advertiser* reported that 'a strong effort is being made to afford the benefit of railway accommodation to Linton and the upper part of Peeblesshire'. As well as being an important feeder to the Peebles Railway at Leadburn, there would be traffic in minerals – ironstone from Macbiehill, freestone from Deepsykehead, as well as the 'extensive and easily-wrought field of limestone along the line'. A meeting of 'the Proprietors, Tenants and others interested in the formation of a Branch Railway from Leadburn, for the accommodation of the Upper District of Peeblesshire, and adjoining Parishes', had been held at Linton on 7th November, 1853. William Forbes of Medwyn was called to the Chair and among the others attending were Sir Thomas Gibson Carmichael of Skirling; William Goldie, Broomlee; Rev. Dr Aiton, Dolphinton; Mr Stodart, Whitfield; Mr Waugh, Roberton Mains; Mr Lawson, Deepsykehead; Mr Brown, Slipperfield; Mr Morgan, Linton; Mr Ferme, Paulswell; and Mr Thorburn, Peebles. Other proprietors from the adjoining Newlands Parish would have been present had the meeting not clashed with a Stated Parochial Meeting. Engineer Thomas Bouch was there and presented a plan for a line running from near the Leadburn Inn to a point near 'the open quarry on the Lands of Broomlee'. He estimated that the cost of the line – some six miles long – would not exceed £16,500, exclusive of the cost of land. John Bathgate appears to have been the moving spirit behind the scheme and he addressed the meeting, which unanimously resolved that it was 'highly expedient' that a branch railway be established between a point in the Lyne Valley most suitable for the entire district, and Leadburn station. A Provisional Committee, with Bathgate as Interim Secretary, was established to have a survey made, to begin preliminary negotiations with the landowners, and to receive applications for shares. A subscription list was started to defray the cost of the survey and other preliminary expenses, but nothing more about the scheme has been discovered.

The Caledonian and Peebles Junction Railway

On 20th August, 1858 the *Peeblesshire Advertiser* reported an attempt to put Linton and Dolphinton on a line from Leadburn to Carstairs, as part of a through route from Galashiels via Peebles and Leadburn to Glasgow. The proposal was for a 20-mile line from Leadburn to

Carstairs, passing through Linton, Dolphinton, Dunsyre and Newbigging, under the name of the 'Caledonian and Peebles Junction Railway' and estimated to cost £70,000 – under £4,000 a mile and 'lower than any railway in Scotland'. It would give the Peebles Railway an outlet to the west of Scotland.

The arguments were the now familiar ones of mineral wealth:

> It passes through a rich mineral district, hitherto unexplored. The valley of the Medwyn water, which it traverses for nine miles, is abundant in mineral resources, lying undeveloped for want of railway facilities. Coal and ironstone are both present, and on Newholm is a mine of manganese. Crossing into Peeblesshire, there is a vast field of limestone, which can be easily wrought, as well as a supply of freestone. A through traffic would also be obtained from Dalkeith, Leith, Galashiels and other places. Glasgow is a great centre of trade and commerce, and any line which ties a district to it cannot fail of developing a good business.

There was widespread support from local landowners, including the 9th Earl of Wemyss, Captain Beresford of Macbiehill, Mr Forbes of Medwyn, Mr Mackintosh of Lamancha, Professor Fergusson of Spitalhaugh*, John Ord Mackenzie and others, as well as the Lockhart family through whose land the southern section of the line would pass for eight or nine miles. The promoters saw it as a better route for Peebles traffic to Glasgow and the west than the recently authorized Symington, Biggar and Broughton Railway (SBBR), protégé of the Caledonian, and its likely extension west to Peebles:

> If it were once made, we will at Peebles be only 27 $^1/_2$ miles from Carstairs, which is as near, if not nearer, than going round by Biggar and Symington; which latter route takes us too far south, and joins the Caledonian [at Symington] at a station where all the trains do not stop. There is no advantage offered by an extension of the Broughton line which is not likewise afforded by the Junction Railway; and the latter has the following additional elements in its favour: it opens up a wider and more populous district, has infinitely more resources in trade and minerals, can be more cheaply made, and forms a tie with the agricultural district centering at Dalkeith. We are not over sanguine in believing that the Junction Railway will, in a few years, be part of a through line from Galashiels to Glasgow, and have the benefit of the traffic from that stirring manufacturing and agricultural district.

It was hoped that the Caledonian Railway would take an interest in the scheme, but the Caley planned instead to help finance its SBBR protégé to

---

* The spelling of Spitalhaugh has varied over time

extend to Peebles, with the intention of continuing from there, along the Tweed, to Galashiels and into the heart of NBR territory. The SBBR opened to Broughton on 5th November, 1860 and to Peebles on 1st February, 1864, the Caledonian having bought it under an Act of 1st August, 1861.

John Bathgate was one of the prime movers of the scheme. On 18th August, 1858 he had submitted a letter to the Board of the Peebles Railway (of which he was Secretary) with a proof list of the Provisional Committee and suggested that the Peebles Chairman should add his name to it; the Board expressed its approval of the scheme. In evidence in an arbitration case between the Town of Peebles and the Caledonian Railway over the valuation of land taken by the Caledonian Railway, held in February and March 1862 and reported in the *Peeblesshire Advertiser* on 3rd and 10th May, 1862, he is reported as saying:

> On 29th July, 1859, Mr Christopher Johnston [sic], the manager of the Caledonian Railway, sent for me to the Tontine Hotel, and intimated that he gave his preference to continuing the Broughton Railway down the Tweed, instead of a project which I wanted to enlist his favour for, of going round by Linton. ... I kept Mr Johnston's preference no secret. I immediately communicated it to sundry parties, because it brought to the ground a favourite scheme of my own. [And later:] The cause of my meeting with Mr Christopher Johnston in July 1859 was this, that I had, along with several others, projected a railway coming down the Tweed to Galashiels, running up the Peebles line to Leadburn, and then going on to Carstairs. I attended a [Caledonian] Board Meeting in Glasgow once or twice, and laid that scheme before the Directors, with several gentlemen from Edinburgh, belonging to the upper part of the county, who wanted a railway there. Mr Johnston was very much struck by the arguments adduced in support of the upper scheme, but he said that as they had embarked £7000 in the Broughton Railway, their view was to go down the Tweed, but he would then give no positive answer, and it was left I suppose in his hands by the Board. On the day mentioned, Mr Johnston sent for me, Mr Cunningham and Mr Gillespie being present, and told me privately in the windows of the Tontine that he was satisfied that the best scheme for the interests of the Caledonian was to come down the Tweed.

No more was heard of the scheme; without Caledonian support, it would have faced serious difficulties. In the event, the Caley didn't get beyond Peebles, which was established by agreement with the North British as the 'front line' between the two rivals. The North British ultimately built the line from Peebles via Innerleithen to Galashiels, where it connected with its main line to Hawick, the final section opening on 18th June, 1866. As part of the agreement, the North British built a connecting line across the Tweed at Peebles to the CR's station on the south side of the river, and this was used for the exchange of freight and livestock traffic.

An advert for the sale of the Broomlee Estate in the *Scotsman* of 30th July, 1859 stated that 'A Railway has been surveyed, and is, it is understood, now likely to be completed from Leadburn to Carstairs Junction, which will traverse Broomlee, and the Linton station will be on the property and within a short distance of the House'. On this occasion, it was not to be, but the idea of a railway through the northern parishes of Peeblesshire was never abandoned.

Early Communications

Such roads as existed in early 18th century Scotland were generally in such poor condition that only travel on foot or on horseback, with armed companions for safety, was possible. From the middle of that century, Turnpike Acts began to be passed by which trustees could borrow money to improve sections of principal routes, the loans being repaid by letting the collection of tolls – on people, vehicles, goods and animals passing through – to the highest bidder. In 1753, the first Turnpike Act applicable to Peeblesshire was passed 'for repairing and widening the several roads in the County of Peebles, leading from Tweedscross [on the Dumfriesshire border] towards the City of Edinburgh by Blyth Bridge, La Mancha, and Wheam [Whim], and by Linton and Carlops, and from Ingleston [Ingraston, on the Lanarkshire border] through Carlops, until all the said roads join the limits of the County of Edinburgh'. The Ingraston to Carlops turnpike ran between Mendick Hill and Slipperfield Loch, west of the present road, to cross the Lyne at Lynedale House, and then on by Fairslacks to Carlops before entering what is now Midlothian. A connecting road from Lynedale down into West Linton – part of the old cross-borders drove road and known as The Loan – emerged opposite the site of what is now the Gordon Arms Hotel, formerly the Hayston Arms Inn. The 1756 toll-house at the south end of West Linton dates from this period, and a coaching inn dating from 1789 stood in what is now Raemartin Square. An 1842 map by F.A. and G.W. Carrington, based on earlier surveys, shows the 'mail road' from Edinburgh to Moffat passing through Carlops and West Linton and on to the village of Blyth, before joining the Tweedscross turnpike at Blyth Bridge.

Under an 1830 Turnpike Act, a number of new roads were authorized in Peeblesshire, principally that on the line of today's A702, skirting West Linton on its route from Carlops to the Lanarkshire border at Dolphinton. It opened in 1833, after which the original turnpike via

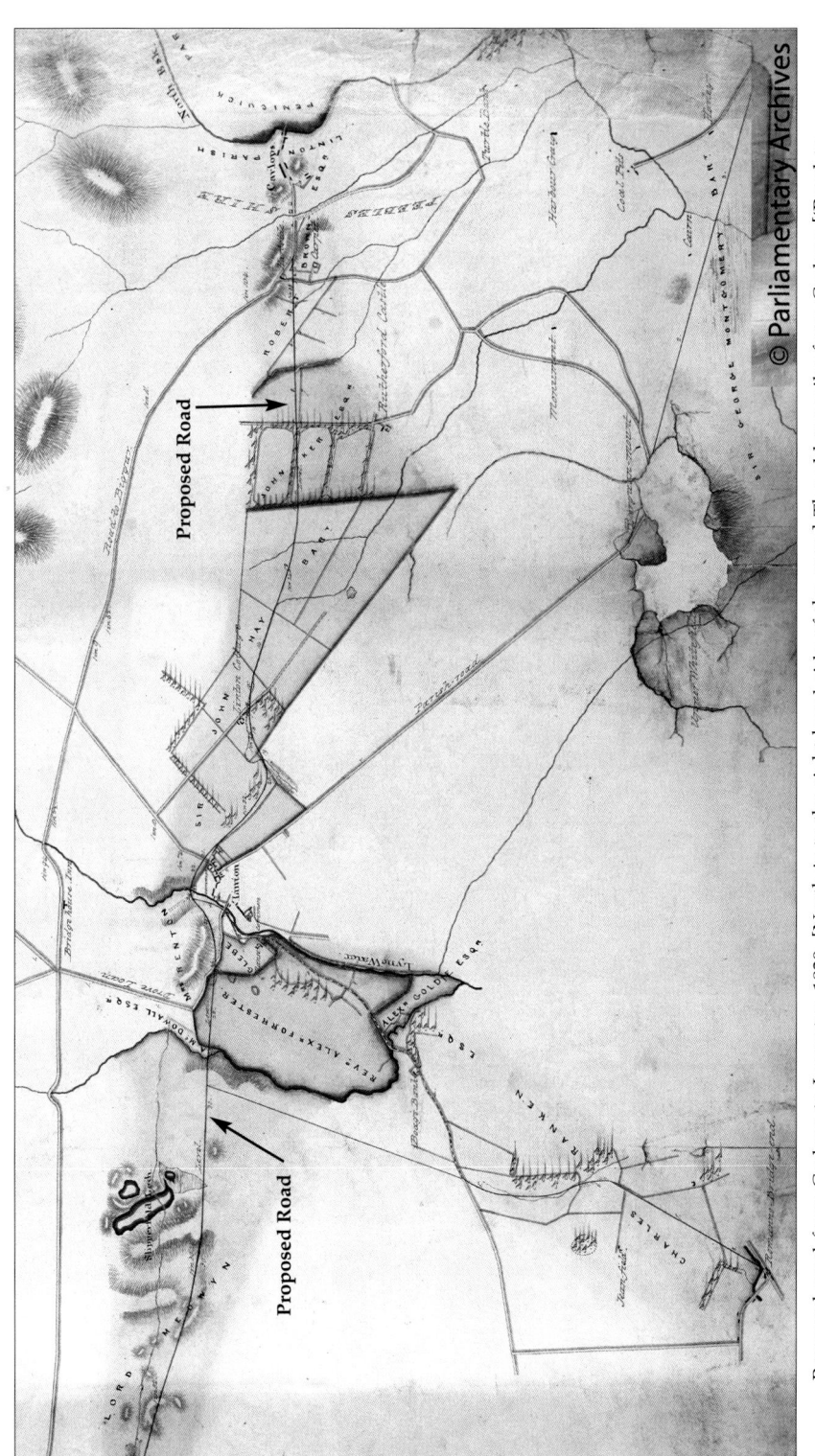

Proposed road from Carlops to Ingraston 1829. [North is to the right-hand side of the map.] The old turnpike from Carlops [Road to Biggar'] runs along the top of the map, crossing the Lyne Water and passing the Bridgehouse Inn. 'Drove Loan' runs down into Linton.
Parliamentary Archives, HL/PO/PB/3/plan74

Looking north towards Carlops on the 1833 road, about a hundred years later. West Linton village lies off to the right, behind the Gordon Arms Hotel (formerly the Hayston Arms), built as a coaching inn to serve the new road. The garage on the left was formerly stables. The Loan, a branch from the old Biggar Road, emerged in front of the telephone box and continued through the village and on to Blyth and Moffat. *Oakwood collection*

Lynedale gradually fell into disuse; the road from Linton to 'Romanno Bridge-end' was authorized by the same Act and other roads were widened and improved. Previously, 'The old road from Edinburgh being very ill directed, the approach to the village, both from the west and the east, was extremely difficult for a carriage of any description; but by a new line lately made and opened last year, various dangerous acclivities were avoided, and, bringing into view the village, which was formerly quite hid from the traveller, it has already been considerably improved in its appearance by new houses being erected, whilst two inns have also been built on this road, one at Linton,* and another at Rutherford, with post-horses and every accommodation which the public would wish.'** In 1834, the village of Linton consisted of 90 houses and had 395 inhabitants, 160 males and 235 females.

At the end of the 18th century, the road from Edinburgh to Moffat via Leadburn and Blyth Bridge ran via Howgate. At Mosshouses, south of Howgate, the Peebles turnpike branched off and ran due south via Craigburn, by-passing Leadburn; it had been repaired and

---

* The Hayston Arms Inn. An Inn may have stood here from the middle of the 17th century.

** *The New Statistical Account of Scotland* (1845), Parish of Linton from the entry by Rev. Alexander Forrester, Minister (May 1834).

widened 'from the Town of Peebles to the King's Eatedge [Kingside Edge] at the confines of the Counties of Peebles and Edinburgh' under an Act of 1771. A later Act authorized the section from Craigburn to Leadburn, where an Inn has stood from at least 1777.* The completion in 1812 of the Telford Bridge across the River North Esk at Penicuik provided a new route south from that town to Leadburn, so forming today's junction of the Penicuik, Howgate, Peebles and Moffat roads. A toll house – now demolished – was erected on the north-west corner of the crossroads at Leadburn.

As roads improved, so Royal Mail coaches and stage coaches provided a limited, though expensive, system of public transport; Edinburgh got its first Royal Mail coach to London in 1786. Williamson's Directory of 1793-94 shows the mail for Howgate, Noblehouse (then a 'Post Town'), Moffat, Dumfries and Portpatrick departing every day at noon, and arriving every morning; the mail for Linton left Edinburgh at 12 noon on Tuesdays and Fridays, and the Biggar mail at the same time on Mondays, Thursdays and Saturdays. By 1820, the Linton mail was dispatched at 8 am on Sundays, Tuesdays and Fridays. In 1829, the Royal Mail coach from Edinburgh to Dumfries and Portpatrick was being run by Edward Piper & Co. from the Black Bull Hotel in Catherine Street, Edinburgh. It ceased to run after the opening, on 15th February, 1848, of the Caledonian Railway from Carlisle, via Carstairs, to Edinburgh and Glasgow.

Coaching's peak year nationally was 1837,** before the industry was gradually killed off by the expanding railway network; by 1850, the only Royal Mail coach left in the Capital served the Border towns on its way to Carlisle. It lasted until 31st August, 1862, shortly after the opening of the Waverley Route, and its last trip was made, ignominiously, on top of a railway wagon.

One name is particularly associated with the coaching era, that of John Croall of Edinburgh, coach-builder and operator, whose life span (1791-1872) coincided almost exactly with the heyday of coaches. He built, owned and operated more vehicles than all the rest of the Scottish proprietors put together. He sold coaches to foreign governments, including the Czar of Russia, and demonstrated one by driving it from Moscow to St Petersburg. At one time he held the Royal Mail contracts for the whole of Scotland and much of northern

---

* *Stories from the History of Howgate: Leadburn* by Alison MacDonald (Howgate Village Historical Society, 2010).

** See, generally, *Stage-Coach to John O'Groats* by Leslie Gardiner (Hollis & Carter, 1961).

England.* He also ran an extensive service of stage coaches. By the early 1830s, his Peebles stage coach left Princes Street at 9 am, as did that of his competitor, Brown's. By 1837, his Dumfries stage coach, later *The Enterprise*, 'the Splendid Light Four-Inside Coach' left Princes Street every 'lawful day' in summer, and every second day in the winter. It ran via the new (1830s) road, by Carlops, West Linton, Dolphinton and Biggar. By the mid-1840s, the service appears to have terminated at Biggar. In 1843, McGregor's and Smart's were advertising an 8.00 am coach from Linton to Edinburgh, taking three hours; the return journey left Edinburgh at 3.30 pm. In 1845, the service was run by Croall & Campbell; the journey time was down to $2\frac{1}{2}$ hours and the service was twice daily, although later adverts show only a daily service. In 1848 *The Enterprise* was serving Penicuik, West Linton and Romanno, the fare to Linton being 3s. inside and 2s. 6d. outside. In 1849-50, Taylor & Co. of 1 North Bridge were running a coach from Linton leaving at 7.30 am and arriving in Edinburgh at 9.30 am. It returned at 4.00 pm and took $2\frac{1}{2}$ hours for the uphill journey. In the summer of 1853, the service was advertised as the 'West Linton, Penicuik and Edinburgh Omnibus'; it left 'Mr Alexander's, Linton' at 7.30 am and returned from 'South Bridge Street (opposite the College Gate)' at 4.30 pm; the route was via Burdiehouse, Penicuik and Carlops. By 1861, the summer service to West Linton via Penicuik and Carlops was two coaches per day, at 7.30 am and 3.00 pm from Linton, and at 9.30 am and 4.00 pm from Edinburgh, with one return journey in the winter, and this pattern continued until 1864. The fare was 2s. inside and 1s. 6d. outside.

Carriers provided a slower but cheaper service for the carriage of goods. Aitchison's Directory for 1794-95 reveals that the Linton carrier arrived in Edinburgh on a Tuesday and left again on a Wednesday. He could be found at his overnight lodgings at Hay's, Canongatehead.

With the opening of the Peebles Railway on 4th July, 1855, coaches connected with the trains at Leadburn. Following a dispute with Croall, the Peebles Railway Board awarded the contract for the Leadburn – Broughton coach in July 1855 to William Hope of 19 Minto Street, Edinburgh, and Romanno Bridge, with a £40 guarantee against loss. An advert of 7th March, 1856 announced that on and after Monday 10th March, Hope & Co., Proprietors, Romanno Bridge, would commence the running of their 'splendid new coach, the *Alma*' between Leadburn, West Linton and Broughton in connection with the Peebles Railway.

---

* *Stage-Coach to John O'Groats, op cit.*

They would also – on and after 1st April – start running a 'Car' from Leadburn to West Linton and Romanno on the arrival of the first train from Edinburgh in the morning, returning in time for the last train from Peebles in the evening. Croall nevertheless competed on the route and the Board resolved to allow Hope two pence for each passenger by his coach who booked to and from Leadburn by rail. In August 1856, the Board entered into an arrangement with both Croall and Hope and the following month Croall was advertising a service from Leadburn to West Linton, Romanno, Dolphington [sic] and Broughton; but both claimed to be losing money on the route and Mr Hope appears to have withdrawn after August 1857. Croall then held out for an increased subsidy from the Board, threatening to withdraw his coach and run it instead between Edinburgh and Blyth Bridge via Penicuik, Carlops and West Linton 'which will be quite away from your line'. The Board had little choice but to concede a subsidy of £65, of which the NBR paid £25. In August 1857, Croall announced that 'the Broughton and Leadburn coaches continue to run as formerly from the Leadburn station of the Peebles Railway on the arrival of the 4.20 pm train from Edinburgh, and from Broughton and Linton in the morning to join the train at Leadburn for Edinburgh at 8.58 am', and that 'the coach to and from Dolphington is withdrawn'. He also ran a coach in 1857 from 'Mr Noble's Coach Office, Blyth Bridge' at 7.15 am to connect with the same train, returning in the evening. Croall was still running the Broughton coach in June 1858 but it is not clear for how long.

Advert for the rail and coach service between West Linton and Edinburgh, July 1861.

On 1st December, 1858 the Board of the Peebles Railway agreed to make an arrangement with the driver of the Linton coach 'to come to Leadburn, but no allowance to exceed £20 per annum, and North British Railway Coy to be applied to for proportion'. The Linton coach driver was Robert Watson, aged 34, and described as a Coach Proprietor in the 1861 Census. Ten years earlier, his occupation was as a Shoemaker. He appears to have run the service between West Linton and Leadburn from then until the opening of the Dolphinton branch railway. On 23rd July, 1861, the North British Railway advertised an 'Important Reduction of Fares between Edinburgh and West-Linton by Rail and Coach Direct'. 'First Class and Inside' cost 2s. 6d.; 'Second Class and Outside' cost 2s., with further information available from Mr Robert Watson.

In June 1862, the coach from West Linton started for Leadburn every weekday at 7.55 am, connecting there at 9.12 am with the Peebles train due in Edinburgh at 9.55 am. It also gave a connection – albeit an hour later at 10.09 am – with the train from Edinburgh that arrived at Peebles at 10.40 am. The return evening coach connected with the 4.20 pm 'fast' train from Edinburgh and left Leadburn for West Linton at 5.02 pm.

In *Peebles and its Neighbourhood with a Run on Peebles Railway* by William Chambers (1st edition, 1856), the connecting coach service from Leadburn was described:

> Here, near the station there is a small well-known inn; and a coach is in attendance to take passengers to West Linton, Romanno Bridge and Broughton. These villages lie in a westerly direction and are all starting points for anglers. At Linton, a large market for the sale of sheep takes place annually in July. At Romanno Bridge situated on the Lyne, there is a small comfortable inn kept by Mrs Hope; and from this spot, anglers may agreeably fish their way down the Lyne and Tweed to Peebles. The stagecoach in proceeding to Romanno Bridge passes Whim, Lamancha, Macbiehill, Hallmyre [sic] and Romanno – gentlemen's seats on the way. A railway from Leadburn to Linton is, we believe, under consideration, and as it would be the means of conveniently bringing lime and sandstone to Peebles, not to speak of other traffic, it would doubtless serve an important local purpose.

Nothing came of that proposed railway to Linton. By the time of the 2nd edition in 1863, a number of changes had been made to the text: the large annual sheep market now 'formerly took place', the small inn at Romanno was no longer kept by Mrs Hope but had become 'exceedingly comfortable', and a railway from Leadburn to Linton was 'now in course of construction'. The old-established sheep market had become a casualty of the lack of railway communication and ceased after 1857.

Chapter Two

Obtaining an Act

Making the Case

In the early days of railways, many companies had had their fingers burned by promoting too many expensive branch lines. The NBR was an extreme example and its policy since then had been to encourage local communities to promote their own branch lines. The NBR might help with the preliminary expenses, and sometimes contribute capital, and there would be an agreement with the local company for the NBR to work the line for a percentage of the receipts, usually under the oversight of a joint committee of Directors; eventually the NBR would absorb the local company as it expanded its empire. The arch rival of the Edinburgh-based North British Railway Company was the Glasgow-based Caledonian Railway Company. For much of the rest of the 19th century they and their expensive Parliamentary Counsel fought each other in Parliamentary Committee, to the despair of their shareholders, and obstructed each other's traffic, to the despair of their customers. Where one promoted a line, the other would oppose it, or build a competing line. Peeblesshire was on the front line, the two companies having agreed on Peebles as a boundary point, with the east coast company determined to prevent encroachment into its territory by its west coast rival, and vice versa. The proposed new branch line was, therefore, seen by the North British as of strategic importance in protecting its territory, and by the Caledonian as a potential threat, should it be extended beyond Dolphinton. It is clear from the generous 4 per cent* offer from Richard Hodgson, the NBR Chairman, that his intention, from the start, was for the NBR to absorb the Dolphinton branch and so protect its front line. However, as we shall see, it suited the promoters to portray it simply as a local undertaking to secure improved communication with Edinburgh (as indeed it would do).

Two weeks after the initial meeting in Edinburgh on 1st August, 1861, Bouch was instructed to conduct a survey of the 'best and cheapest line betwixt the termini', and a deputation of Messrs Mackenzie, Forbes and Gordon, with Bouch and Bathgate, was appointed to confer with Richard Hodgson. It received Hodgson's assurance of support, but he asked that publicity for the proposed arrangements with the NBR be

---

* Although in October 1864 he was telling his opposite numbers in the Edinburgh & Glasgow, and Glasgow & South Western, companies that he hoped to acquire a lease of the LL&DR for 3 per cent on the capital of £40,000 (*see Chapter 9*).

avoided meantime. The less that the Caledonian – or perhaps his own long-suffering shareholders – knew, the better.

A Circular, with a form of application for shares in 'The Leadburn, Linton and Dolphinton Railway' was issued on 16th September to the local proprietors, tenants and other members of the Provisional Committee. It painted a positive picture:

> Several of the Proprietors in the parishes of Linton and Newlands, and vicinity, having felt the increasing necessity of Railway accommodation for the district, held recently a meeting in Edinburgh, when the prospect of success was so encouraging, that they resolved to proceed with the promotion of a local railway; and a Sub-committee was formed, to invite the co-operation of all interested, as members of a Provisional Committee, and take other steps requisite for the prosecution of the scheme.
>
> It is proposed that the Line shall start from the Leadburn Station of the Peebles Railway, and pursue an easy route by La-Mancha and Coalyburn to the neighbourhood of Linton, and thence on to Ingraston Loan-end, near Dolphinton – a distance of about ten miles – accommodating the inhabitants along the Line by Stations at the most convenient and central points, and passing close to the Lime and Coal Field. The Engineer states that, from the nature of the ground, the works will be of the most favourable description – even more so than the Peebles Railway – the earthwork of the whole ten miles scarcely amounting to the average of a single mile of railway works generally. In consequence, the estimated cost is unusually low, and will not exceed £3,500 per mile. The present low price of iron is a favourable circumstance.

There followed a lesson in railway economics:

> It is a very common error to suppose that the profitable return on a Railway depends wholly on the traffic, whereas it is dependent on the relation of the traffic to the capital cost. If a Line can be cheaply constructed, a very moderate amount of traffic ensures a lucrative return. For example: the Caledonian Railway has a traffic of £78 per mile per week, yet it pays no higher dividend than the Peebles Railway, which has only a traffic of £13 per mile per week. A traffic on the proposed line of one half of that on the Peebles Railway would ensure at least 4 per cent., and the per-centage would rapidly rise with the development of the resources of the district.

The estimates of prospective traffic were encouraging:

> The supply of Limestone is inexhaustible. There are [sic] also abundance of Freestone, several Coal seams, Ironstone, Fireclay, and other minerals. The rental of the district accommodated amounts to £30,000, which ensures a considerable traffic in agricultural and dairy produce. The Woods, by being brought within reach of the market, would also add to the traffic. There are numerous residences in the neighbourhood of the proposed Line, besides a

large tenantry and several villages, which afford a sufficient index of the passenger traffic. All these circumstances, combined with the low capital cost, and the fact that the extreme point of the Line would be brought within an hour and ten minutes' travelling from Edinburgh, prove undoubtedly that one-half of the rate of the Peebles Line is too low an estimate of the traffic. In assuming that the traffic would yield £6 10s. per mile per week, an under instead of an over-estimate is made. Scarcely any line in the kingdom, however small, pays less than £10 per mile, and there is none with so low a yield as £6 10s. There is, therefore, the utmost confidence that, by the capital being kept low, the undertaking will be remunerative.

But 'hearty support' was essential:

The line can only be proceeded with by all the proprietors and tenants giving their hearty support, and there is every expectation that a satisfactory arrangement will be made for leasing the Line. The scheme being purely local, must depend in the first place upon the united effort of proprietors, tenants, and residents in the district. … If they will come well forward in organizing the undertaking, they will be in a position to obtain such terms from the leasing Company as will be mutually beneficial, and obviate the hazard of loss.

The shares were to be £10 each, which would bring them within reach of a wide range of the local population. Calls for payment, in instalments, would be spread over a period of about two years. As requested by Hodgson, no mention was made of the North British Railway interest.

A public meeting was called for Friday 27th September, 1861, in the Somervail School, West Linton, to galvanize local support. John Ord Mackenzie of Dolphinton House took the Chair. He referred to the Caledonian's original proposal for connecting Edinburgh with the West Coast route, which might well have brought the railway through Linton, and to other unsuccessful attempts to open up the district, but now it was up to themselves to make the line, and everyone must help. The benefits were obvious to all, and he was hopeful that they were at last to be successful. 'The time occupied in transit, now so tedious by coach, would be so short as to render Linton almost a suburb of Edinburgh'. He was supported by William Chambers of Glenormiston, partner in the eminent Edinburgh publishing firm of W. & R. Chambers, future Edinburgh Lord Provost (after whom Chambers Street is named), and Chairman of the Peebles Railway Company. Chambers explained that if the line were cheaply made, there was no reason why it should not become as successful as the Peebles line, particularly in light of the local mineral wealth, an asset which the Peebles line lacked. Instead of carriers' carts twice a week, Peebles now had four trains each way daily, with numerous trucks filled with goods, and the weekly market which had dwindled away now attracted buyers from Edinburgh and elsewhere; the same benefits could follow for Linton. Passengers would be comfortably and rapidly carried on their journeys, and by means of the electric telegraph could communicate instantaneously with any part of Great Britain.

John Bathgate followed Chambers, 'proving from unquestionable data that the undertaking had every prospect of success' and referring to the traffic likely to arise from the important mineral resources. Even the lead mines near Linton, last worked a hundred years ago, could be re-opened were the railway to be built. The financial prospects were good: the Peebles line drew £13 per mile per week; assuming the proposed line drew only £6 a week 'which was very far under the mark', that would yield four per cent 'with the sure prospect of an increase'. He reported that Mr Mackintosh of Lamancha had shown an excellent example in not only subscribing £1,000, but also in agreeing to take shares in exchange for the land to be taken for the railway. Mr Forbes of Medwyn promised to do the same, and a resolution that the proposed undertaking was 'deserving of every encouragement, and those present pledge themselves to support it by every means in their power' was carried with acclamation.

John Bathgate (10th August, 1809 – 21st September, 1886)

John Bathgate was born in Edinburgh, and moved to Peebles when his father became Master of the Peebles Burgh School in 1822. He trained as a solicitor and practised in Peebles from 1835 to 1863. Besides being a Writer and a Notary Public, he was Procurator Fiscal, Agent for the Union Bank of Scotland and founder of the local paper the *Peeblesshire Monthly Advertiser and Tweedside Journal*, forerunner of the *Peeblesshire Advertiser*. He was a local Councillor until appointment as part-time Town Clerk, Clerk to the Commissioners of Supply (forerunners of the County Council), to the Trustees for the County's Turnpike and Statute Labour Roads, and to the Heritors of Peebles Parish Church, an elder of the Kirk, and much else besides. Together with publisher William Chambers, and banker and mill owner Walter Thorburn, he was instrumental in the formation of the Peebles Railway Company, of which he became Secretary.

The Parliamentary agents for the Peebles Railway Bill, Messrs Dodds & Greig, wrote to Bathgate, commenting on 'the kindness and

Portrait of John Bathgate.
From the collection of Scottish Borders Council administered by Live Borders (Tweeddale Museum & Gallery).

handsome feeling we have all along experienced from the Directors and yourself. What with this constant urbanity of intercourse and perfection of every arrangement, we have never had more satisfaction in conducting business'.

As is recounted later, he left Peebles for New Zealand in 1863 having been 'head hunted' to become the Colonial Manager of the Bank of Otago in Dunedin, South Island. There he became MP for Dunedin and a Minister in the New Zealand Government, before resigning to become a District Judge.

Prospectus and Shareholders

The Provisional Committee met on 23rd October, 1861 and appointed as Provisional Directors Messrs Mackenzie, Forbes, Gordon, Woddrop and Rev Dr Aiton, along with Messrs Charles Alexander of Whitfield, Captain George Robert Beresford of Macbiehill, James Mackintosh of Lamancha and John Forrester WS of Edinburgh. Also appointed was Peter Redford Scott of Deanshouses, through whose land the railway would run for $1\frac{1}{4}$ miles, but no more is heard of him; he died in May 1865. The meeting heard that almost £15,000 had already been subscribed. The Prospectus was finalized, with the capital fixed at £40,000. It began: 'The north-western part of Peeblesshire has for several

PROSPECTUS.

Leadburn, Linton, and Dolphinton Railway.

CAPITAL £40,000, IN 4000 SHARES OF £10 EACH.

THE north-western part of Peeblesshire has for several years felt the pressing want of Railway communication. Its resources have hitherto remained dormant, while the rest of the district has been advancing in an extraordinary degree, from the advantages of local railways. Seeing that the Peebles Railway has amply fulfilled the expectations of its promoters, and yields a 5 per cent. dividend, with the prospect of an increase, the principal land-owners, and others interested, have had a meeting, and resolved to establish a local railway, communicating with the Peebles Railway near the summit level at Leadburn. By its means this portion of the county will be brought into immediate connection with Edinburgh and Dalkeith, as well as the county town of Peebles, and a stimulus given to its capabilities, including water-power and a mineral field almost entirely undeveloped.

The stream of passengers being chiefly to and from the capital, any line having Edinburgh near one extremity cannot fail to possess a remunerative passenger traffic. The neighbourhood to be traversed possesses more mansion houses, with resident families, than any other part of the county, and has also a numerous and respectable tenantry, besides the villages on the route. The extreme point of the line would be brought within an hour and ten minutes of Edinburgh, and the present passenger traffic, which is considerable, requiring the accommodation of stage coaches as well as other conveyances, be greatly increased.

In addition to the ordinary traffic in agricultural, pastoral, and dairy produce, to be afforded from lands amounting in rental to £30,000 a year, very valuable water power would be brought into immediate employment, ensuring the addition of manufacturing production. But it is to the transit of minerals the promoters look with confidence for a return much beyond what is necessary to yield a remunerative dividend to the shareholders. The extent of mineral wealth will be best judged of by the following extracts from a report obtained from Mr WILLIAMSON, Mining Engineer, several years ago:—"The portion from West Linton passes over coal, ironstone, "and limestone, on the estates of Macbiehill, Lamancha, and Whim. Besides the minerals in the carboniferous "strata, there are hematite and lead in the metalliferous rocks at Macbiehill; and at West Linton, on the Earl "of Wemyss' property, there is lead." Besides the coal at present partially wrought, and the limestone, which is inexhaustible, there are very valuable quarries of sandstone, and beds of fireclay. The latter has been recently tested, and is found to be of the best quality. There cannot be a doubt that the traffic in lime, for which there is a large demand in the lower parts of Peeblesshire and elsewhere, would be very considerable, and the same thing may be said of sandstone for building purposes.

If to these great natural capabilities, rendering a large traffic a matter of certainty, be added the important fact that the proposed Line can be made at a cost remarkably low, then the remunerative character of the undertaking is at once obvious. The course of the Line will run through the south-west corner of the carboniferous basin of Mid-Lothian, to the confines of Lanarkshire—a distance of ten miles—on a very uniform level, and wholly on the surface. The earthwork will scarcely exceed the simple formation of the bed for the rails, amounting to little more for the whole ten miles than the average earthwork of a single mile of railway. There is no viaduct or tunnel, or heavy work of any kind. There is only one small river to cross, which can be done by a bridge of an inexpensive character, and altogether, making a high estimate in the circumstances, the cost of the undertaking will be £35,000; but, to allow an ample margin for all contingencies (including cost of land) the capital will be fixed at £40,000, or £4000 a-mile—a cost one-third below the Peebles Railway, which has been often quoted as an economically constructed and successful railway. Almost all the proprietors throughout the district, and the tenants generally, are shareholders and cordial supporters of the undertaking. In addition to the shares in the line taken by the land-owners, they have agreed almost without exception to take shares for the value of their land required. From this unusually favourable conjunction of circumstances, the promoters feel justified in inviting the co-operation of the public generally to enable them to carry through the project to a successful issue.

In the Bill power will be taken to enter into agreements with the North British Railway Company for the working and maintenance of the Line, and apportionment of the traffic, whereby the expense of workshops and plant will be avoided. By joining at Leadburn outlay on a terminal or junction station will be saved.

Looking at the low capital cost, and viewing the undertaking without reference to its peculiar resources, it may be safely estimated that the revenue will not at first be less than £7 per mile per week. No thoroughfare leading directly to the capital has so low a traffic as that. The Peebles line draws £13, or nearly double; and it is no exaggeration to value the anticipated revenue at the sum stated. The traffic, estimated at £7 per mile per week, allowing 50 per cent. for working, would pay 4 per cent. £10 per mile per week would yield upwards of 6 per cent. If the advantages of the Line as a mineral line be considered, there are grounds for anticipating even a higher return.

The greater part of the capital required has already been subscribed for in the district, and the remaining portion is open to public subscription, for which immediate application by intending subscribers is requested.

Provisional Committee.

JOHN ORD MACKENZIE, Esq. of Dolphinton—*Chairman*.
CAPTAIN BERESFORD, of Macbiehill.
W. FORBES, Esq. of Medwyn.
W. FERGUSSON, Esq. of Spittlehaugh.
RICHARD GORDON, Esq. of Halmyre.
JAMES MACKINTOSH, Esq. of La Mancha.
JOHN WHITE, Esq. of Drummelzier and Netherurd.
W. A. WODDROP, Esq. of Elsridgehill and Garvald.
REV. DR AITON, the Manse, Dolphinton.
JOHN FORRESTER, Esq., W.S., Edinburgh.
CHARLES ALEXANDER, Esq., Whitfield.
ARCHD. ALEXANDER, Esq., Banker, Linton.
ROBERT BLACK, Esq., Westfield, Dolphinton.
THOMAS BROWN, Esq., North Slipperfield.
CHARLES LAWSON, Esq., Deepsykehead.
W. MORGAN, Esq., Merchant, Linton.
SIMON RITCHIE, Esq., Blyth.
JOHN WATSON, Esq., Ingraston.
&c.   &c.

THOMAS BOUCH, Esq., C.E., Edinburgh, *Engineer*.
JOHN BATHGATE, Peebles, *Solicitor and Interim Secretary*.

Bankers.

THE BANK OF SCOTLAND.
THE UNION BANK OF SCOTLAND.

Applications for Shares may be made to WM. BELL, Esq., Sharebroker, Edinburgh; ROBERT ALLAN, Esq., Sharebroker, Edinburgh; GEORGE MACCALLUM, Esq., Sharebroker, Edinburgh; JOHN BATHGATE, Peebles; or any of the Committee.

years felt the pressing want of Railway communication. Its resources have hitherto remained dormant, whilst the rest of the district has been advancing in an extraordinary degree, from the advantages of local railways'. The Peebles Railway had 'amply fulfilled' the expectations of its promoters. Every town or village of any significance was getting a railway and West Linton and district were impatient for one too. Dolphinton would be but 70 minutes from Edinburgh, and there would be a link to Dalkeith and Peebles. With a 'numerous and respectable tenantry', besides the villages on the route, and the mansion houses with their resident families, passenger traffic was assured.

The mineral resources made 'a large traffic a matter of certainty' – coal, ironstone and limestone on the estates of Macbiehill, Lamancha and Whim; haematite and lead at Macbiehill, and lead at West Linton, together with quarries of sandstone and beds of fireclay. The earthworks would be light with no tunnel or viaduct, and only one small river to bridge (the Lyne Water at West Linton). The estimated total cost was £35,000 with a further £5,000 as contingency. At £40,000 for 10 miles, the cost per mile would be one-third below that of the Peebles line which had been constructed on the 'cheap railway principle'. There was already strong local support: 'Almost all the proprietors throughout the district, and the tenants generally, are shareholders and cordial supporters of the undertaking. In addition to the shares in the line taken by the land-owners, they have agreed almost without exception to take shares for the value of their land required.'

Powers would be taken in the Bill to make an agreement with the NBR to work and maintain the line, and so there would be no expense on workshops or plant. By joining the Peebles Railway at its Leadburn station, the expense of a junction station would be avoided. Revenue was 'safely estimated' at not less than £7 per mile per week (£70 per week for the 10 miles) which, after allowing 50 per cent to the NBR for working the line, would pay 4 per cent on the capital invested. £10 per mile per week would yield upwards of 6 per cent, and the likely mineral traffic could push that even higher. As with so many railway prospectuses, the forecasts of future prosperity were to prove hopelessly optimistic.

Notice was given in the official *Edinburgh Gazette* of 5th November, 1861 of the intention to apply to Parliament to promote 'A Railway commencing by a Junction with the Peebles Railway, at a point at or near the Leadburn station on the Line of said Railway, in the Parish of Penicuik and County of Edinburgh, and terminating at a point in a plantation at or near Ingraston Toll-Bar in the First District of Peeblesshire Turnpike Roads, in the Parish of Linton and County of Peebles ...'

On 11th December, shares to the value of £15,220 were allotted, exclusive of those to be given in exchange for land, the value of which was currently being negotiated. Leading the list was Engineer Thomas Bouch with shares worth £2,000 taken in full payment of his fee; this was a useful device to increase the take-up of the share capital, while reducing the cash outlay, and a similar condition was often imposed on the contractor and suppliers. John Ord Mackenzie, the Earl of Wemyss and March, William A. Woddrop of Garvald House, William Fergusson of Spitalhaugh, James Mackintosh of Lamancha, and Captain G.R. Beresford of Macbiehill, currently at Curragh Camp, Ireland, had each pledged £1,000. Richard Gordon of Halmyre had pledged £600, with £500 each from John Bathgate, John White of Drummelzier, and William Forbes of Medwyn. The amount per share required as the initial deposit was fixed at 30 shillings.

The shareholdings ranged from Thomas Bouch's 200 shares to Robert Tennant, farmer, of Howieson Hall, who took one share. The list names all the local lairds, plus a few from further afield. Many Linton tradespeople were subscribers: Margaret Rough, grocer; Thomas Thomson, baker; Archibald Alexander and John Alexander, both merchants; Robert Alexander, flesher; William Morgan, draper; Patison Bain, shoemaker. Others included Ebenezer Blacklock, teacher, Newlands; James Palmer, schoolmaster, Kirkurd; Richard Cleghorn, smith, Dolphinton; Charles Lawson, quarryman and builder, Deepsykehead; John Borthwick, butler, Garvald House. The capital ultimately raised from shareholders came to £20,291 10*s*.; £208 10*s*. was not paid up when called. Of the local population, 29 farmers provided £1,950, 14 tradesmen and merchants £900, 8 lawyers £1,280, 11 lairds £6,750, and others (15 in number) £4,340. Taking into account that the annual wages of a working man at that time ranged from £30 per annum, unskilled, up to £100, skilled, the company was remarkably well supported.

Encouragement came from the Board of the Peebles Railway. Not only was the proposed line a good investment in itself, and would act as a useful feeder for the Peebles Railway, but the Board entertained the hope that 'there is every likelihood of someone extending it to Carstairs, in which case it will become a junction line connecting us with the Caledonian system in the west. When that ensues, the advantage to us need not be dwelt upon'. A number of Peebles Railway Directors took shares, including William Chambers of Glenormiston and Sir G. Graham Montgomery of Stanhope (the current and former Chairmen), and Peebles mill owner and banker, Walter Thorburn. Likewise, some Linton people were shareholders in the Peebles Railway, including landowners William Forbes and James Mackintosh, and merchant Archibald Alexander, who was also the Bank Agent and Postmaster; Richard Gordon of Halmyre was also a Director.

Dirty Work by the Caledonian

By the time the Provisional Directors met again in Edinburgh on 2nd January, 1862, the necessary Petition to bring in the Bill had been lodged in Parliament and a provisional working agreement with the NBR, described below, had been negotiated. Richard Hodgson had again 'expressed his desire to further the interests of the undertaking to the utmost of his power'. The agreement was ready to be signed at the LL&DR Directors' meeting on 3rd February, but it was reported that a Director of the Caledonian Railway had been in touch with William Forbes, requesting a meeting that day; signature was delayed while Messrs Mackenzie, Mackintosh and Forbes went off with John Bathgate to meet three Caledonian Directors and their General Manager. A subsequent memorandum summarized the discussions:

> After some conversation Mr Hill for the Caledonian Railway Company proposed that the Promoters of the Leadburn line should go on with their Bill striking out the enabling Clauses in favour of the North British and enter into no agreements with the North British Railway Company and the Caledonian Company would bring in a Bill next year to complete the connection to Carstairs and take over the Leadburn branch at its Estimated Cost of Forty thousand pounds (£40,000) or – let the Leadburn Bill be withdrawn and the Caledonian would bring in a Bill next year to make the entire line from Carstairs to Leadburn – the Local Promoters finding Forty thousand pounds (£40,000) and the Caledonian working the line in perpetuity.
>
> The alternative offers not being considered expedient it was resolved to complete the Agreement with the North British and it was accordingly signed.

A through line to Carstairs, giving access to the west of Scotland, as well as to the east, was exactly what the promoters of previous schemes – John Bathgate in particular – had wanted, and Bathgate had previously shown willingness to work with the Caledonian. But it was not to be. Perhaps the LL&DR Directors were doubtful as to their ability to raise £40,000, as later events were to prove, and were counting on the North British to fund the shortfall. The threat of having the Caledonian Railway on its doorstep at Leadburn would have led to a major

Parliamentary battle with the NBR that could have derailed the LL&DR's plans.

The Caledonian response was to lodge a Petition in Parliament against the LL&DR Bill, and so Parliamentary Counsel had to be engaged, and a deputation from the Board had to travel to London at its own expense, to give evidence to the House of Commons Select Committee proving that the scheme was for a local railway line, and was not a threat to the Caledonian. Mr Mackenzie, Captain Beresford, Mr Gordon, Mr Woddrop, Mr Mackintosh, and the Rev Dr Aiton all went. Sir Graham Graham-Montgomery and Professor Fergusson of Spitalhaugh were also prepared to join the Deputation, being already in London. Sir Graham was MP for the County, and Professor Fergusson was Surgeon to Her Majesty.

A series of letters between John Bathgate and the Caledonian Railway Solicitor, Robert Mackay WS, in the days immediately before the Bill was due to go before the Commons Select Committee, reveal the fears – amounting almost to paranoia – of the Caledonian. It regarded the LL&DR line as 'aggressive' and 'a covert scheme for invasion of their proper territory' through a future extension of the line west of Dolphinton. It would withdraw its Petition against the Bill if the LL&DR would drop the provisions for a working agreement with the NBR, which it saw as 'a hostile party who has for years been attacking and abstracting Caledonian traffic, and who engaged not to go west of Peebles …'. (Needless to say, the North British held a similar opinion of the Caledonian!)

John Bathgate was having none of this and strongly refuted the allegations. The LL&DR was a local undertaking, got up by local landowners for the purpose mainly of securing railway communication with Edinburgh, and there was absolutely no intention of extending the line westwards. The Caledonian, apparently reassured by this, and by an assurance from Richard Hodgson that the NBR did not intend to subscribe to the capital of the LL&DR but merely to work the line, and that it had no aggressive intentions towards the Caledonian, eventually abandoned its Petition and the Bill passed the Commons unopposed. LL&DR witnesses had gone to London, and Counsel had been engaged, quite unnecessarily. It was unlikely that the Caledonian's Petition would even have been considered by the Select Committee: the LL&DR barely came within 10 miles of the Caledonian at Carstairs, and was stated to be only a local undertaking, as its witnesses would have proved.

Thereafter, events moved swiftly. The Bill went to the Lords Select Committee, again unopposed, passed through all its stages, and received the Royal Assent on 3rd June, 1862. When the Directors met on 18th June, a copy of *The Leadburn, Linton, and Dolphinton Railway Act, 1862* was laid on the table. The whole process, from the meeting of the 'Gentlemen Interested' on 1st August, 1861 to Royal Assent had taken just 10 months. The capital of the company was confirmed at £40,000 and there were the usual borrowing powers of one third of the capital (£13,300) which could be exercized once the whole capital had been subscribed for, and one half of it paid up. The qualification to be a Director was set at the holding of £300 worth of shares. Messrs Mackenzie, Forbes, Mackintosh, Beresford, Fergusson, Gordon, Woddrop, Forrester and Alexander were named in the Act as Provisional Directors with full powers to carry the undertaking into effect. Rev. Dr Aiton, a cleric widely known beyond his Dolphinton parish which he served for 40 years until his death in May 1863, didn't hold the necessary £300 worth and had been replaced by Professor Fergusson. These nine were to be reduced to a maximum of six at the first General Meeting of the Company held following the opening of the line. The Directors chose John Ord Mackenzie as their Chairman, and John Bathgate was appointed Secretary. The Act empowered the LL&DR and the NBR to enter into agreements for the working, maintenance and management of the Railway, subject to the future agreement of both sets of shareholders and of the Board of Trade.

The first General Meeting of the shareholders of the newly incorporated Company was held in the Somervail School on 19th July, 1862. Seventeen persons were present. The Directors' report and the accounts were adopted and a first call of £2 per share agreed. The Provisional Directors were confirmed in office (other than Charles Alexander, who did not stand for election, being replaced by John White of Drummelzier and Netherurd) and the Auditors appointed – Kenneth Mackenzie CA of Edinburgh and Archibald Alexander, merchant, Linton.

The newly incorporated Company was about to get down to business.

Chapter Three

Building the Railway

Thomas Bouch and the Cheap Railway Movement

For a small railway line such as the LL&DR, it was essential to contain its capital costs if it was to survive. In particular, it had to avoid, if possible, excessive Parliamentary expenses in promoting and defending its Bill, and the cost of land had to be kept to a minimum; if the landowners would take shares in exchange, rather than cash, so much the better. More importantly, construction costs had to be kept low. So far, the LL&DR had been successful, despite the Caledonian's Parliamentary obstruction.

The anticipated volume of traffic on many local branch lines simply couldn't justify construction to main line standards, and so the 'Cheap Railway Movement' had been born. Without it, many branch lines – in Scotland, in particular – would never have been built. The principal exponent of the 'Movement' in Scotland was the Engineer, Thomas Bouch. He 'established himself by catering for enthusiastic but poverty-stricken local patriots, tailoring his lines to the limited capitals available'.* Economy was achieved by having a minimum of earthworks, steeper gradients, tighter curves, lighter rails and chairs, fewer sleepers, lower speeds and usually lower land costs. Bouch also restricted his fee as compared to the standard of the time. His charge of £2,000 to the LL&DR represents £200 per mile, considerably less than charged by other engineers. His first 'cheap' line had been the St Andrews Railway, opened in 1852, and his reputation had spread. The Peebles Railway – 'To be formed on an Economical Principle' – was satisfied with what he had delivered, and that was recommendation enough for the LL&DR. Bouch later became Consulting Engineer to the North British Railway and engineered many of its schemes.

Thomas Bouch in 1879.
NRS/Department for Transport under Open Government Licence v3.0.

---

* C.J.A. Robertson 'The Cheap Railway Movement in Scotland' in *Transport History* Vol 7 No. 1 (1974).

Choosing the Contractor

The first business of the Board was to appoint a contractor and get the line built. A Press advert of 5th September, 1862 invited tenders to be submitted by the end of the month for the construction of the line of 9 miles and 69 chains*. Eight tenders were submitted to the Board meeting on 11th October, ranging from £21,873 2s. 4d. to £26,855 12s. 1d. The lowest was from John Waddell, Rosebank, Bathgate. Three of these were remitted to Bouch to examine and report, the Chairman being authorized to accept the preferred tender, and 'the successful offerer to become a shareholder'. Waddell's offer was accepted and it was reported to the Directors meeting on 26th November that he had already begun work on the line. One hundred shares were allotted to him, to be paid from the 10 per cent retention fee for the contract. This was to be Waddell's first major construction project, at the age of 34; his younger brother, George, was employed as his Manager. Tenders for rails and chairs were likewise referred to the Engineer and Chairman, and a contract was concluded with Messrs Bolckow & Vaughan, Middlesbrough, for rails at £6 per ton and chairs at £3 15s., delivered at Leith. They, too, were required to become shareholders and were allotted 100 shares in part payment.

Press advertisement inviting tenders for the construction of the line.

> **LEADBURN, LINTON, & DOLPHINTON RAILWAY.**
>
> *COUNTY OF PEEBLES.*
>
> **CONTRACT FOR WORKS.**
>
> The DIRECTORS are prepared to receive TENDERS for the CONSTRUCTION of this RAILWAY, in one Contract—the Length being 9 Miles 69 Chains.
>
> The Rails, Fishplates, and Bolts will be supplied by the Railway Company.
>
> The Drawings and Specifications may be seen at the Office of Thomas Bouch, Esq., C.E., 78 George Street, Edinburgh, on and after Tuesday the 16th inst., from whom Duplicate Schedules of Measurements and Forms of Tender may be obtained on payment of Thirty Shillings. An Assistant Engineer will be at Leadburn Station of the Peebles Railway on Tuesday the 23d inst., at Ten o'clock A.M., for the purpose of accompanying intending Offerers over the Line.
>
> SEALED TENDERS, addressed to John Bathgate, Esq., Writer, Peebles, must be lodged on or before Tuesday the 30th Inst., at Ten A.M. The Directors do not bind themselves to accept the lowest or any offer.
>
> Edinburgh, 5th September 1862.

John Waddell (16th August, 1828 – 17th January, 1888)

John Waddell, the son of a farmer, was brought up at Gain in the parish of New Monkland, near Airdrie. Although he retained a lifelong interest in agriculture, his chosen career was as an engineer and contractor

---

* The Parliamentary Plans show the line as 9 miles and 71 chains; the NBR Distance Tables of 1920 show 9 miles and 70 chains. There are 80 chains to a mile.

Depiction of John Waddell, from his memorial in the Dean Cemetery, Edinburgh.
Author

despite having no formal training. His first major contract was the construction of the Leadburn, Linton & Dolphinton Railway, from which he and his firm went on to greater things. He worked with Thomas Bouch on several more projects – the Penicuik Railway, the Edinburgh, Loanhead & Roslin Railway, connecting lines for the first Tay Bridge (and the recovery of the wreckage of Bouch's bridge for the NBR after the Tay Bridge disaster of 28th December, 1879), the North British Arbroath & Montrose Railway, Bouch's first Forth Bridge (abandoned after the fall of the Tay Bridge), and the Edinburgh Suburban & Southside Junction Railway, Bouch's final project before his death at Moffat on 30th October, 1880. Waddell tendered, unsuccessfully, for the replacement Tay Bridge. Amongst many other projects, he constructed the Cleland and Midcalder Railway, the NBR's Coatbridge branch, the connecting railway lines to the Forth Bridge, the North Eastern Railway bridge across the Wear at Durham, and the Whitby & Scarborough Railway. Other major projects included the Mersey Tunnel, the James Watt dock at Greenock and the bridge over the Thames at Putney. He also built the Caledonian Railway's Dolphinton branch, of which more later.

John Waddell was for many years Provost of Bathgate, where he lived until moving to Edinburgh in the early 1870s. Latterly, he was a Director and financier of a number of companies and Chairman of the Burntisland Oil Company, the Rosewell Coal Company and the Edinburgh Northern Cable Tramways Company. He was widely known for his success in breeding Clydesdale horses.

John Waddell had a reputation for kindliness, and this is borne out in the curling medal that he presented in 1865, to be competed for annually between the West Linton and Newlands Curling Clubs, in appreciation of the kindness received by himself and his men when laying the railway. The story goes that during a period of severe winter weather, when work on the construction of the line was suspended, a curling match was organized between Waddell's men and a local team. The medal has now been contested by the two clubs over 155 years, the first occasion being in January 1865 on Slipperfield Loch, when the Linton club won by 46 shots. The inscription on the medal reads:

> Presented by John Waddell Esq
> Provost of Bathgate
> And Contractor for the LL&D Railway
> To the West Linton Snr & Newlands Water
> Curling Clubs
> To be played for annually
> The Secretary of the winning club
> retaining it till again competed for
> 1865

It was remitted to the Secretary to arrange with the Chief Constable at Peebles as to 'the appointment of Constables during the progress of the works – the Company defraying the necessary expenses'. It was not uncommon for disturbances – or worse – to occur amongst the 'navvies' on railway construction sites, particularly on pay day, but no reports of such conduct have been discovered. The company's accounts for the half-year to 31st July, 1863 include expenditure on Police wages and uniform. On 15th January, 1864 a cheque was issued for 'Police' for £53 4s. and a further one on 6th July that year for 'Constables Wages' of £22 16s.

Completion of negotiations for the purchase of land took until the beginning of 1866. The shareholders were told that, of the 11 proprietors, all, with two or three exceptions, had agreed to take shares in respect of the value of the land, and of any damages due to them. The Directors acknowledged the liberality experienced in their negotiations with landowners and the 'equitable spirit' of the affected tenants. William Forbes of Medwyn would have wished to take shares in exchange for his land, but it had been conveyed to Trustees, under a Marriage Contract, for the benefit of his children, and the Trustees could accept only an equivalent amount of land for any

The curling medal presented in 1865 by John Waddell, to be competed for annually by the West Linton Senior and Newlands Water curling clubs. *Author*

surrendered; the solution was to feu the land to the LL&DR. The Trustees also required the company to make a siding on the Medwyn estate, at the company's expense, as a condition of their consent. The Directors responded that they would willingly give facilities for a siding to be built at the expense of the estate, although they did later agree to bear the cost of making it, if and when required. Mr Mackintosh of Lamancha also required a 'small siding near my Coal Pits, Freestone and Lime Quarries, as agreed on'. The company was happy to allow this at his cost. There is no evidence of these, or indeed any, sidings having been provided for local proprietors.

The nine shareholders who attended the second General Meeting at 9 Hill Street on 25th March, 1863 were told that Waddell 'had commenced vigorously to the work' and expected to have the line finished by the end of the year. Thomas Bouch, who had appointed John Carline as his resident engineer, confirmed that fair progress had been made, despite the unfavourable winter weather. Over a quarter of the earthworks had been removed, the masonry of the public road bridges was complete at Leadburn and Whim, and in progress at Cowdenburn and Coalyburn. Two miles of permanent fencing had been completed, and laying of the first three miles of the permanent way was about to begin. The *Peeblesshire Advertiser* of 18th July reported that permanent rails were now in place for three miles from Leadburn to Cowdenburn, where the quarry that supplied the ballast was located, and that an engine was continuously running with ballast wagons to supply the southern part of the line towards Broomlee, which ran on soft and peaty soil. On the extension to Dolphinton, material would have to be excavated from the nearby hillside to supplement that excavated from cuttings, so as to form the trackbed.

At the Board meeting on 5th August, 1863, John Bathgate intimated his resignation, on appointment as Colonial Manager of the Bank of Otago, New Zealand. Generous tributes were paid to him by the Directors:

> On accepting the resignation of Mr Bathgate as secretary of this Company the meeting deem it right to express their great regret at losing the valuable services of that gentleman to whom, in a great measure, the Company owes the position it now holds, and the realisation of the long-deferred hopes of railway communication by the inhabitants of the district through which their line passes. The Directors, in name of the company, now tender to Mr Bathgate their best thanks for his unwearied exertions on their behalf, and in their individual, as well as their official capacity, beg to convey to him their warmest wishes for his success in the new and distant sphere to which he has devoted his energies for the future. They earnestly trust that in his public life, as well as in his private relations, he may be amply blessed with that measure of prosperity of which in the opinion of this Meeting, he is so deserving.

THE LEADBURN, LINTON & DOLPHINTON RAILWAY COMPANY'S REPORT.

No. 3.   SATURDAY, 24th OCTOBER 1863.

NOTICE IS HEREBY GIVEN, That the Third General Meeting of the LEADBURN, LINTON, AND DOLPHINTON RAILWAY COMPANY, will be held within the SOMERVAIL SCHOOLHOUSE, WEST LINTON, on SATURDAY the 24th day of OCTOBER current, at TWELVE o'clock Noon, for the purpose of receiving a Report on the affairs of the Company.

By Order,

J. D. BATHGATE, *Secretary.*

Peebles, 2d October 1863.

REPORT by the Directors of the Leadburn, Linton, and Dolphinton Railway Company, to be submitted to the Third General Meeting of the Shareholders, to be held at Linton, on Saturday 24th October 1863.

1. Since the last Report the Works have been proceeding in a very satisfactory manner, as will be seen on reference to the Report by the Engineer appended hereto, and the Directors have every hope that the Line will be opened for traffic by the end of December or early in January.

2. No additional shares have been taken up since the date of last Report, but the Directors have every expectation that the whole Capital will be ultimately subscribed for. They have completed the arrangements approved of by the Special Meeting of Shareholders, held at Linton on 12th September 1863.

3. The amount due on Shares subscribed for has been called up, with the exception of 10s. per Share, which will also be called up shortly.

4. One third of the Directors retire at this time, but are eligible for re-election. One of the Auditors also retires, but is eligible for re-election.

5. It will fall to this Meeting, in terms of the Statute, to fix the remuneration of the Secretary and the Auditors.

6. A Statement of the Accounts, brought down to 31st July last, duly certified by the Auditors, is hereto appended.

7. Mr John Bathgate having, in consequence of his appointment as Colonial Manager of the Bank of Otago, resigned the office of Secretary to this Company, the Directors appointed his brother, Mr James D. Bathgate, Writer, Peebles, as Secretary in his room. In accepting the resignation of Mr Bathgate the Directors placed the following upon their minutes:—" On accepting the resignation of Mr Bathgate as Secretary of this Company, the

meeting deem it right to express their great regret at losing the valuable services of that gentleman, to whom, in a great measure, the Company owes the position it now holds, and the realisation of the long-deferred hopes of railway communication by the inhabitants of the district through which their Line passes. The Directors, in name of the Company, now tender to Mr Bathgate their best thanks for his unwearied exertions on their behalf, and in their individual, as well as their official capacity, beg to convey to him their warmest wishes for his success in the new and distant sphere to which he has devoted his energies for the future. They earnestly trust that in his public life, as well as in his private relations, he may be amply blessed with that measure of prosperity, of which, in the opinion of this meeting, he is so deserving."

JOHN ORD MACKENZIE,
Chairman.

ENGINEER'S REPORT.

78A GEORGE STREET,
Edinburgh, 12th October 1863.

To the Directors of the Leadburn, Linton, and Dolphinton Railway.

GENTLEMEN,

The following is a short summary of the progress of the works up to this date:

Of the Earthwork about 96,000 cubic yards, or nineteen-twentieths of the whole have been excavated.

The Turnpike and Public Road Bridges, four in number, are finished, with the exception of the one near Boagsbank, which only requires the malleable iron girders, and timber roadway to complete it.

The Bridge over Cairn burn is also finished. That over the Lyne water requires the girders and timber roadway. Tarth-water Bridge is not yet commenced, but this is a very small work.

Two occupation Bridges over the Railway, and six cattle creeps have been built. One over occupation Bridge and one cattle creep are in progress, and two occupation road Bridges over Railway, and two cattle creeps are yet to build.

The approaches to Public Road Bridges and Level Crossings are, with the exception of fencing and metalling, complete.

About eight miles of permanent fencing are erected complete, and three-fourths of a mile with posts only.

Six and a quarter miles of the permanent way are laid, five and one-half miles of which have been ballasted, and the greater portion of the remainder is ready for the ballast.

The Station Buildings are let, and will be commenced immediately.

Since my last Report, the progress made by the Contractor has been most satisfactory, and as the quantity of work now to execute is very light, I see nothing to prevent the line being opened by the specified time.—I am &c.,

THOMAS BOUCH.

The Leadburn, Linton, and Dolphinton Railway Company.

STATEMENT of RECEIPTS and EXPENDITURE on CAPITAL ACCOUNT, to 31st July 1863.

RECEIPTS.

To Capital—			
For Deposit and Calls from Shareholders, per last account,	£8419 10 0		
For Do. to 31st July last,	5093 0 0		
		£13,512 10 0	
To Interest from Banks, per last account,	£1 18 2		
To Do. to 31st July last,	115 14 0		
		117 12 2	
Balance due on Bank Account to 31st July,	£2368 5 2		
Less Balances on hand,	74 13 4		
		2293 11 10	
		£15,923 14 0	

PAYMENTS.

By Preliminary and Parliamentary Expenses,			
per last account,	£799 12 0		
Do. to 31st July last,	425 0 0		
		1224 12 0	
By Engineering Expenses, per last account,	£300 0 0		
Do. to 31st July last,	1700 0 0		
		2000 0 0	
By Expense of Works—			
Paid Contractor to account,	£7662 0 0		
Paid for Rails,	4411 10 10		
Paid for Carriage of Do.	424 15 6		
		12,498 6 4	
By Sundries—			
Paid Police Wages, Clothing, Advertising, &c., &c., up to 31st July last,		200 15 8	
		£15,923 14 0	

Edinburgh, 16*th October* 1863.—We have examined the above State, with the Books, Accounts, and Vouchers from which it is made up, and have found the same to be correct.

Kenneth Mackenzie, C.A., *Auditor.*
Archd. Alexander, *Auditor*

'It was resolved that James Duncan Bathgate, Writer, Peebles be elected Secretary to the Company in room of Mr John Bathgate resigned.' James Bathgate was John Bathgate's business partner and half-brother.

The meeting of shareholders on 24th October, 1863 was told that the works were proceeding in 'a very satisfactory manner', with the Directors still hoping that the line would be open for traffic by the end of December or early in January. Bouch reported that 95 per cent of the earthworks had been excavated, and three of the four Turnpike and Public Road Bridges were finished, the fourth requiring only the iron girders and timber roadway to complete it. The bridge over the Cairn Burn at Broomlee Mains was finished, that over the Lyne Water (immediately south-west of Broomlee station) required only the girders and timber roadway, with the Tarf Water [West Water] Bridge still to be started. Two occupation bridges over the railway, and six cattle creeps, had been built, with one occupation over-bridge and one cattle creep in progress; two occupation road bridges over the railway, and two cattle creeps under, were yet to be built. The approaches to the public road bridges and level crossings were, with the exception of fencing and metalling, complete. About eight miles of permanent fencing had been erected, and three-quarters of a mile had posts only. Six and a quarter miles of the permanent way was laid, of which five and a half had been ballasted, and most of the remainder was ready for ballast.

Bouch considered the progress made by the Contractor as most satisfactory, and saw nothing to prevent the line being opened by the specified time. The meeting 'separated' in a mood of optimism, unaware of the dark cloud that was gathering over the railway and its works.

The Fatal Accident at the Tipperwell Embankment

Less than a week later, there was a disastrous set-back.

FATAL RAILWAY ACCIDENT NEAR PENICUIK was the headline in the *Scotsman* of Friday 30th October, 1863.

> Yesterday afternoon, a disastrous accident occurred to the express passenger train on the Peebles Railway, near Penicuik, by which one boy – the son of Charles Tennant, Esq. of The Glen – lost his life, and six or seven persons were seriously injured …

Five heavily loaded wagons being hauled up the Dolphinton branch from its junction with the Peebles line at Leadburn had broken loose;

The Illustrated London News portrayal of the Tipperwell Accident on 29th October, 1863.
National Railway Museum / Science and Society Picture Library

gathering speed on the falling gradient, they burst through the 'chock-block' designed to prevent runaways, then through the locked points at the junction and on to the main line, and continued their headlong dash until brought to a sudden and devastating halt in a fatal collision with the oncoming 4.20 pm fast passenger train from Edinburgh to Peebles.

The North British Railway report by James Bell (Senior), the NBR's Engineer-in-Chief, wasn't concerned with the human casualties:

> Collision on the Peebles Railway between Leadburn and Penicuik Stations on 29th October, 1863.
>
> Mr James Bell CE reports. 30 Oct. 1863.
>
> The Line at Tipperwell embankment on the Peebles Branch where the Accident took place last night was cleared for the traffic at 7 o'clock this morning.
>
> It appears the trucks which caused the Accident (4 loaded with Sleepers and one with Cast Iron Beams) broke adrift from an Engine on the Dolphinton Line about half a mile from Leadburn station. The gradient falls towards Leadburn, and the wind being blowing a gale at the time, the Trucks gained a high speed, and carried away the choke block at the Station, and continued their course down the Peebles Line for a distance of 3615 lineal yards when they came in contact with the 4.20 pm fast Passenger Train from Edinburgh to Peebles. The gradients on the portion of the Line over which the Trucks passed vary from 1 in 64 to 1 in 173. The damage done to the Road is only two Rails broken, but the Engine, Carriages, and Trucks were damaged to a considerable extent. Three of the Trucks were broken to pieces and three of the Carriages were very much damaged.

BUILDING THE RAILWAY

The official report of the investigation by Captain H.W. Tyler, RE of the Board of Trade, Railway Department, was published on 25th November:

> The Linton line is connected with a coal-siding on the west of the Leadburn station, by a pair of points, 28 yards to the south of the passenger platform; and there is a chock-block 50 yards south of those points. The coal-siding joins the main-line of the Peebles railway at the south end of the passenger platform by a second pair of points, which, as well as the former pair, lead towards Edinburgh.
>
> The Linton line rises on a gradient of 1 in $67\frac{1}{2}$ for 800 yards from Leadburn, and on a gradient of 1 in 150 for 400 yards further; and the Peebles line falls towards Edinburgh from Leadburn on gradients of 1 in 64 for about half a mile, 1 in 80 for about 500 yards, and 1 in 173 for about 1450 yards.
>
> At 2.25 on the afternoon in question, five waggons, the first loaded with iron girders, and the remaining four with wooden sleepers, reached Leadburn for the Linton line, and were placed upon that line ready to be taken away by the contractor's engine. The main-line points were locked, and the chock-block was turned across the Linton line by the station porter, after the waggons had been placed on that line; and a 'spragg' was fixed in the wheel of the last waggon, as a further means of security, by or under the direction of the station master. The contractor's engine came down for the waggons at about 4 o'clock, but the breaksman who ought to have accompanied it remained at Cowdenburn, $2\frac{1}{2}$ miles from Leadburn.

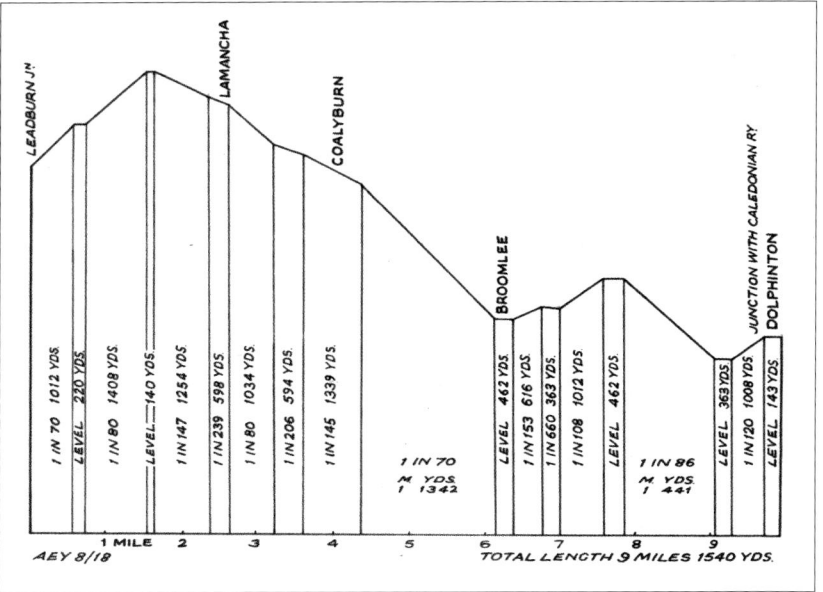

Gradient Diagram of the LL&DR, redrawn from the 1899 NBR diagram. The diagram is slightly at odds with Captain H.W. Tyler's accident report (*above*).

A stone-mason, who left off work at 12 o'clock in consequence of the bad state of the weather, and who was in the habit of occasionally riding backwards and forwards on the engine when his work was over, made use of it on this occasion to get down to the Leadburn inn; as did also three other men, foremen of navvies; but these men remained at the inn when the engine driver, the fireman and the stone-mason rejoined the engine at 4.45.

According to the stone mason's evidence, the men remained at the Leadburn Inn for half or three-quarters of an hour, 'taking about two glasses of whiskey apiece'. Then, with the late October daylight fading, it was out into the gale for the journey back towards Linton.

The five waggons having been attached to the engine by the fireman, the driver proceeded to take them towards Linton at that hour. But the wind was strong, and the rails were slippery; and the sand was blown away as fast as he applied it. The engine slipped, therefore, all the way up, until, at 1,000 yards from Leadburn, it came to a stand altogether. In the absence of the breaksman, the engine driver got off the engine and scotched the wheels of the foremost waggon with stones. Observing then, he states, that a link of the coupling between that waggon and the engine was twisted, he withdrew the hook of the coupling; and finding that the waggons began to move back towards Leadburn, he applied the break of that which was next to him, and stopped them, and called to the fireman to 'let the engine down steady'. He saw the fireman climbing over the tank at the back of the engine (which was a tank engine) at the same time as the stone-mason (or, as he says, some one) slacked off the break, and opened the regulator. The engine ran back upon him and against the waggons; knocked him on one side, and pushed them down towards Leadburn; and crushed the fireman between the tank and a girder which projected from the waggon behind it. The engine-driver ran after the waggons shouting to the fireman to follow with the engine. Having caught them, he jumped upon the first, and clung to the break of it until they approached the Leadburn station; but he dropped off before they reached the chock-block, under the belief that they would be thrown off the line by it, and that he would thus run great risk. He fell on his head and was much hurt. As soon as he recovered himself, he returned to the engine, which had followed the waggons to within a short distance of the station.

The 'chock (or 'choke') block' was a strong wooden beam that could be pivoted across the rails on inclines and sidings and secured with a padlock so as to prevent wagons being blown down the line by a gale, or otherwise set in motion; the chock block at Leadburn was of the patent type used by the NBR, and provided with a cast-iron shoe, designed also to derail any runaways, but on this occasion the block was set too high.

The waggons, however, instead of being thrown off the line, knocked the chock-block on one side, and continued their course along the rails. They passed from the Linton line to the Leadburn coal-siding, and from that siding to the main line; and they forced open the main-line points (which were locked) as they went through. The station-master heard them approaching, and saw them run by at a speed of 15 or 20 miles an hour. He went to his telegraph instrument, and endeavoured to attract the attention of the next station, Penicuik [later 'Pomathorn'], 2½ miles distant in the direction of Edinburgh; but before he was able to do so, he found (in the course of about a minute and a half) that his instrument failed to work; and he concluded rightly that a collision had occurred between the runaway waggons and the train which was then overdue from Edinburgh.

The station porter was opening the gates of a level crossing near the station [at its northern end, across the Howgate road] in anticipation of the arrival of that train when the waggons approached him. He was in some doubt as to the course which he ought under these circumstances to adopt, but he decided upon letting them through, under the belief that if he kept his gates closed they would probably be broken to no purpose.

The waggons finally met the 4.20 pm fast passenger train from Edinburgh to Peebles at two miles from Leadburn, while they were travelling at a speed which must have been very great upon the falling gradient of 1 in 173 before referred to. The passenger train consisted of an engine and tender, five carriages, and a break-van. It left Penicuik about 5.13, nine minutes late, and was travelling at a speed of 15 or 20 miles an hour up this gradient, when the fireman suddenly saw the waggons 20 or 30 yards before him. He attempted to turn on his break, but of course without any good result. The engine-driver, who had just turned to look at his steam-gauge, saw nothing of the waggons until he struck them. They were both much hurt, the driver having been thrown against some part of his engine, and the fireman to the top of the carriage behind it; and the guard, who was riding at the tail of the train, was stunned in the first instance by the shock.

Two of the waggons ran in under the engine and were broken up, and a third, in front of them, was set on fire.

Three of the passenger carriages were much damaged, the second having mounted the third, and having been crushed by the first; the van and the carriage in front of it only, were in a condition to return to Penicuik. One passenger, a little boy, was unfortunately killed on the spot, five others are stated to have been injured, and all, perhaps 20 or 30 in number, must have been more or less hurt or shaken.

Seven-year-old Charles Tennant, son of Sir Charles Tennant of the Glen, a Director of the Peebles Railway, later Deputy Chairman of the North British Railway, and a shareholder in the LL&DR, had been travelling with his governess, Augusta Saye. He was killed; she was relatively uninjured. One passenger, a Mr Hodgson, from New Shildon, County Durham, was so badly injured that the NBR later settled his claim for damages and expenses for £1,000 – a very large sum in those days. At the NBR Board meeting on 14th July, 1865, the Secretary was authorized to offer a free pass to Mr and Mrs Tennant of the Glen on condition of their abandoning all claim for pecuniary compensation in respect of the death of their son. The pass was to be for the NBR's lines then existing, and so excluded the lines of the Edinburgh & Glasgow Railway with which the NBR was about to amalgamate, just two weeks later, on 1st August!

The Procurator Fiscal had begun an immediate inquiry after the accident. Both the brakesman, John Macnamara, and the contractor's engine driver, William Dudley, were arrested and brought before the Sheriff for judicial examination, charged with culpable violation of duty, and committed to prison. Captain Tyler RE was dispatched north to carry out the Board of Trade investigation.

At the LL&DR Board meeting on 9th November, a letter was read from the NBR's solicitors intimating that the NBR held the LL&DR liable for the damage caused to its plant &c, and 'the Secretary laid upon the Table correspondence between the Manager of the North British Railway and Mr John Bathgate in reference to the connection of this Line with the Peebles Railway'. It transpired that Thomas Bouch had recommended that catch points be installed at the coal siding at Leadburn to derail runaways, and that Bathgate had transmitted the recommendation to the NBR General Manager. The NBR had either ignored or overlooked the request and fitted a chock block instead. This, Captain Tyler concluded, was a 'serious oversight'; such an accident should have been anticipated, and adequate precautions taken:

> Looking to the mode in which operations are usually carried on by the servants of a contractor on a line in course of construction, it was not a very extraordinary circumstance that the waggons in question should run away, but it was a serious oversight to form the connection at Leadburn or to allow it to be formed, between very steep gradients on both lines, without a locked safety-switch for the protection of the traffic on the Peebles Railway. It is chiefly to the want of this simple addition that the occurrence of the accident must obviously be ascribed.

The report added that the contractor's fireman – Robert Donald – had been too badly injured to be interviewed, and he was not expected to recover; however, no record of his death has been discovered.

Meeting on 4th November, the Board of the Peebles Railway resolved that 'looking to the late distressing accident near Penicuik anxiously request that the North British Railway Company will now adopt all proper means to prevent the possibility of such an accident occurring in future, and in particular recommend that a throw off siding be placed at the junction of the Dolphinton line'.

At the next LL&DR Board meeting on 7th December, there was laid upon the table a Summons at the instance of the NBR against the company and John Waddell, concluding for payment of £1,000 for damage to plant. John Ord Mackenzie's partner, William Ramsay Kermack, undertook the negotiations with the NBR's solicitor, John Wood, and the LL&DR decided to defend the action. In this they were successful, the NBR being allowed to abandon its action against the LL&DR in February 1865 on payment of the latter's expenses. However, the NBR continued the civil action against Waddell, and the case was heard before a jury in March 1865. The Lord Justice Clerk, in summing up, laid considerable stress on the NBR's failure to provide a 'throw-off siding', and the jury, after an absence of only two minutes, returned a unanimous verdict for Waddell. This was in the days when any degree of contributory negligence on the part of the pursuer would entirely defeat the pursuer's claim and so, even if Waddell (as being legally responsible for the actions of his men) had been negligent – as may or may not have been the case – the slightest negligence on the part of the NBR wholly defeated its claim against him. Nowadays the NBR might have been successful, while having the amount of its claim considerably reduced because of its own 'contributory negligence' in not providing the 'throw-off' siding.

On 15th February, 1864, the driver, William Dudley, appeared at the High Court in Edinburgh charged with culpable homicide and culpable violation of duty, principally on the grounds of having undertaken the fateful journey without a brakesman, and having left his engine to attend to the couplings. Technical objections, taken by his defence counsel as to the way in which the indictment had been framed, were sustained by the Court, and the Crown deserted the case *pro loco et tempore*. Dudley was dismissed from the bar. Although he could have been re-tried on an amended indictment, no record has been found of a retrial. Among the witnesses who had been listed to give evidence for the defence were Mrs Dalgleish of the Leadburn Inn, James Young and James Gowans, well-known railway contractors, and the locomotive superintendent of the Edinburgh & Glasgow Railway, William Steel Brown, and his assistant, William Stroudley.

Meanwhile, the new line remained unopened, heavy winter rains being blamed, but the *Peeblesshire Advertiser* of 11th March reported that 'the stations at Cowden-Burn, Colly-burn, and West Linton, are all up and roofed in, while the present terminus at Dolphinton, which is to be entirely a wooden erection, is being put up' and Bouch assured the shareholders on 23rd March that the line would be ready for opening, at the latest, by the second week of April 'provided the weather continues

THE LEADBURN, LINTON, & DOLPHINTON RAILWAY COMPANY.

Secretary's Office

PEEBLES, _____ 186_

Mr McNemach reported that Mr Wood had proposed to him as Agent for the Co that the various actions of damages should be compromised on the footing of the North British, Messrs C, Mr Waldie & Co contracted paying each one third but he (Mr McNemach) had stated that the Co could not agree to this and referred Mr Wood to the previous communication wh had been made by the Sec to the Sec of the North British to the effect that while the Directors of this

Co declined all liability in connection with such claims they were willing that the claims should be settled by the North British Co without inquiry being claims of wh the said Co might have acquired. This Co in the footing that this Co will [not?] under any circumstances state any objections to the terms on which such claims might be compromised or settled, to which no reply had been made, but to which this Co was still willing to adhere. Approved J.

good'. The required notice requesting an inspection had been given to the Board of Trade.

Agreements with the North British

In February 1862, prior to obtaining its Act, the LL&DR had entered into an agreement with the NBR for the maintenance and working of the line. The LL&DR was to construct the line and all ancillary works, and to form the station at Leadburn 'so as to permit a convenient exchange of passengers, parcels, carriages, waggons' etc. between the LL&DR and the Peebles Railway – in effect, building another face to the existing platform. The Company's 1862 Act empowered the two companies to enter into agreements for the maintenance, management and working of the railway after its completion, but subject to the approval of the Board of Trade and the shareholders of both companies; and so another agreement, to confirm and supplement the former, was required.

The LL&DR was to make the alterations to the station at Leadburn and, when completed, hand over control to the NBR to work, maintain and manage, the necessary staff being provided by the NBR; the LL&DR retained ownership of the land it had purchased there. The NBR would be entitled to a payment of £100 per annum for providing maintenance and staffing, but the charge would be suspended during the continuance of the working agreement between the companies. The NBR would be entitled to 'terminals' – a handling charge levied per passenger, or per animal, ton of goods, minerals, etc for loading, unloading, storage and delivery – on all traffic received from or delivered to the public at Leadburn station. For example, 'for every third-class passenger, one penny', 'for every parcel, dog or calf, one penny', 'for every ton of minerals, of every kind, eightpence per ton'. As soon as the line was opened, the NBR would enter into possession for the purpose of working the line for an initial period of 10 years. As was usual in such agreements, the LL&DR would be responsible for maintaining and repairing the works for the first six months to the satisfaction of the NBR's Engineer – during which period any defects were likely to become apparent – with the NBR assuming responsibility thereafter. The NBR would not be required to run more than four trains daily, each way. The traffic would be managed by a joint committee of two Directors from each company but the NBR would be responsible for the appointment and control of all the staff, with the exception of the Secretary and those involved in the 'direction' of the LL&DR. The NBR appointed Chairman Richard Hodgson and Director Mark Sprot to the joint committee, the LL&DR representatives being Messrs Mackenzie and Forrester. Out of the gross revenue, the NBR would first pay the cost of cartage at the stations, together with taxes and other public burdens. The LL&DR would then receive 50 per cent of the balance, from which it would pay the salary of the Secretary, together with Directorial expenses, feu duties, interest on loans for works, and dividends to shareholders. In practice, none of the LL&DR Directors took a fee for their services; the Secretary's remuneration was £60 per annum, with an allowance of £15 per annum for a clerk. The Auditors declined a fee until the railway could pay a dividend. No dividends were ever paid by the LL&DR.

The agreement was approved by a Special Meeting of the shareholders at 9 Hill Street on 23rd March, 1864. Of the 13 present, seven were Directors. John Waddell was there too. This was a fairly typical attendance; most shareholders appear to have been content to leave the affairs of the company in the hands of the Directors. The NBR shareholders approved the working agreement on the same day.

Sites for Stations

The Directors agreed in November 1862 that there should be a 'Passenger Station' at Cowdenburn, where the line crossed under the road to Moffat (now the A701), and a 'Passenger and Mineral Station' where the road crossed the line at Coalyburn. A change of name from 'Cowdenburn' (the hamlet where the station was situated) to 'Lamancha' (the name of the estate of Director James Mackintosh) was agreed at their meeting on 12th September, 1863. 'Coalyburn' became 'Macbie Hill' in the June 1874 timetable. The principal station, 'West Linton', was to be at the crossing of the Broomlee road, some half a mile south-east of the village, 'and that a footpath be made alongside the Railway thereto from the old turnpike road leading to Blyth Bridge [the Bogsbank road]'. The footpath does not appear to have been made.

Before the line opened there was a spirited correspondence in the *Peeblesshire Advertiser* about the name for the station at Linton. William Forbes of Medwyn wrote 'there are so many Lintons in the United Kingdom – one in Cambridge, one in Yorkshire, one each in Huntingdon, Devon, East Lothian and Roxburgh, besides our own, and there may be others. I find my letters occasionally dancing all over Britain ... I propose that Linton should resume its ancient name of

Linton Roderick – there will be no difficulty with the Post Office authorities: all that is required is for the inhabitants to hold a meeting, form a resolution to restore the old name, and transmit a petition to the Secretary of State who will at once instruct the Post Office'. Someone replying from Romanno Bridge with the *nom de plume* of 'An Old Bookworm' declared there was no good reason for asserting its ancient name was Linton Roderick. It should be Lyntoun. The Leadburn Linton & Dolphinton Board was not impressed, and called the station 'West Linton' but, in August 1864, shortly after opening, the NBR wrote and 'urgently pressed a change of name': there was already a 'West Linton' station on its Border Union Railway, between Carlisle and Longtown (later renamed 'Lineside', then 'Lyneside'). The LL&DR assented, renaming the station 'Broomlee for West Linton' at its meeting on 23rd August.

Bouch's plans for the stations were generally approved, but with 'such alterations as he may deem expedient, having a tendency to reduce the cost'. Money was tight and there were to be no extravagances. The Chairman reported to the Board in October 1863 that he had arranged with shareholder Mr Charles Lawson of Deepsykehead for the immediate erection of the booking offices at Lamancha, Coalyburn and West Linton; the price is not recorded. These were erected and roofed in by March of the following year. Lawson's tender of £187 7s. 6d. for the station master's house at Linton, 'doing the whole work in a substantial tradesman-like manner', was also accepted – on 20th May, 1864, just six weeks before the line would open. Bouch was ordered to provide plans immediately for conveniences at this station. Plans for the station houses at Lamancha and Coalyburn, costing less than £150 each, were called for in July 1864 – after opening! When plans were produced the following month, they were 'ordered to be reduced within the limit mentioned at last meeting'. The Directors subsequently approved of 'the smallest plan' but it was agreed to delay their erection until the following spring. By the end of March 1865, they were under construction; from the payments made, it appears that these too were built by Charles Lawson. As we shall see, the stations and their facilities were less than basic! Lawson also tendered successfully for the engine shed at Dolphinton (£182 14s.) and goods shed at West Linton (£133 14s.).

As outlined in Chapter Nine, the Caledonian Railway was planning a railway line from Carstairs to Dolphinton. It obtained its Act on 11th May, 1863 but the line did not open until 1st March, 1867. In January 1863 the LL&DR decided to 'delay entering into the question of a joint station with the Caledonian Railway Company at Dolphinton'; the following October it was agreed to erect a 'temporary station' at Dolphinton. In between times, the Caledonian Minutes of 9th June, 1863 record the receipt of a letter from John Bathgate suggesting 'joint station arrangements', the matter being remitted to General Manager Christopher Johnstone to report. In July 1865, it was remitted to Johnstone to meet Mr Blyth, the CR's Consulting Engineer, on the ground, 'to arrange for a cheap station' for the CR. The LL&DR Directors returned to the matter in October 1865 when they considered 'the expediency of arrangement being made with that Company [the Caledonian] for a Joint Station there'. The Chairman and Mr Woddrop were delegated 'to further the arrangements in every possible manner', and the Secretary was instructed to let the Caledonian know and 'to express their readiness to meet any authorized party on behalf of the Caledonian Coy as soon as convenient', but there is no further reference to the matter in the LL&DR Minutes. The Caledonian Minutes of 10th October, 1865 record a letter from James D. Bathgate proposing a meeting as to a joint station at Dolphinton; the matter was remitted to Johnstone and Blyth, but there is no record of any further activity in the matter. It would seem that the Caledonian's Dolphinton branch was intended to block infiltration by the NBR into Caley territory rather than to provide a convenient service to the public.

Each station required a clock, and an offer by James Ritchie & Son of Edinburgh to supply 'four timepieces of the best quality of workmanship and construction to go for eight days with one winding', showing the time upon two dials, one facing outside, each 15 inches diameter, for £9 each, was accepted in April 1864.

Cowans, Sheldon & Co. provided a turntable at Leadburn and one at Dolphinton for £584 8s. The 1922 NBR *Appendix to the Working Time Tables* shows these as being 42 feet long. A loading bank crane was approved for West Linton, and one for Coalyburn, at a cost of £25. Each station was to have a 'steelyard' – a large straight-beam balance weighing machine – at a cost of £26 each.

The NBR agreed to share the cost of a water tank to be erected at Leadburn. So far as the station houses were concerned, a supply of water for Dolphinton could be brought in by gravitation; the West Linton water supply came from a well in the station house garden, operated by a hand pump still in use when the line closed; and it was remitted to Mr Mackintosh to get water brought in for the station at Lamancha at a cost not exceeding £3 if possible, 'also a wire fence round the garden'. The drinking water for Macbie Hill was latterly brought in daily by train.

The Inspections and Opening of the Line

Before a passenger-carrying line could be opened to the public, it had to pass an inspection by an Inspecting Officer from the Railways Department of the Board of Trade, the inspectors being drawn from the ranks of the Royal Engineers. Captain Frederick H. Rich (later Colonel, and Chief Inspecting Officer) intimated that he would inspect the line on Saturday 21st May, 1864. Secretary J.D. Bathgate had arranged with the NBR to provide engines – although only one was supplied – for the inspection. Unfortunately, matters did not go to plan and the Captain's verdict was that the line 'cannot be opened for passenger traffic without danger to the public using the same by reason of the incompleteness of the works'– the standard formula.

The most serious faults related to some of the cast-iron girders on bridges, four of which appeared to be honeycombed and others being poorly cast. One girder would have to be replaced, and the original broken up on site when the Captain came to re-inspect the line, so that he might make a judgment as to the probable condition of the others. Three of the larger bridges couldn't be adequately tested for deflection under the weight of traffic, as only one locomotive had been supplied by the NBR. Some of the girders were not standing vertically, the bottom flanges having been deflected outwards; transverse girders would be required to keep them in place. Lamancha station was on a gradient of 1 in 92 – unsafe for a station in the event of a runaway – and much steeper than shown on the authorized plans; it would have to be improved to at least 1 in 250. Coalyburn station was on a 1 in 121 gradient, and it too would have to be altered. West Linton station was on a gradient of 1 in 173 – quite unnecessarily so according to the Inspecting Officer, as the adjacent sidings were on the level, but as it was situated at the foot of the incline from the summit of the line, he did not require it to be altered. None of the signals was complete, so far as the fixing of the lamps, and the distant signal from Leadburn would not act properly, owing to the very temporary framing to which the gear was fastened. The chairs used to hold the rails in place were very light and the Captain did not consider them sufficiently large or strong to secure the safety of the permanent way; additional, heavier chairs should be inserted next to every joint in the rails. Clocks were required at the stations (already ordered); and there had been a deviation of the line near Lamancha station outwith the limits authorized by Parliament for which the landowner's assent to the encroachment had to be provided.

The inspector noted that a house had to be provided for the crossing keeper at the level crossing at Linton station, as the station did not afford such accommodation. This requirement was laid down in the LL&DR's Act, subject to a fine of £20, and a daily penalty of £10 thereafter, if the company failed to erect the lodge or appoint a crossing keeper. Despite this, it was 1889 before the NBR decided to erect a lodge. Perhaps the station house adjoining the level crossing was accepted as satisfying the requirements of the Act.

Deficiencies in construction were not uncommon on new lines and Bouch's resident engineer, John Carline, set about correcting them. Captain Rich re-inspected the line on 30th June and expressed himself satisfied in his letter to the Board of Trade, written from Dolphinton the following day. The chairs had not been altered, having turned out to be slightly heavier than those first inspected and, as the line was not a main line, and would not be worked at high speed, Captain Rich was prepared to accept them; Chairman John Ord Mackenzie had undertaken to have all renewals made with heavier ones. It was stipulated that the points of the cross-over road to the North British main line at Leadburn should always be kept locked against the branch trains except when in use for the transfer of goods and carriages. The line, being a single line with no passing stations, was to be worked by Train Staff – possession of the physical staff being the driver's authority to occupy the line.

The text of the Inspection Reports (not fully decipherable) is reproduced in Appendix One.

Under its agreement with the NBR, the LL&DR was responsible for the maintenance of the line for the first six months, but it asked the NBR to carry this out on its behalf. The NBR agreed to do so for the sum of £35 per mile and, on Bouch's recommendation, the offer was accepted.

With his work completed, John Carline sought a Testimonial from the Board, and 'the Chairman was authorized to state to Mr Carline that the Directors had much pleasure in testifying to his zealous attention as Resident Engineer on the line in the course of its formation during the last two years and it ... will afford this Board much pleasure to learn that Mr Carline meets with that success in his future career of which they consider him so well deserving.' Born in North Yorkshire, Carline had worked for Bouch for nine years, both in England and Scotland. He went on to become Surveyor to the Lewisham District Board of Works for over 30 years. In March 1877 we find him writing to Bouch, asking that he propose him for Associate Membership of the Institution of Civil Engineers; at that time, Bouch was abroad for the sake of his health. Carline was duly elected on 4th December, 1877. He died at Melrose on 26th September, 1905 and his

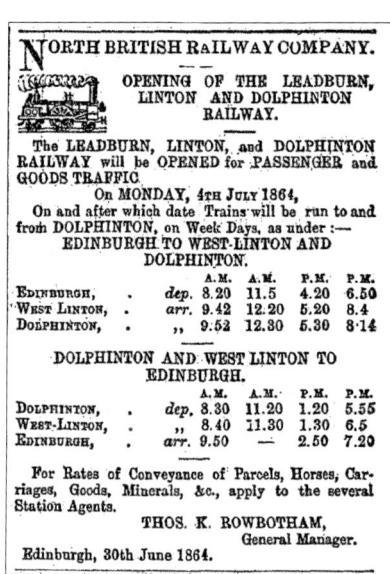

Press intimation of the opening of the line on 4th July, 1864.

obituary talks of his work in 'successfully carrying the line over Leadburn Moss, one of the deepest mosses in the south of Scotland'.

Having passed its re-inspection on Thursday 30th June, 1864, the line entered into the possession of the NBR, which lost no time in opening it to the public on Monday 4th July. There were no formal celebrations to mark the event, but the day must have lived long in the memory of the local population at a time when travel outwith one's immediate locality was very much the exception.

The *Peeblesshire Advertiser* predicted a great future for the line once the Caledonian had built the extension to Carstairs, 'after which there will be an unbroken line of railroad from Dalkeith to Glasgow. The Dolphinton line, therefore, which is at present a small offshoot of the Peebles line, will shortly form a central part of an important trunk line of railway, by which the inhabitants of Peebles, by going as far as Leadburn, will have a ready communication with the west country lines.' The Caledonian had different ideas!

A Short Period of Independent Existence

At the General Meeting on 22nd October, 1864, the number of Directors fell to be reduced from nine to six in terms of the Company's Act of 1862 and Messrs White, Beresford and Fergusson intimated their intention to retire. John White was later re-appointed on the death of Richard Gordon of Halmyre on 22nd May, 1865. Gordon, a prominent landowner, a Director of the Peebles Railway and a supporter of the several proposals for a railway to Linton, had been kicked by his horse and had sustained a severe fracture of the leg below the knee. The local doctor was called, and the local minister set off for Edinburgh by train, returning with a physician, Professor Syme. Amputation followed that evening and, as so often happened in those days, death quickly supervened.

The Caledonian was still apparently making overtures to the LL&DR (not recorded in the LL&DR Minutes), probably in an unsuccessful attempt to persuade it to sever its connection with the NBR. The Minutes of the Caledonian Railway, always frustratingly brief, only hint at what was happening:

> General Committee 8/11/1864. Mr Ainslie [Director] reported and was authorised to communicate with the Directors of the Leadburn & Dolphinton and give them the opportunity of meeting the Committee here on Tuesday next at one o'clock in reference to the offer he is authorised to make.
>
> Board 29/11/1864. Mr Ainslie reported his & Mr Mackay's [CR Solicitor] meeting of yesterday with representatives of the Leadburn Linton & Dolphinton Coy & a memorandum of the meeting and accompanying letter from Mr Mackay also letter from Mr Forbes of Medwyn were read. The working agreement between the LL&D and the North British was also produced. Remit to Mr Ainslie & Mr Mackay, and to report from time to time.

By July 1863, the financial difficulties that would eventually bring to an end the company's independent existence had already begun to make themselves felt. There were insufficient funds to complete the line and the Directors resolved to borrow £25,000 from the Union Bank of Scotland. As additional security for the loan, they agreed to give their personal guarantees, subject to the company agreeing to relieve them of their obligations. A Special Meeting of Shareholders held in the Somervail School on 12th September, 1863 approved the arrangements, at the same time expressing its thanks to the Directors 'for the great interest they have shewn in the prosecution of the undertaking'.

At the Half-Yearly meeting of shareholders in October 1863, the Directors still had 'every expectation that the whole capital will be ultimately subscribed for', but it was a hopeless expectation. Against the authorized share capital of £40,000, only £20,500 was eventually issued, of which £208 10s. wasn't paid when called. Payments on capital account would eventually total £45,553 – a cost of some £4,550 per mile against the estimate of £4,000 – to which had to be added £3,014 for interest charges on the loan of £25,000:

Preliminary & Parliamentary Expenses	£1,274
Engineering Expenses	2,000
Expenses of Works	37,648
Expenses of Stations	1,402
Sundries	400
Expenses of Management	225
Land Compensation	2,287
Tenants' Claims	317
TOTAL	45,553
Interest on bank loan (to 31/1/1866)	3,014

As for Revenue, that had been estimated in the Prospectus at not less than £70 per week, of which rather more than half would be retained by the NBR under the terms of the working agreement. The shareholders were told on 22nd October, 1864 that the revenue for the first month of operation (July 1864) was considered satisfactory, and that the return for August showed a considerable increase. But the LL&DR's share for the first seven months of operation, to the end of January 1865, worked out at only £11 13s. 4d. per week. There was a slight improvement in the half-year to 31st July, 1865, but only to £13 11s. per week. The Directors continued to hope that as the resources of the district became more developed, larger returns could be expected, and indeed these rose to £15 per week for the half-year to 31st January, 1866.

Meanwhile, the interest due on the bank loan was accumulating. On 13th October, 1865, the Secretary of the Union Bank of Scotland wrote to require that the sum outstanding – £27,137 10s. – be reduced to the original sum of £25,000. It was left to the Chairman to negotiate with the Bank, and a meeting was called for 22nd November to hear the outcome. But there had been developments: the Chairman had agreed with Adam Johnstone, the NBR's Solicitor, to the promotion of a Bill to allow the NBR to amalgamate with, or lease, the railway. The Directors agreed unanimously to seek amalgamation and notice was given in the official *Edinburgh Gazette* of 24th November, 1865. Whether this situation had all along been anticipated, or was now reluctantly forced upon the company, is not clear; the continuing efforts of the Directors to secure additional shareholdings suggest the latter.

The meeting of Directors on 10th January, 1866 unanimously approved a Draft Minute of Agreement for the amalgamation. Under a Bill to be promoted by both companies in Parliament, the amalgamation would, unusually, be backdated to 31st July, 1865, with the NBR paying off the LL&DR debts of £28,600. LL&DR shareholders would become holders of Leadburn Preference Stock and receive, half-yearly, beginning in March 1866, a dividend equivalent to the dividend paid on NBR Ordinary stock for the immediately preceding half year. The NBR would be entitled to issue the unsubscribed LL&DR share capital and also to exercise the borrowing powers in the LL&DR's 1862 Act. Mr Forbes reminded the meeting of the obligation to provide a siding on his land, should it ever be required, but the Chairman had already intimated this to the NBR. The Directors signed and sealed the agreement on 30th January.

The dividend that the LL&DR shareholders would receive in March 1866, for the half-year to 31st January, 1866, was at the rate of 3 per cent per annum, as declared for NBR Ordinary shareholders for the half-year to 31st July, 1865. Unfortunately, there were to be no more dividends for NBR Ordinary shareholders until March 1872. The NBR's books of account had been systematically cooked on the instructions of Chairman Richard Hodgson, albeit for no personal gain, but largely to hide the huge cost over-run on the construction of the Border Union Railway (from Hawick to Carlisle). Revenue expenses were being charged to capital, or lost in suspense accounts, in order to justify the payment of a dividend. The company was facing a massive shortfall of £1.875 million. Chairman Hodgson, a majority of the Board, the accountant, James Lythgoe, and the General Manager, Thomas Rowbotham, were all casualties and left the company. The NBR was hard up for most of its existence, and the LL&DR shareholders would have fared very much better had they thrown in their lot with the Caledonian! It would take a former Caledonian Director – the new NBR Chairman, John Stirling of Kippendavie and Kippenross – to rescue the North British.

On 15th June, 1866, a Special General Meeting was held at the premises of Messrs Mackenzie & Kermack WS at 9 Hill Street, Edinburgh. Only six shareholders were present: Chairman John Ord Mackenzie*, Directors John Forrester WS of Edinburgh, William A. Woddrop of Garvald and John White of Drummelzier, shareholder Alexander Cunningham of Newholm, and Secretary James D. Bathgate. Forty-eight other shareholders had sent in proxies in favour of the Chairman. Under Parliamentary Standing Orders, a meeting of shareholders was required to consider and approve the amalgamation Bill, as presently pending in Parliament. 'A copy of the Bill referred to was submitted to the Meeting and read and the clauses explained. It was then moved by John Ord Mackenzie Esq seconded by John White Esq and unanimously Resolved That the Bill or Act now submitted to the Meeting entitled Act to Amalgamate the Leadburn Linton and Dolphinton Railway Company with the North British Railway Company be approved of.'

The Act received the Royal Assent on 16th July, 1866 and the LL&DR ceased to exist as a separate company.

---

* John Ord Mackenzie died on 14th March, 1902, four days short of his 91st birthday, the 'father' of the Society of Writers to Her Majesty's Signet (the WS Society), of which his father had been Deputy Keeper of the Signet.

Chapter Four

Along the Line

The Route Described

The LL&DR made its junction with the Peebles Railway at Leadburn, situated just north of the Peeblesshire county boundary in the County of Edinburgh (later 'Midlothian'), and at a height of some 860 feet above sea level, in an area of bleak moorland. The Peebles Railway had a single-platform station there to serve its single line; the station was on the west side of the line, backing on to the Howgate road and opposite the Leadburn Inn. The LL&DR shared the station with the Peebles Railway: as the Inspecting Officer had put it, the intention was 'to deposit the passengers at the outer side of the passenger platform at Leadburn'.

Leaving Leadburn, the LL&DR line ran parallel to, and on the west side of, the Peebles branch, each line spanning the Peebles road on its own adjacent bridge some 175 yards south of the Leadburn crossroads; after another 350 yards or so, the Peebles line continued due southwards while the LL&DR struck off south-westwards. The summit of the Peebles branch lay immediately to the south of this point, at around 920 feet. The LL&DR continued to climb steeply over Leadburn Moss, at 1 in 70 and 1 in 80 gradients to the summit of the line at Mitchell Hill, 985 feet above sea level, a mile and a half from Leadburn. From there it was downhill on gentler gradients, over meadow and arable land, passing Whim Farm where it crossed over the Black Yett road to Eddleston, then turning westwards to reach the station of Lamancha, 2 miles and 52 chains from Leadburn. Originally to have been called Cowdenburn, the station lay a few yards south of that settlement, where the line crossed under the Moffat road (today's A701).

The line continued to fall, at gradients of up to 1 in 80, to the next station at Coalyburn, later 'Macbie Hill', where a section of moorland again intervened. It was 4 miles and 10 chains distant from Leadburn, and situated about a mile north of the entrance to Macbiehill House, a bridge over the railway carrying the minor road that connected the Moffat Road at Whitmuir with Upper Whitfield and the Biggar road south of Carlops. From Coalyburn, the line turned south-west again and continued on a falling gradient, including a mile and three-quarters at 1 in 70, before crossing the road connecting West Linton to the Moffat road (today's B7059) on the level and immediately reaching the principal station on the line – Broomlee – situated 6 miles and 29 chains from

Leadburn. Broomlee lay a little over half a mile south-east of the village of West Linton.

Continuing south-westwards, the Lyne Water was crossed just beyond the platform end; the railway then bridged the ford at the point where the Bogsbank Road crossed the West Water, locally known as 'the Splash'. Skirting the southern edge of the White Moss and turning westwards, it crossed the minor Thief's Road near Hyndfordwell on an ungated crossing. Another ungated crossing of the track from Felton followed as the line again turned south-westwards to parallel the southern tail of the Pentlands and the Biggar road to Dolphinton (A702), having climbed slowly for a mile and a half, and descended for a similar distance at 1 in 86, through pasture and arable land. A final moderate ascent over Ingraston Moss and another ungated level crossing over an old cart road brought it to the southern terminus of the LL&DR at Dolphinton, 9 miles and 70 chains from Leadburn. The village of Dolphinton proper lay across the county boundary in Lanarkshire, some two-thirds of a mile away; the LL&DR stopped some 600 yards short of that boundary.

The Stations

We have already seen how little money was spent on constructing the station houses and booking offices. The May 1893 report by Major F.A. Marindin of the Railway Inspectorate of his inspection of the new signalling arrangements on the line (described in Chapter Eight), makes reference to the condition of the stations. By this time an additional platform had been laid in at Leadburn. He described the stations thus:

> Leadburn Junction – the junction of the Dolphinton branch. This station has two platforms, with good accommodation, and a footbridge crossing the platforms. Requirement. Nil.
>
> La Mancha Station. The accommodation for passengers is wretched, being a mere shed, with no conveniences whatever for ladies. Requirements. A loop with second platform and proper accommodation; improvement of existing platform.
>
> Macbie Hill Station. This is a similar station to La Mancha, but the accommodation is even worse, for there is not even a urinal. Requirements. A loop with second platform and proper accommodation for passengers; improvement of existing platform.
>
> Broomlee Station. This is a station with one platform and goods sidings. The accommodation for passengers is insufficient, as there is nothing but a shed, with no conveniences for ladies. Requirement. Improved waiting room accommodation.

Dolphinton Station. The terminus. The single platform at this station is short and low, and there is no waiting room accommodation worthy of the name, there being no convenience whatever for ladies.

Requirements. Improved accommodation for passengers and improved platform.

The NBR's Works Committee had ordered the painting of the branch stations in April 1874, at a cost of £35, but there would have been precious little to be painted!

As explained in Chapter Eight, the second platforms at Lamancha and Macbie Hill referred to by Major Marindin were not required. The NBR submitted plans in October 1894 showing proposed improvements, and Major Marindin inspected the work at the beginning of December 1895. He reported that the stations at Broomlee and Dolphinton 'have been practically rebuilt, and the whole of the stations ... , formerly very inadequate as to accommodation, are now in a very satisfactory state.' It is not clear what authority the Board of Trade and its Railway Inspectorate had to require improvements in the passenger accommodation of stations already open for business. In October 1896, as part of a long-running dispute with the NBR for a better station, Berwick Town Council sent a 'memorial' to the Board of Trade, seeking its support. The Board's reply was that it had no power to require the NBR to make improvements. The Town Council of Musselburgh

An undated view of the Dolphinton branch bay platform at Leadburn, with the run-round loop nearest the camera. *Bill Lynn collection*

68   THE LEADBURN, LINTON AND DOLPHINTON RAILWAY

received a similar reply in March 1903 after it complained about the narrowness of the station platform there. No matter! Passengers on the LL&DR got their improved facilities.

Leadburn Station

Dolphinton branch trains to Leadburn ran into their own dock platform, on a new west face to the existing platform. The line terminated at a turntable beside the station buildings and station access road, and a parallel loop line, with a short siding at its southern end, allowed the engine to run-round its train. Branch trains could also access the Peebles

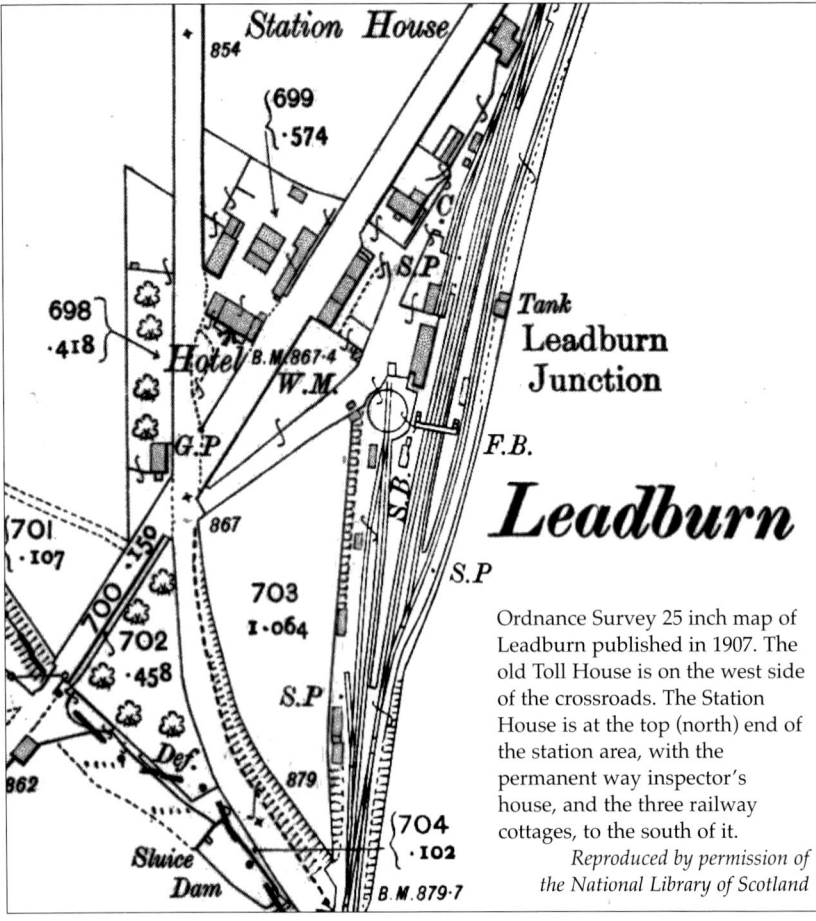

Ordnance Survey 25 inch map of Leadburn published in 1907. The old Toll House is on the west side of the crossroads. The Station House is at the top (north) end of the station area, with the permanent way inspector's house, and the three railway cottages, to the south of it.
Reproduced by permission of the National Library of Scotland

main line platform from a facing crossover. Initially the station access road came off the crossroads of the Peebles and Moffat roads, but in 1947 the LNER sold 100 square yards of land to the County Council to improve the crossroads while also improving access to the station.

The first station at Leadburn, opened with the Peebles line on 4th July, 1855, appears to have been a very basic affair. The *Peeblesshire Advertiser* of 20th October, 1877 reported a fire in the booking office, with 'a temporary booking office in course of erection until a new station can be provided'. The NBR's Works Committee recommended the erection of new offices at a cost of £460, to be charged against its Insurance Fund. The cause of the fire is supposed to have been the high wind which caused some coals to fall from the fireplace; there is no suggestion that the desire for a better station had played any part!

On 10th September, 1892 the same newspaper described the altered layout at Leadburn in connection with the installation of the block signalling system – in particular, a second platform, a new signal box, and a passing loop:

> The most extensive alterations occur at Leadburn Junction, where a handsome, towering cabin has been erected to accommodate the 38 levers and switches now concentrated within it. At this station also, a goods shed, a reserve siding and a platform for detraining of passengers with the down* trains are all in course of construction. An overhead bridge will afford a means for crossing from the one platform to the other.

The new signal box was on the down (to Edinburgh) platform beside the footbridge; its predecessor had been beyond the south end of the down platform. In its final incarnation, the main station building on the down platform was a rectangular brick structure with a hipped slate roof; on the new up platform there was a timber waiting room with hipped slate roof. A siding ran behind the up platform and there were two sidings and a goods shed at the north end of the down platform with a 30 cwt crane. The water tank was towards the north end of the up siding, with a water column at the north end of the down platform and, presumably, one at the north end of the Dolphinton bay platform.

NBR staff records exist for the period from 18th April, 1874. At that date, the Leadburn 'Agent' (which is what the NBR called its station masters) was James Brown. He was paid £52 per annum and had a rent-free house. There was also a signalman, a signal porter, porter, and two female

---

* Actually, the 'up' trains. From Edinburgh to Peebles and Dolphinton (and London!) was the 'up' direction, and to Edinburgh was 'down'. Before October 1867, it was the other way round.

gatekeepers for the level crossings at Easterdeans and Earlyvale on the Peebles line between Leadburn and Eddleston. James Brown was dismissed and replaced from 27th October, 1879 by James Wilson, who had come from Middleton on the Wansbeck line. He resigned, aged 62, on 5th June, 1909.

The station house was located at the north end of the station, close to the level crossing carrying the Edinburgh – Peebles line over the Howgate road. A little to the south, between the Howgate Road and the station access road, was a house ('Station Road Cottage') built for the 'Travelling Foreman' in the Engineer's Department, authorized in July 1893 by the NBR Works Committee; the estimated cost was £190. A block of three railway cottages, dating from 1859, lay immediately to the south of that.

The 1901 Census gives a picture of the small railway community. In the Station House was station master James Wilson, aged 53, originally from Manor, Peeblesshire, with his wife and son, still at school. In Station Road Cottage was permanent way inspector Adam Kerr, aged 44, with his wife, school-age son, and his daughter, who at age 17 was a 'Pupil School Teacher'. Mr Kerr formerly resided at Venture Fair level crossing cottage, north of Leadburn, where his wife was gatekeeper; he features in Press reports over a number of years, describing the efforts to keep the Peebles and Dolphinton branches open during periods of severe snow. In one of the three railway cottages was Robert

The three Leadburn railway cottages and the permanent way inspector's house, with the station access road in the foreground. The Leadburn to Howgate road is beyond the cottages.
Alison MacDonald collection

Leadburn looking to Edinburgh on 13th June, 1953. The replacement brick signal box is being built around the frame of the existing box. A brake van stands in the former Dolphinton dock platform which by this time has lost its edging and the run-round connection has been removed.　　*J. L. Stevenson*

Leadburn in the snow. Class 'B1' 4-6-0 locomotive No. 61332 on a Peebles passenger train on 8th February, 1958.　　*Stuart Sellar*

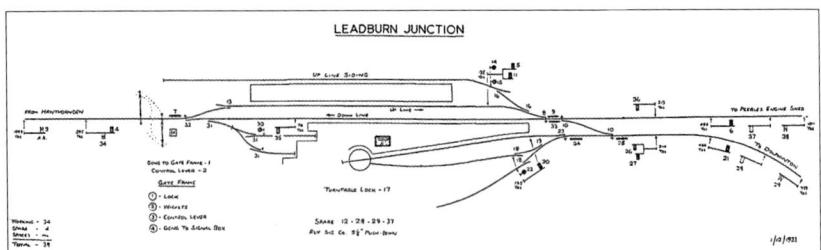

The Leadburn Junction signalling diagram drawn on 1st December, 1933, shortly after the closure of the Dolphinton branch to passenger traffic.
Forbes Alexander/Rae Montgomery collection

Borrowman, aged 57, a railway surfaceman, and his wife; in another was railway signalman Robert Johnston, aged 44, with his wife and five school-age children, and a boarder – 26-year old David Wilson; in the third cottage was foreman platelayer James Anderson, aged 30, and his wife Christina, from West Linton.

James Wilson was replaced by John Reid, previously at Rosslynlee, who also acted as sub-postmaster. By January 1919 his salary was £80 per annum, with rent of £7 10s., but it had risen to £230 on 1st August, 1919, following the very substantial post-First World War increases awarded that year to reflect the soaring cost of living.* A popular and well kent figure, John Reid retired on 30th September, 1930 at the age of 64 after 21 years at Leadburn. A ceremony of the kind that took place in small communities all over the country, on the transfer or retiral of their station master, was held in the booking-office at Leadburn when 'Mr Reid was waited upon by the staff and presented with a wallet of notes upon the occasion of his retiral'. The contributions had come from the staff and the travelling public alike. The staff ledger records 'No succ[essor] req[uired]' and the station came under the supervision of Mr Greig at Broomlee from 6th October, 1930 until the Dolphinton branch closed; Peebles took over supervision from 8th May, 1933. Mr Greig's LNER notebook records that in March 1932 the Rev. Mr R.H. Glendinning, Howgate, was given permission to hold evening meetings at Leadburn booking hall once a month 'fire and light provided'. The station closed to passenger traffic on 7th March, 1955** and, along with the Peebles branch, to all traffic on 5th February, 1962.

---

* During the War, War Bonus and War Wages had supplemented the basic wage.

** Passenger trains continued to stop to exchange the single line token, but passengers were forbidden to join or alight as the station was officially closed!

Leadburn station looking south in the 1930s. After crossing the Peebles road, the Peebles and Dolphinton lines ran parallel for 400 yards before diverging.

Bill Lynn collection

A view of the 'Farewell to Peebles' SLS Railtour at Leadburn on 3rd February, 1962 with class J37 0-6-0 locomotive No. 64587 (ex-NBR 467 of 1918).

WAC Smith/Transport Treasury

Notice of the withdrawal of passenger services from Leadburn station.

J.L. Stevenson

Leadburn featured in a newspaper article of 23rd June, 1944 entitled *From the Whim Road* by Alex Aitken MA, who for many years wrote about the district and its railway under the pen name of *A Linton Plooman*:

Leadburn Junction. Surely none who knows it will deny that Leadburn merits a paragraph and a heading all to itself. It just misses being in Peeblesshire but the postal authorities have always associated it with our county. Were it not for the railway there would not be much in the place, for only the inn, on the Midlothian side of the line, and the farm, on the Peeblesshire side, would remain. Doubtless the cross roads suggested to the railway planners that this was the place for the far-off horizons. Long ago the finger post contented itself with saying that Moffat was 39 miles off, but now the sign more grandiosely reads "Fork right for Carlisle". As a junction Leadburn cannot have been held in the kindliest remembrance by the travellers who were forced to wait connections there by the vagaries of old-time compilers of railway time-tables. Leadburn seems to have exerted a most malign influence over them. Forty minutes to wait was quite a common sentence. To be fair, however, the waiting room was commodious and airy and clean if not always well appointed in the matter of a fire. Kindly men about the place usually saw to it that adequate warmth was supplied, though not always in the official fireplace. A crack in the office, or the porters' room, made many a long waiting period seem all too short. During a miners' strike of 1912 the time-tables excelled themselves, for then travellers between Peebles and the Dolphinton branch had to wait close on three hours at Leadburn. Only necessary journeys were undertaken, but great arguments were settled. Now Leadburn has lost its position as a junction for passengers, and its waiting room, still as bright and commodious, must be largely untenanted, save when it serves as a church for the neighbourhood if the old happy arrangement still subsists between the Company and the minister of Howgate.

The other memorable feature about Leadburn is its bridge. The branch passengers often found themselves compelled to cross it, and that could be a hazardous enough venture on a stormy January night. But not in high summer.

The crews of two SMT buses pose for the photographer at Leadburn Crossroads, probably in the early 1930s. Ahead lies the road to Penicuik, with the Howgate road branching off to the right. Bus SC 2071 was a Maudslay of 1928, withdrawn in 1935/36. The prominent building is the Leadburn Inn. *Alison MacDonald collection*

Looking north from the Down platform of Leadburn station towards the level crossing over the Howgate road in 1960. *Tom Pyemont*

BR class 'J37' 0-6-0 No. 64607 (ex-NBR 301 of 1919), working the Hardengreen local goods, on the crossover at the north end of the up platform at Leadburn station on 11th November, 1961. The station house is on the left, the up line siding is on the extreme right, and the gates of the level crossing over the Howgate road are in the centre background.

Rae Montgomery

Former BR Mark 1 coach used as a dining extension at the rear of the Leadburn Inn, photographed in 1985. The Leadburn Inn was totally destroyed by fire on the morning of 12th November, 2005 when a car travelling north on the Moffat road failed to negotiate the junction, embedded itself in the building, and exploded. The Inn was subsequently rebuilt.

Bill Roberton

Of all the stations in Scotland that I know Aviemore alone equals the view from Leadburn. If it surpasses it that is only because the Cairngorms are grander than the Pentlands nor do our southern hills have anything like the Larig Ghru to show ...

Lamancha Remembered was the title of a letter to the Press on 18th May, 1979 and Leadburn was remembered in it too:

> I well remember the cry: 'Leadburn, Leadburn – change for Lamancha, Macbiehill, Broomlee and Dolphinton'. Out we got and crossed the line – no one ever used the footbridge – to the other side where the little tank engine, 'Dumpy' we called it, was being pushed laboriously round on the turntable and coupled up ready to take us the remaining two miles home.
>
> Leadburn was said to be the highest junction in Britain, about 800 feet, the same as Arthur's Seat. The station was dominated by what looked like an elevated greenhouse. It was actually the signalbox, but how the signalman managed to see out was a mystery, as all the window space seemed totally blocked by potted geraniums.

The demolition of the Peebles branch bridge at Leadburn on 6th November, 1962. Health and Safety was obviously less of a consideration in those days!

The Scotsman Publications/Evening Dispatch

On the evening of Saturday 7th June, 1890, the station was the scene of an armed battle between two opposing forces, one of which occupied the station and came under fire from the other. But it was just the Volunteers on exercises and no blood was spilled.

'Leadburn' or 'Leadburn Junction'? The NBR never quite made up its mind. The company's Working Time Tables for the Peebles line and for the branch had it as 'Leadburn Junction' throughout. In the Public Timetables, it was initially 'Leadburn' for the branch and 'Leadburn Junction' for the Peebles line, but 'Junction' was dropped from the latter in the late 1880s. The main station name board had it as plain 'Leadburn'.

Lamancha Station

Known previously as Romanno Grange, the rather unusual name for this property on the road to Moffat is explained by a former owner having at one time lived in the Spanish province of La Mancha. (The 'ch' in the name is pronounced locally as a hard 'k'.) James Mackintosh, a

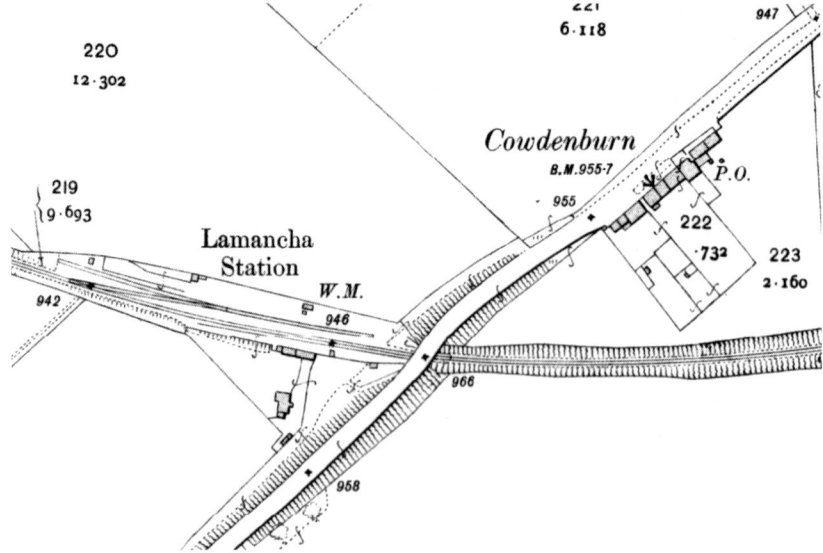

Ordnance Survey 25inch map of Lamancha published in 1908. The line from Leadburn (to the east) passes under the Moffat Road (later A701). The station house is to the south of the station buildings, and a weighing machine is shown on the north side of the line. The station is located a few yards south-west of the hamlet of Cowdenburn, which boasted a Post Office. *Reproduced by permission of the National Library of Scotland*

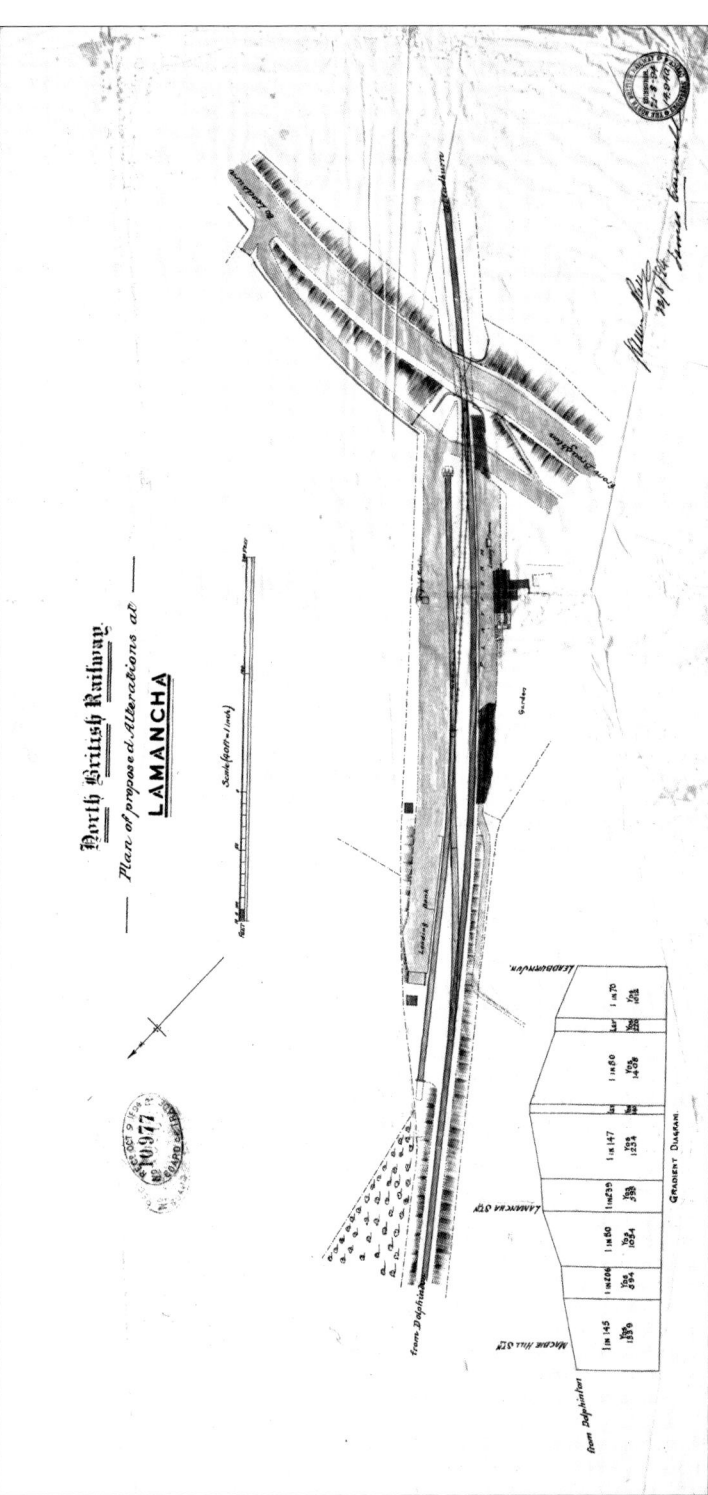

NBR August 1894 plan of Lamancha station showing the proposed additional station buildings, the platform extension, and the removal of the crossover at the east end of the station. The loading bank is at the west end of the yard.
Reproduced by permission of the National Archives, Kew, Ref MT 6/718/1

The presence of the station nameboard suggests that this view was taken while the station was open, or shortly afterwards. However, the long building behind the station nameboard, not shown on earlier plans or later photographs, is a puzzle and appears different from the wartime extension seen in the photograph on page 81. The small wooden building with windows and gable roof in the centre of the image presumably housed the ground frame. *Bill Lynn collection*

Director of the LL&DR, acquired it in 1832. He sunk coal pits, built lime kilns, and brick and tile works, and provided a school.*

The revisions to the 1858 Ordnance Survey 6-inch map show the platform and its rudimentary stone and timber buildings on the south side of the running line, and there is a loop line on the north side with short sidings off it. The NBR's 1894 plan for the improvements required by Major Marindin shows the removal of the points at the east end of the loop, so converting it into a siding with access from the west end only. This was in connection with the restrictions on shunting on the steep gradient, described in Chapter Eight. Other improvements included extensions to both ends of the platform, lengthening it to 300 feet, and the addition of a ladies' waiting room and urinals etc at the west end of the existing booking office and waiting room block. The locking frame, to control the points, is shown on the platform to the east of the station buildings. There is a loading bank at the west end of the siding and a weighing machine in the yard. The station house was set back at right angles from the south side of the line, with access from the Moffat road.

Lamancha station never figured prominently in the records of the North British Railway, but on 16th September, 1897 the NBR Works

---

* From *Pentland Days and Country Ways* by Will Grant (1934).

Committee considered its water supply: 'The Committee approved of permission being granted to Mr James McIntosh, Lamancha … to lay a water pipe across the Railway near Lamancha station, subject to the usual conditions, the Company to contribute a sum not exceeding £12 towards the cost, to pay half the cost of maintenance of the pipe from the spring to the Company's communication [sic] and Mr McIntosh to provide free of charge by means of a connecting pipe of agreed upon dimensions, to be laid by the Company, a continuous and efficient water supply to that Station.'

Lamancha was the least busy of the four branch stations in terms of 'Merchandise and Livestock Forwarded and Received', and broadly comparable to Macbie Hill in terms of passengers booked (*see Appendix Two*). For the year ended (y.e.) 31st July, 1874, the first for which records survive, it booked 2,412 passengers. Its best year was y.e. July 1898 when 3,703 passengers were booked, but in the y.e. June 1932, the last full year of operation, it booked only 1,456. The period from 1897 to 1901 saw a boost in passenger numbers and mineral tonnage on the branch, this being the time of construction of the large-capacity aqueduct to carry water from the great Talla Dam on the headwaters of the River Tweed to Fairmilehead, to supply the City of Edinburgh, over 30 miles distant. The Talla scheme was inaugurated on 20th May, 1905 when the valves were

Lamancha station buildings looking towards Leadburn on 30th May, 1954, with the A701 road bridge in the background. The building nearest the camera, consisting of ladies waiting room and WCs etc, was erected as part of the improvements to the original 'wretched' facilities, ordered by the Board of Trade. The long building between the station house and the road, of which no trace now remains, may have housed the railway administrative offices for the Admiralty traffic during the Second World War.

CJB Sanderson/ARPT

opened to divert the Talla Water into the bed of the reservoir, and officially opened on 28th September. Lamancha benefited to a lesser extent than the other stations, being more distant from the construction sites.

Lamancha station was chosen by the newly formed Penicuik Homing Pigeon Society for the first race of young birds on 4th June, 1887. Special trains often carried hundreds of pigeons up to a few hundred miles across Britain before release, but this would have been a much more modest affair, with perhaps just a basket or two of birds transported in the branch brake van to the starting point for the five-mile race back to their lofts; Eskbank station would be the Society's next venue.

The Census for 1871 records that Lamancha's agent was George Pryde, aged 54, a native of Stow, a widower living alone, and that the station house had three rooms with one or more windows. The NBR staff records for April 1874 give his salary as £52 per annum with a free house, but no other staff. He died in service on 3rd November, 1888 at the age of 72 after 40 years' service, the last 20 of which were spent at Lamancha. Death in service was by no means unusual: it was 1st June, 1905 before all salaried staff were required to retire at 65. As for wages staff,* it was not until 13th December, 1906 that the Board decided that all those aged 79 and over must retire, after which the 'age limit' was gradually reduced to 65. Pryde's successor was Alex Thomson, formerly a signalman at Galashiels; he was aged 51 in April 1891, and living at the cottage with his wife Agnes. There is no record of his departure, but James Rae, formerly a shunter at Portobello, replaced him on 25th February, 1901 at £70 per annum with rent of £5. On the night of the April 1911 Census, six adults shared the small cottage: James Rae; his wife Elizabeth; son William (29), an NBR surfaceman; son James (21), a postman; son Arthur (18), a joiner; and daughter Mary (16). The station acquired a porter – James Kyle – appointed on 14th October, 1917 at 18s. per week. When James Rae retired on reaching the age limit of 65 on 18th October, 1919, he was still earning £70 per annum, and paying rent of £5, but he received a backdated increase to £200 per annum under the 1919 cost of living settlement.

The post was filled from 26th November, 1919 by Mrs Louisa MacKinnon, variously described as 'Female Agent' and 'Station Mistress'. She was the widow of the former agent at South Queensferry. Her wage was £1 per week, which rose to £2 17s. 6d. under the cost of living increase and later to £3 1s. 6d. The services of the porter were

---

* In general, 'salaried staff' grades were appointed on an annual salary and 'wages staff' on a weekly wage.

Lamancha looking towards Dolphinton, probably taken in the 1930s shortly after closure.
Lens of Sutton Association

dispensed with on 9th March, 1922, 'No successor' being recorded in the ledger. Mrs MacKinnon was transferred to Kirkbank station on 25th April, 1928 to replace the agent there and Lamancha, too, came under the supervision of Mr Greig at Broomlee. His official notebook records 'Lamancha station closed 2/7/28' per a General Manager's circular – a date slightly later than that of Mrs MacKinnon's departure – and later 'Lamancha closed 28/5/29' – when it closed to goods traffic, no goods statistics being recorded after June 1928. Passenger trains continued to call, tickets presumably being supplied by the guard in the same way as for Macbie Hill (*below*). Mr Greig's notebook also records the granting of permission in August 1930 to Mr James Taylor, the new tenant of the station house, for the use of Lamancha ladies lavatory!

In January 1928, on the appointment of a woman – Miss Mary Cochrane – to replace her father as station master at nearby Eddleston, an LNER official gave a statement to the Press Association:

> Most of them were appointed before the railway amalgamation, and their stations are mainly on the old West Highland line and the North British. They are principally the daughters or widows of railwaymen who held the posts before them. Mind you, they are women – not 'flappers'* – and they are efficient stationmistresses in every sense of the word. They are supplied with a

---

* 'Flappers' were a generation of young Western women in the 1920s who wore short skirts, bobbed their hair, listened to jazz, and flaunted their disdain for what was then considered acceptable behaviour – *Wikipedia*.

uniform, and on the collar and cap is the word 'Stationmistress'. They take complete charge. As a rule there is not much passenger traffic at their stations but timber and other goods is handled, and they give a hand with the manual work when necessary. They have porters under them and keep order about the place. They receive the same pay as men in similar posts, and they are treated in every way as if they were men. There has been no difficulty with any unions about them.

Lamancha Remembered, referred to above, recalled these days:

> But Leadburn was a Waverley Station compared with Lamancha; there we felt really at home. We had a station mistress, Mrs McKinnon. Her husband had been killed on the railway and she had been given the smallest station on the line in lieu of pension. She doubled as porter, and could handle heavy trunks with the best of them. Arriving in good time for the morning train we would meet her taking down her washing which had been hung out in the waiting-room overnight.
> While exchanging local gossip she would then open the office and produce our tickets. She never had any change in the morning as the day's takings were always sent off by the last train. Usually we hadn't either, so we got our tickets 'on tick' and paid when we returned in the evening. No one awaited the train's arrival more eagerly than Mrs McKinnon's dog, which trotted up to the engine in expectation of a piece from the driver.

Lamancha station house and buildings before the line was lifted in 1961.
NRS/Department for Transport under Open Government Licence v3.0.

Coalyburn (later Macbie Hill) Station

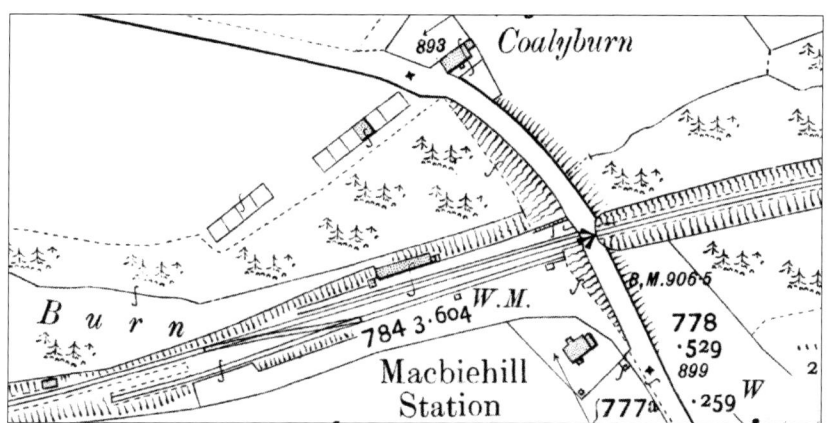

Ordnance Survey 25 inch map of Macbie Hill station published in 1908. Leadburn lies to the north-east (*right*). The Station House is on the access road to the yard, with its weighing machine. The station buildings are on the opposite side of the line and, beyond them, a row of miners' cottages, a few remains of which can still be seen today.

Reproduced by permission of the National Library of Scotland

'Coalyburn' was shown as 'Coalyburn (Macbie Hill)' in the October 1872 timetable, and 'Macbie Hill' in the June 1874 timetable;* it retained that style in timetables until closure, although 'Macbiehill' (which was the more common usage and the name of the estate) appeared in other NBR documentation.

The platform and station buildings were on the north side of the running line; access was by a flight of steps from the road bridge above. The revisions to the 1858 Ordnance Survey 6-inch map show the small station building on the north side of the line with a loop and siding on the south side. As with Lamancha, the NBR's 1894 improvement plan shows the removal of the points at the east end of the loop and its platform was also to be extended to 300 feet, with the addition of a 'Ladies' Room etc'. It also had a loading bank and weighing machine, but it also boasted a 2 tons 10 cwts crane. The station agent's house was at the yard entrance, on the south side of the line.

The existence of several coal seams at Macbiehill had been relied on by the promoters of the LL&DR in its Prospectus. Coal had long been

---

* The Railway Clearing House *Minutes of Goods Managers etc Conference* quote 25th May, 1874 as the effective date of change.

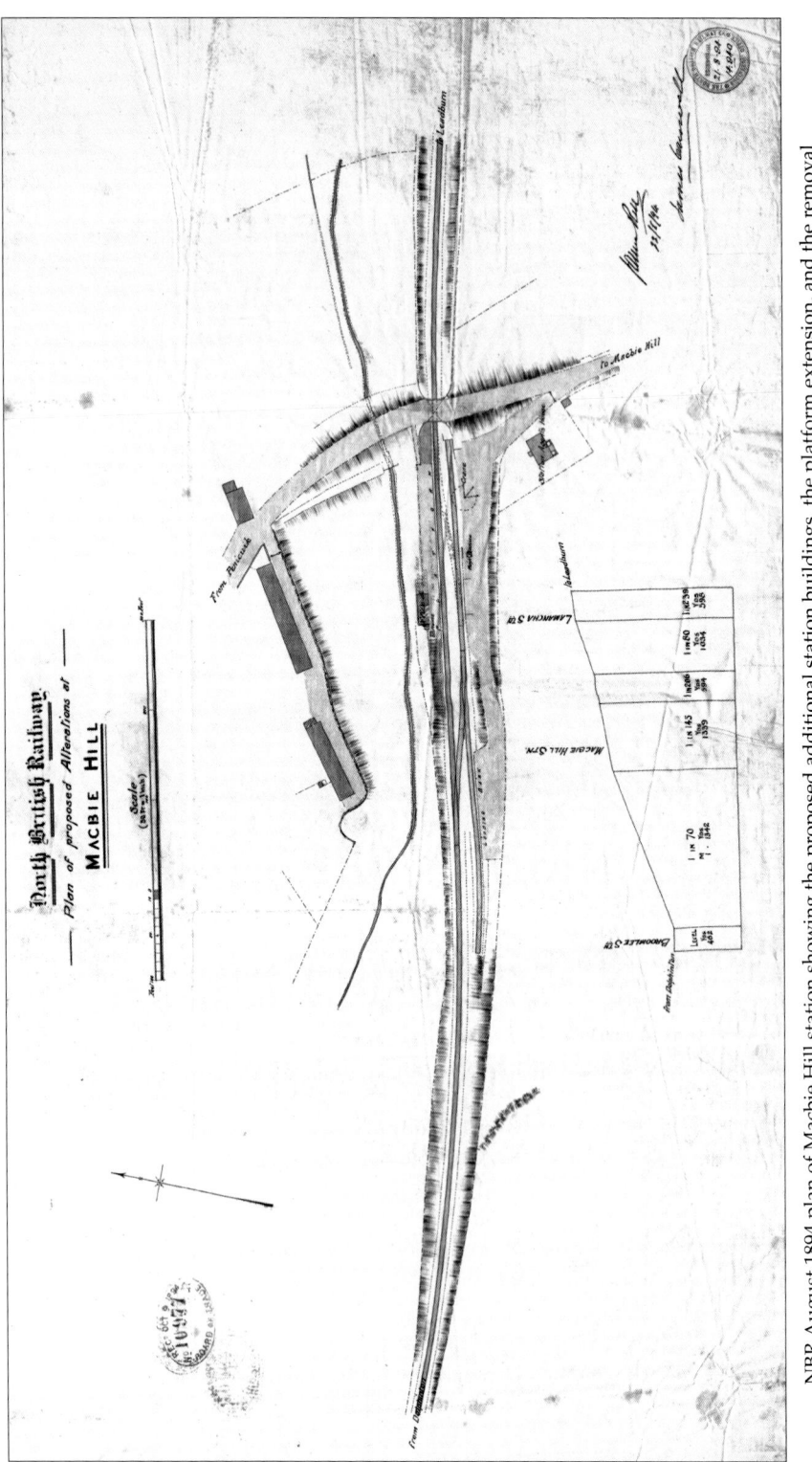

NBR August 1894 plan of Macbie Hill station showing the proposed additional station buildings, the platform extension, and the removal of the crossover at the east end of the station. The crane is at the foot of the yard access road, alongside the siding, with the loading bank to the west. The Coaly Burn runs to the north of the station buildings.

Reproduced by permission of the National Archives, Kew, Ref MT 6/718/1

mined on the Macbiehill estate, at a number of sites including Harlawmuir and Coalyburn, and at times by a workforce of some 50, including many women and children.* The mines were shallow – about 15 feet deep. The *List of Mines*, published annually by HM Inspectors of Mines, has entries for Macbiehill from 1890, when the Yeats family was working variously at 'Harleymoor', Whitfield, Corbie and, for a long period, at Bents, south of Macbie Hill station. The maximum number employed by them, in 1914, was six men underground and two on the surface, but latterly it was down to three – three generations of the Yeats family. John Yeats Senior died in September 1922, and John Black took over the lease of the Bents workings in 1925 and 1926; these are shown as abandoned in 1927. The Macbiehill Coal and Lime Company then worked at Harlawmuir until September 1930 before going into liquidation.

It is thought unlikely that much coal from the mines in the area was carried by rail and none of them was rail-connected; being on the edge of the Midlothian coalfield, the coal deposits were not of high quality and no household coal was produced, much of the output being used in the kilns in the nearby limestone quarry or for boiler coal. The lime, however, was said to be of excellent quality. Certainly by October 1920, the coal was being carted exclusively to the lime kiln, also worked by the Yeats family, with the finished product being dispatched by rail.** The lime works were being advertised for sale in June 1925, on the death of the former lessee: 'High-grade Limestone in plenty, suitable for Building, Agriculture and Road Metal. Open-cast quarries, face a Mile in Length; near Macbiehill station, L&NE. Small Coal Mine attached.' When the downgrading of the station was announced in November 1930, the view of the local paper was that 'the decay of the lime trade in the district has proved the crowning factor in deciding the fate of Macbiehill, or Coalyburn, as they used to call it. Even the coalmine, however, is today derelict and the lime-kiln cold'. Freestone from the nearby Deepsykehead Quarries, owned by Charles Lawson – who constructed most of the early buildings for the railway – may also have gone from the station in the early years of the railway. At their peak, the quarries employed around 100 men, but they appear to have ceased operating in 1873.*** The freight statistics (Appendix two) show that the

---

* See 'The Peebles-Shire Miners' by J.B. Fleming in *Scots Magazine* May 1990.

** See 'Lilliputian Mining' in the *Scotsman* of 27th October, 1920 and 'Scotland's Smallest Coal Mine', *ibid* 19th June, 1922.

*** Historic Environment Scotland website.

Macbie Hill station looking towards Leadburn on 30th May, 1954. As at Lamancha, the loop has been reinstated. The station buildings are semi-derelict.
CJB Sanderson/ARPT

By 23rd May 1959, the station buildings at Macbie Hill had been demolished and only the platelayers' bothy survives. The remains of the goods loading bank are on the right.
DW Ronald/Rae Montgomery collection

mineral tonnage handled at Macbie Hill – whether sent or received – considerably exceeded that of the other stations on the branch until *circa* 1920, suggesting that there may have been a significant traffic in coal, lime or stone.

On 10th September, 1896, the NBR General Manager reported to the Works Committee that permission had been granted to the Edinburgh & District Water Trust to form an aqueduct under the Dolphinton branch, 'on the usual conditions, a nominal rent of 20s. a year being charged for the privilege'. It was to pass under the railway between Macbie Hill and Broomlee, just under a mile north of the latter. Contract No. 2 of the great Talla waterworks scheme, let to John Best of Edinburgh, got under way towards the end of 1896 with a contract period of three years and was for the 5-mile section of aqueduct between the valleys of the Lyne and North Esk, partly in tunnel and partly in cut and cover, commencing at a siding north of Broomlee station. The longest and deepest tunnel commenced west of Macbiehill, where the aqueduct struck off north-eastwards.

Macbie Hill booked fewer passengers than Lamancha in most years until the late 1890s, when numbers soared, almost certainly the result of the aqueduct work on Contract No. 2. Mineral traffic also shows a considerable increase during this period, as does coal traffic, coal being

Macbie Hill station, looking towards Dolphinton through the arch of the bridge carrying the road from Whitmuir to Upper Whitfield and Carlops, in May 1936.
National Railway Museum / Science and Society Picture Library

used for the steam-driven machinery. For the year ended 31st July, 1874, Macbie Hill booked 3,001 passengers. Its best year was y.e. July 1899 when 6,227 passengers were booked, but in y.e. June 1932 it booked only 1,156. The number of livestock (mainly sheep) handled at Macbie Hill was exceeded only by Broomlee, there being extensive grazing land on the Macbiehill estate. There was timber traffic too: Mr Greig's LNER notebook records that a timber loading platform was completed on 22nd May, 1924.

The first agent recorded for Macbie Hill is James Paterson Douglas,* also on £52 and a rent-free house. He was in post on Census night, 2nd April, 1871, living with his wife and two young children; two more children were added to the family during his long tenure. He died in Edinburgh in February 1899, aged 61, after a long illness, having been replaced by Andrew Mounsey** formerly a signalman at Longtown, by 6th April, 1898. In April 1901 he was living in the small station house with his wife, and three 'scholars' (school age children) – his son, daughter and nephew. He transferred to Penton from 29th April, 1907 and was replaced by Mrs Jane Somerville,*** wife of foreman surfaceman Philip Somerville, both aged 42 and with a one-year-old son. Mrs Somerville's remuneration was minimal – only £5 4s. per annum (2s. per week), doubling to £10 8s. (4s. per week) from 1st January, 1918 but then to £1 18s. 6d. per week (£100 per annum) with the cost of living rise. Mr Greig's notebook records 'Macbiehill Platform bell sent Cowlairs 30/6/25'. Cowlairs in Glasgow was the main locomotive works of the NBR (by then the LNER).

The NBR had an unenviable reputation for dirty carriages, untidy stations, and unkempt and uncivil staff. On his arrival in Edinburgh from the Cambrian Railways in November 1891 to take charge of the North British Railway, Scots-born General Manager John Conacher set out to change this. One of his measures was to introduce an annual competition for the Best Kept Stations, with 'Premiums' awarded in four classes. While the other stations on the branch won the occasional award, Macbie Hill did particularly well under Mrs Somerville, winning one of the 20 First Class Premiums of £4 in 1908, a Second Class premium of £3 in 1907, and Third or Fourth Class Premiums in 1913, 1914, 1915, 1916, 1917, 1920 and 1924.

---

* He is 'James Paterson' in the NBR staff records; his death is registered in the name of Douglas, but his widow's death is in the name of Paterson!

** 'Mounsery' in the Census.

*** 'Sommerville' in Census.

In November 1930, the LNER had announced that 'on and after 1st December, 1930 Macbiehill station will be treated as a siding for goods traffic under Broomlee station, and passenger train parcels and miscellaneous traffic will not be dealt with. Passenger trains will, however, continue to call at Macbiehill, and passengers joining at that place will be supplied with tickets by the guard on the train.' The duties of ticket seller, collector and inspector were now all undertaken by the guard, although by that time there were few fares to collect. The 'office' consisted of a steel cash box transported in the guard's van. Macbie Hill then also came under the supervision of Mr Greig at Broomlee. Mrs Somerville became waiting room cleaner at 5s. per week; she retired on 30th June, 1931 and was replaced briefly as cleaner by a John Duncan. Permission for the Rev. James T. Hall to use the waiting room at Macbie Hill is recorded in Mr Greig's notebook around June 1923.

As well as Philip Somerville at Macbie Hill and William Rae at Lamancha, the surfacemen who maintained the track at the time of the 1911 Census included William Scott, living in the Old Toll House at Romanno Bridge, and William Blake – with his wife and six young children – living at Tile House, Newlands (two rooms with windows). George Brunton was at Whim Cottages, and Walter Finlayson and Alexander ('Eck') Niddrie were living in West Linton. Eck Niddrie, Philip Somerville and a Frederick Dickson are shown in the photo taken *circa* 1909 (*page 100*). Their predecessors included Richard Brunton, whose death at Mitchell Hill at the age of 72 was recorded in the *Peeblesshire Advertiser* of 17th December, 1887; he had worked on the branch since it opened.

Crime came to Macbie Hill on 6th January, 1929. It was discovered on the Monday morning that the station had been forcibly entered during the night. While considerable damage was done to property, the intruders were unsuccessful in their attempt to secure money, as apparently nothing had been taken. A nearby hut had also been entered and tools removed, which had then been used in an attempt on the station house.

Jimmy Brown of Dolphinton remembers his Army basic training at Dreghorn Camp in the early 1940s, and the overnight exercises on the moor near Macbiehill. While the officers and NCOs bedded down in the disused station waiting room, the recruits had to dig trenches for their overnight shelter.

A Linton Plooman wrote a piece for the *Peeblesshire Advertiser* in September 1943. Seeing a paper luggage label for 'Macbie Hill' stuck on the glass door of a typing agency in St Giles Street, Edinburgh, no doubt purloined by some small boy from the set of pigeon holes in the booking office at Waverley, he decided to set out for that very place:

> When the men of the 1860s made the railway to Macbiehill they had great hopes that the mineral wealth of the land would be developed, and that farming would be improved. They felt that they were making a lifeline for the countryside, and they had the experience of other places to fortify their belief. But it did not work out that way. The mineral wealth was not developed; it shrank to vanishing point some time before the railway finally died after sixty-four years of working. Agriculture did develop, though I do not think that dairy farming was one of the ways in which these pioneers envisaged the improvements to come about. In any event few of the farms on the higher parts of the route 'put on dairies', and most of them went over to 'a pickle sheep' with disastrous results to the amount of employment the land provided for men bred on it ... Even were there a station at Macbiehill today, there would be few passengers for it for the land is empty, the houses roofless or in ruin. ... Macbiehill was not a holiday resort and, though it was actually the nearest station to Carlops, few people for that place travelled to it by reason of the difficult road connecting the two places ... And it had one drawback; drinking water had to be brought from Leadburn, and the familiar black watering can was often the principal luggage of the day. It did not use a label!

It is worth noting here a proposal, reported in the *Peeblesshire Advertiser* on 26th February, 1887, for an extension of the branch railway from Edinburgh to Glencorse, with stations at Penicuik, Kerswell [Carsewell], Brunstane [Brunston], Carlops and West Linton to join the Dolphinton branch a little beyond Broomlee. The justification for this unlikely scheme was the presence of minerals at Brunston, Harlaw Muir, Newhall and Rutherford, and potential passenger traffic to Habbie's Howe, near Carlops, the scene of Allan Ramsay's play *The Gentle Shepherd*, and a spot very popular in the 19th century with visitors from Edinburgh. Much of the proposed route appears to follow that of McCallum and Dundas' survey for a line from Carlisle to Edinburgh running south-east of the Pentland Hills, described in Chapter One. Unsurprisingly, no more was heard of the scheme.

Broomlee Siding (1)

In September 1898, a short siding was laid in for Contract No. 2 of the Talla scheme, already referred to, $1\frac{1}{2}$ miles south-west of Macbie Hill, and three-quarters of a mile short of Broomlee. It was on the east side of the line, in the trailing direction for trains heading from Macbie Hill

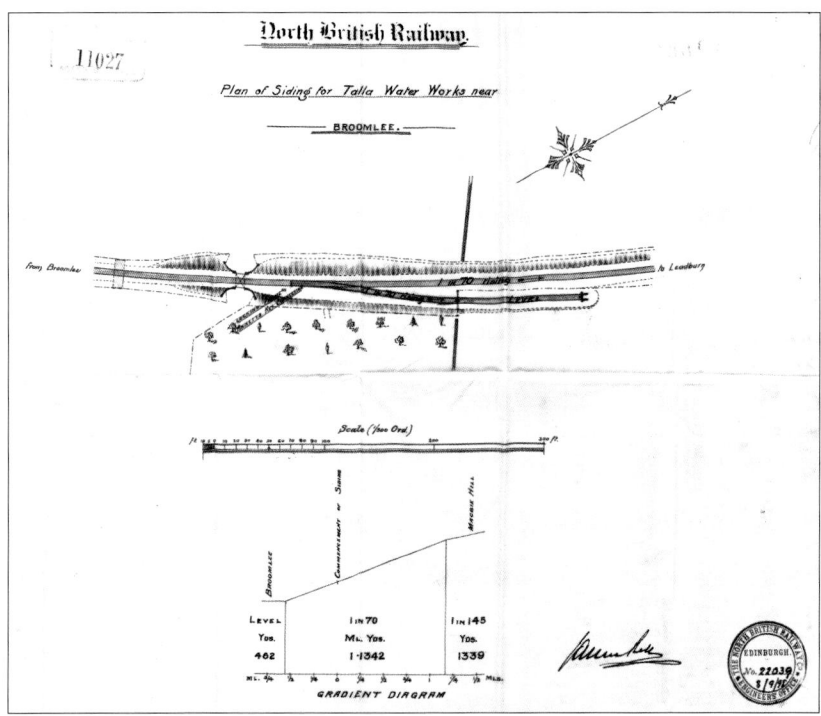

1898 NBR plan of the siding north of Broomlee for the Talla Aqueduct Works.
Reproduced by permission of the National Archives, Kew, Ref MT 6/850/3

towards Broomlee, and was located approximately at grid reference NT165516; the aqueduct crossed under the railway at grid reference NT169523.* The siding was on a 1 in 70 gradient, and so catch points were provided to derail any runaways and protect the main line. Colonel Sir Francis Marindin (as he now was) of the Railway Inspectorate reported on 2nd October that the points were worked by a 2-lever ground frame, locked by the train staff. Subject to an undertaking being given by the NBR that the siding would be worked only by trains having the engine at the Broomlee end, the works were approved.

A 3-foot gauge 0-4-0ST locomotive named *The Duke*, and possibly later named *Penicuik*, is believed to have operated the contractor's narrow gauge works railway on this section of the aqueduct.** The line is referred to in the *Scotsman* of 23rd August, 1897 in a report of an

---

* Information from Scottish Water.

** Information from *Contractors' Steam Locomotives of Scotland* by Russell Wear and Michael Cook (Industrial Locomotive Society, 1990).

accident in which a workman had a narrow escape when a cement wagon left the rails: 'At one part of the Broomlee – Macbiehill section of the new Edinburgh water extension scheme a deep gully is bridged over by a trestle bridge which carries a railway used for the conveyance of cement and other material …'

The main construction site of the Talla dam was served by its own 7-mile standard gauge railway from Broughton, on the Caledonian Railway, to Victoria Lodge, a mile south-east of the village of Tweedsmuir on the A701. The earthworks for that railway are still clearly visible from the road.

Broomlee (for West Linton) Station

Approaching Broomlee from Leadburn, the Cairn Burn was crossed on the approach to the goods yard. The stone-built goods shed was on the right, and the gatekeeper's cottage on the left, both accessed from Station Road, which the train crossed on the line's only gated level crossing. Immediately across the road, on the right, were the signal box and the single-platform Broomlee station immediately adjoining it. If one believes the *Southern Reporter* article reproduced in Chapter Five, passengers on 'mixed' trains

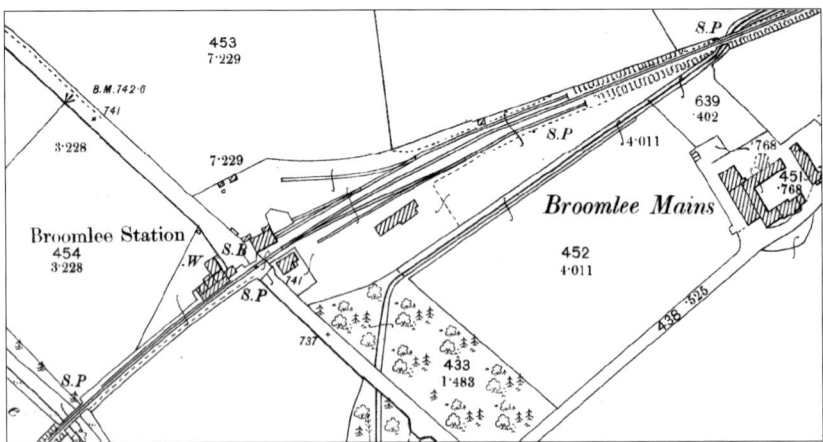

Ordnance Survey 25 inch map of Broomlee published in 1898. Leadburn lies to the north-east (right) and West Linton village is to the top left. The station buildings, signal box and station house are to the west of the road at the level crossing, with the goods shed immediately across the road, and the gatekeeper's house opposite that. The sawmill building is on the south side of the goods yard sidings.

Reproduced by permission of the National Library of Scotland

The approach to Broomlee from Macbie Hill in the early 1920s. The gatekeeper's house is on the left (with a young Jean Fleming in the garden), and the goods shed on the right. Beyond the level crossing is the signal box and the station with its canopy. The village of West Linton lies along the road to the right, from which there is a vehicle entrance to the goods yard.
WLDHA collection

In this early postcard, Station Road winds down to Broomlee station, with Broomlee House beyond and Broomlee Mains opposite. The railway from Leadburn crosses the Lyne Water on its way to Dolphinton.
T.C. Atkinson collection

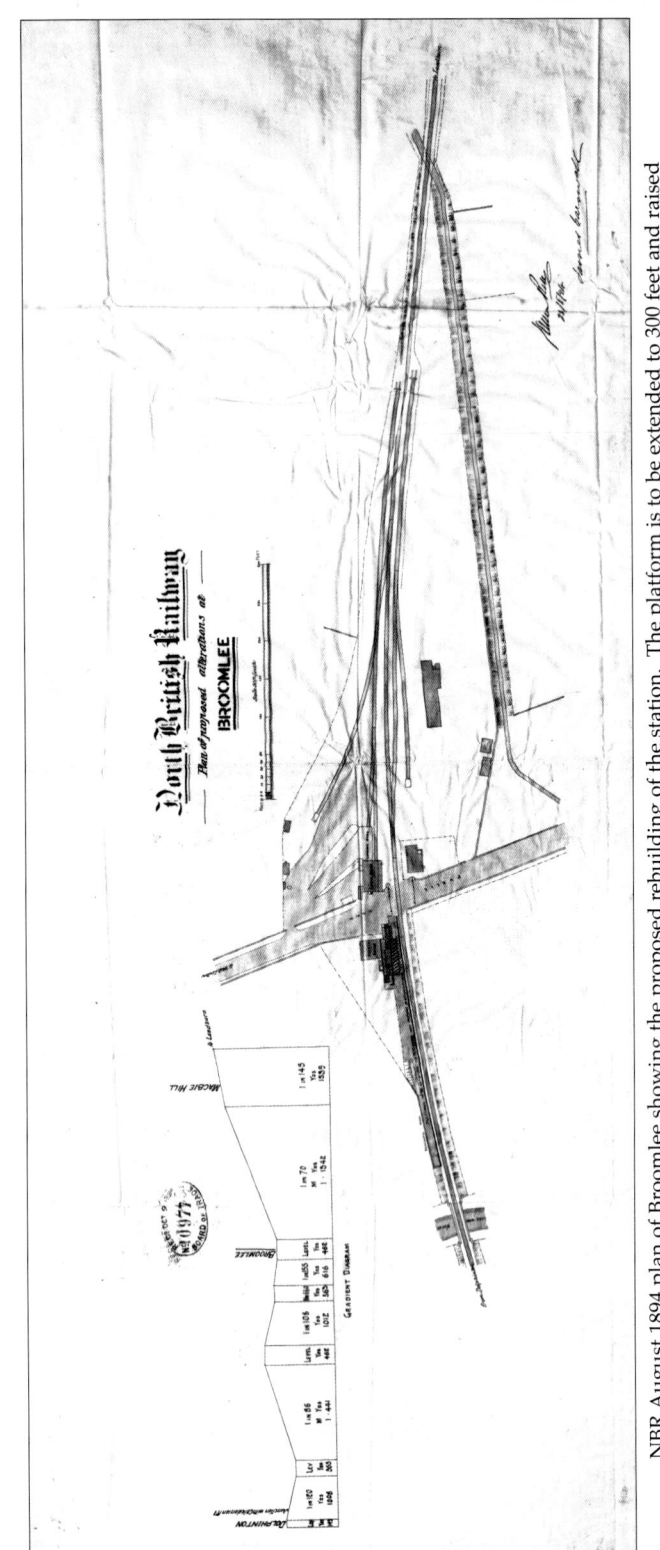

NBR August 1894 plan of Broomlee showing the proposed rebuilding of the station. The platform is to be extended to 300 feet and raised to 2 feet 6 inches. *Reproduced by permission of the National Archives, Kew, Ref MT 6/718/1*

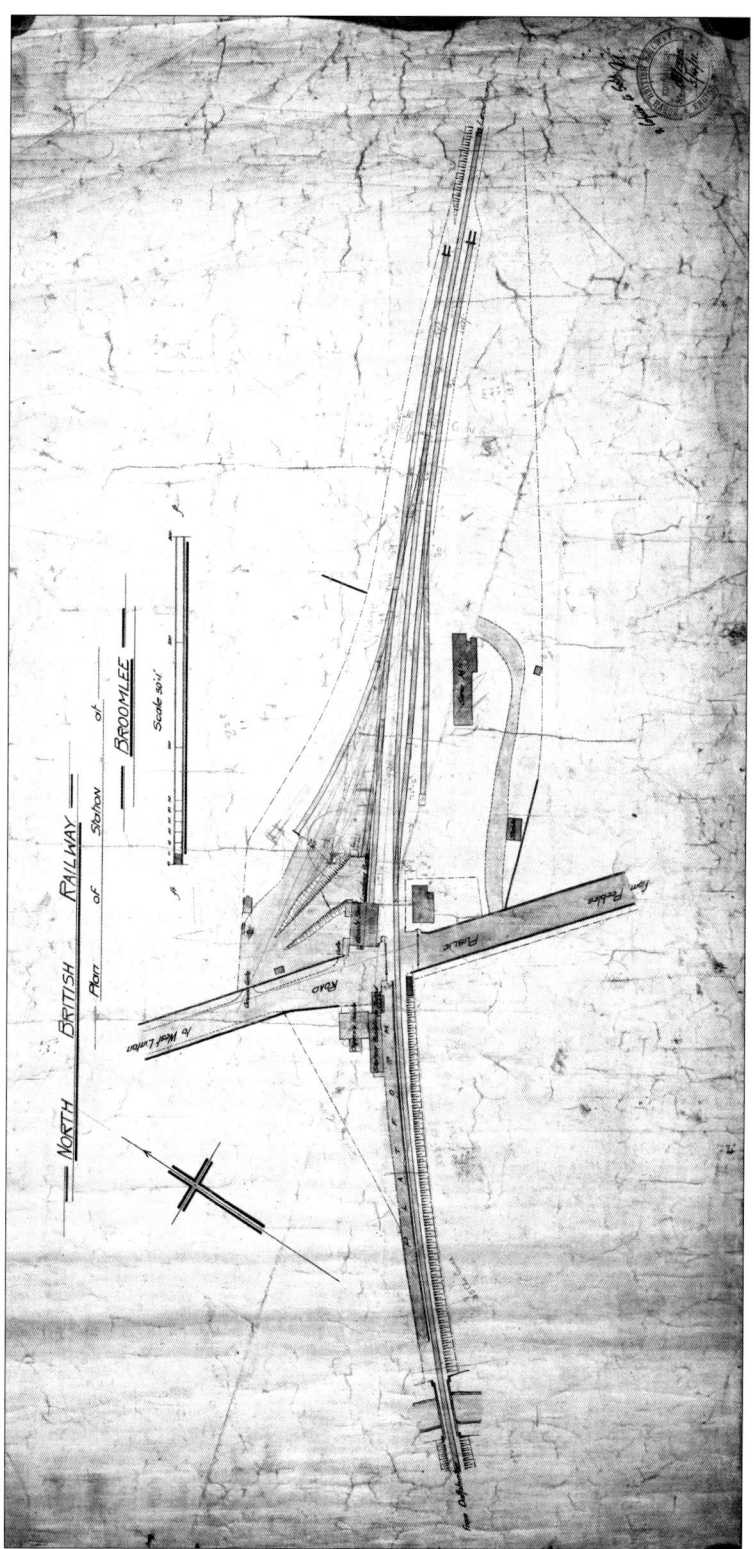

NBR April 1911 plan of the Broomlee station layout, with some scribbled notes and costings, possibly relating to the 1915 extension to the goods yard. *NRS/Department for Transport under Open Government Licence v3.0.*

could first be subjected to some protracted shunting of wagons in the goods sidings, and the young and the fit would jump out and be in the village half a mile away before the train had reached the station platform!

Broomlee was the principal, and the busiest, station on the branch, serving West Linton and its hinterland (population of West Linton parish in 1891: 1,005). The revisions to the 1858 Ordnance Survey 6-inch map show only the running line and one (unconnected!) siding. The station building, with the station house at right angles behind it on the public road (later Station Road), was on the West Linton village (north-west) side of the single line; the entrance to the goods yard was on the opposite side of the road, towards the village. The NBR's 1894 improvement plan shows a ladies room and WCs, added to the existing 'Waiting Shed' and booking office, within a rebuilt structure with horizontal timber boarding and a full-length platform canopy; the platform is raised in height to 2 feet 6 inches, and extended to 300 feet in length. By this time, Broomlee had acquired its signal box. As can be seen from the plan, there was no run-round loop at the station, and the sidings in the goods yard were not extensive. For those passenger trains from Leadburn that terminated at Broomlee before making the return journey, the engine would have had to propel its coaches a short distance back up the main line (which was on a slight gradient), leave them there and go into a siding, and wait for the coaches to be run back by gravity before coupling-on to the other end of the train – the practice known on the railway as 'running by'. The October 1922 *Appendix to the Working Time Tables* shows Broomlee as having a 'siding in which a train not conveying passengers may be refuged to allow any train (Passenger or Goods) to pass'.

The NBR Works Committee approved the extension of the loading bank and siding at Broomlee, estimated to cost £220, in May 1915. The NBR's 1911 plan appears to be annotated in pencil with the positions of possible new sidings, but the exact layout has not been discovered. This development may have been in connection with the extensive forestry operations during the First World War when 'the railway proved useful in the war time in order to help denude our wooded slopes of their trees'. In June 1920 the Committee approved the renewal of the bridge over the Lyne Water at Broomlee. The successful tenderer was the Brandon Bridge Building Co. Ltd, and expenditure of £1,935 1s. was authorized. In September, the Committee accepted the tender of Messrs P. & W. MacLellan for the renewal of another two bridges on the branch, one of which was to feature in the accident described later.

The number of passengers booked at Broomlee was larger than the combined total of the three other branch stations. For the year ended

31st July, 1874 it booked 12,205 passengers. Its best year was y.e. July 1899 when 20,001 passengers were booked, this being at the height of the work on two Talla aqueduct contracts based on Broomlee – the Lyne to North Esk contract referred to above, and the Broughton – Broomlee contract described later; the tonnage of goods and mineral traffic carried was likewise inflated. For y.e. July 1901, passenger numbers were 16,647, but by y.e. June 1932 had declined dramatically to just 4,091.

Goods were brought in for the local merchants, and for the farmers in the surrounding countryside, and unloaded into the goods shed to await collection. The 1904 Railway Clearing House *Handbook of Railway Stations* lists a 1-ton crane at Broomlee. On 17th January, 1919, the NBR Board signed a contract with Gilbert Millar, 'with regard to parcel delivery at West Linton'. He was one of two coal merchants based in the station yard, where there was a weighbridge to weigh the empty carts in and the loaded carts out. Miss Jane ('Jean') Fleming (1914-1991), daughter of Broomlee signalman John Fleming, recalled her 'Life on the Leadburn Line' in a *Scots Magazine* article of August 1988: 'Goods wagons were backed into the sidings and coal trucks into coal merchants' yards. Broomlee had two yards and coal was shovelled out by hand and riddled to remove dross before being bagged.' Leslie's Saw Mill private siding, listed in the 1904 *Handbook*, was on the south side of the yard, and the *Peeblesshire Advertiser* regularly advertised an 'Annual Sale of Sawn Wood' at Broomlee station Saw Mills. The 1930-31 Valuation Roll lists the occupants of the yard as Gilbert Millar, coal agent, West Linton (coal depot and office), Charles Lawson, builder, Romanno (coal depot), and James Leslie, Broomlee, (coal depot and office, and sawmill site). Following James Leslie's death, his daughter sold the coal business to Peebles coal merchant Edward Marshall in 1934.

The transport of sheep, particularly in the second half of the year, cattle, and a few pigs, swelled the station's earnings; there were horses too, although horseboxes were classed as 'coaching' (i.e. passenger) traffic, and numbers are not separately identifiable. Milk, in churns, was sent away daily on the first train. Jean Fleming again: 'Entrance to the platform for the first train of the day had to be negotiated between horses and farm carts. The farm hands had brought the morning's milk in large churns and were collecting the empties to take home.' In *A Bairn in the Borders**, she recalls that one of the largest poultry farms in Britain was about three miles from the station and that many hundreds of 'Day Old Chicks' were sent off by train every day to places all over the country. As a young child, she 'used

---

* Moray House Publications (1991)

to enjoy peeping into the cardboard boxes, through the ventilating holes, at the lovely little bundles of yellow fluff going "Cheep, cheep, cheep"!'

The 1871 Census records that Broomlee's agent was William Rae, aged 48, a native of Selkirk, living in the station house with his wife and five daughters, and that the station house had four rooms with windows. The NBR staff records for April 1874 show that he was earning the standard £52 per annum with a free house. The only other member of the station staff recorded was a signal porter. In the 1861 Census, William Rae had been a porter at Stow. A keen amateur gardener, he is recorded on a number of occasions as being a prize winner, and one of the judges, at the West Linton Horticultural Society's annual Flower Show. Details of his departure from Broomlee are not recorded, but as he was in his early 70s when replaced on 8th June, 1893, he most probably retired; he died at Bordlands Lodge, age 74, on 16th May, 1896 and is interred at West Linton.

Rae's successor was Robert Speirs, age 30, married with a young daughter, and formerly a foreman at Alloa. Two other daughters were born at West Linton. Mr Speirs moved to Fountainhall on 31st March, 1904 and was replaced by Joseph Joss, aged 31, from Aberdour, whose salary by 1911 was £70 per annum less £5 for rent. However, the 1911

Photographed outside the station house at Broomlee, *c*.1910, are (*back row l. to r.*) Tom Cowe, clerk; Bob Miller, signalman; Joe Joss, station master; John Fleming, signalman. In the front row are Philip Somerville, foreman surfaceman with Eck Niddrie and Fred Dickson, surfacemen. *WLDHA collection*

Andrew Headridge, Broomlee station master from 1914 – 1918.
WLDHA collection

Andrew Headridge with Mrs Headridge and daughters Rachel, Cathie, Jean, and Wilma (born at Broomlee on 6th October, 1916), shortly before his death at Reston in September 1920. His widow, Jane, became station mistress at Rosslynlee and, later, at Gordon.
WLDHA collection

Census shows Joss living not in the station house but in the sizeable Horseshoe Cottage on Main Street (10 rooms with one or more windows) with his wife, daughter, two lodgers and a visitor. The staff ledger records: 'Absconded 24.8.14' and elsewhere 'Dismissed – dishonesty 24.8.14'. On his death, he is described as a retired accountant.

Joss was succeeded from 23rd September, 1914 by Andrew Headridge, aged 34, formerly a clerk at Dunfermline Lower station, who moved into the station house with his wife and three daughters; a fourth daughter was born in 1916. Still relatively young to hold a station master's appointment, and with the prospect of a promising career, he transferred to the larger junction station of Reston on 3rd July, 1918 but died there in September 1920, aged just 40, as a result of the 'flu pandemic; his widow Jane was appointed station mistress at Rosslynlee on 1st December, 1920 and was there for 13 years before being transferred to Gordon in February 1933, retiring in 1943. Andrew Headridge had been replaced at Broomlee, in a swap, by the agent at Reston, John Lawson, formerly station master at Tayport, on £85. His daughter, Ethel Lawson, served as 'Temporary Female Passenger Clerkess' at Broomlee during 1918/1919 until her services were dispensed with as male employees returned from the War. John Lawson died in service, aged 61, on 16th January, 1923.

The final Broomlee station master was George Greig. He arrived on 4th June, 1923, aged 50, after nine years' service at Greengairs, the possessor of a gold watch presented to him by the traders there on his departure. A native of Dalkeith, he had entered the service of the company on 14th March, 1887 as a messenger in the Electrical Engineer's Department at Eskbank, transferring to Hardengreen as a clerk a year later and to the Goods Department in 1896. He served as a clerk at Dalkeith from January

George Greig, Broomlee station master from 1923 to 1933.
Marion Moore collection

Alex Aitken on Mr Greig's official 'Excelsior' motorbike, supplied in October 1930, at Broomlee station.
Marion Moore collection

1906 until his transfer to Greengairs as goods agent. His marriage in 1901 to Elizabeth Thomson, a railway telegraphist, took place in the Station House at Eskbank where his future father-in-law was station master. At Broomlee, the youngest of their three sons, Frank, supplemented his pocket money by carrying visitors' luggage the half mile or so to the village, accompanied by Spot, the dog. George Greig's salary was £210 per annum, rising to £230 in 1927. As we have seen, he assumed responsibility for the stations at Lamancha, Macbie Hill and Leadburn, and later Dolphinton too, and so needed transport to travel around his area. The staff ledger records: 'Rural Motor Cycle supplied 6.10.30'. Following closure of the station, and branch, from 1st April, 1933, Mr Greig was appointed agent at Scotland Street, Edinburgh from 8th May. He retired at the end of June 1935 and died on Christmas Day, 1957, at Hope Lodge, West Linton, at the age of 85, 'a much loved figure in the community'.

The inspection report in May 1864 had stated that 'There is a public level crossing near Linton station, where it is necessary to provide a house, for the man in charge to live in, as the station affords no such accommodation'. The house doesn't appear to have been provided at that time, as the NBR's Works Committee approved the erection of a gatekeeper's lodge at its meeting on 10th January, 1889; it was on the

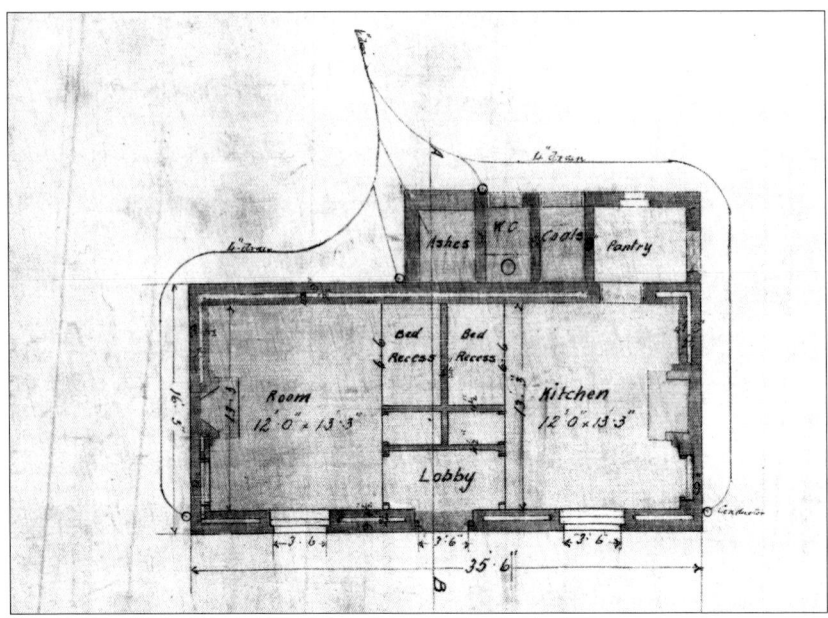

Extract from NBR May 1890 architectural drawing for the belated erection of a gatekeeper's lodge at Broomlee.
NRS/Department for Transport under Open Government Licence v3.0.

Broomlee gatekeeper's cottage with Mrs Fleming, wife of signalman John Fleming, and daughter Jean. *WLDHA collection*

opposite side of the line from the goods shed, and adjacent to Station Road. The expense was estimated at about £150. A new signalman/gateman post was filled on 26th May, 1890 by the appointment of John Fleming, formerly a surfaceman at Peebles, and the family occupied the gatekeeper's lodge. He remained in post until his retiral on 2nd March, 1929 after 41 years of railway service. A second signalman was in post from December 1899.

A clerk was appointed on 5th July, 1898 – 'temporarily during continuance of Edinr. Water Works'; the post was made permanent in November 1905, and one of the incumbents was Luke Mounsey, nephew of the Macbie Hill station master. A second clerk's post was established in April 1912.

The NBR staff register lists: 'Men & lads left to join Colours' in the First World War. Three went from Broomlee: George Durrant, clerk, was called up on 5th August, 1914, two days after Britain declared war on Germany; John Wilson, porter, on 28th February, 1917; and John Dickson, clerk, on 9th October, 1917. All three returned safely in 1919,

Broomlee station c.1908 – 1909. Road traffic must have been light when the crossing gates were closed for this group photograph. Standing at the back are (l. to r.) John Fleming, signalman; Peter Small, driver; Andrew Simpson, guard; Bob Bonnar, fireman; Bob Miller, signalman. Seated are Bob Fell, fireman; Joe Joss, station master, and Tom Cowe, clerk. In the background is Hurst 0-6-0 goods locomotive No. 203 (withdrawn in 1909).

W Hennigan collection per Bill Lynn

Durrant going to Peebles, and the other two back to Broomlee, Dickson as clerk in February 1919 and Wilson as signalman in December 1919. During 1917-18 there were two passenger porters, one of whom was a female, Annie Fleming, a cousin of Jean Fleming. By 1930, there were the agent, George Greig, passenger clerk, Joseph Charters, two signalmen, and a passenger porter, the latter post being shown as vacant after 1930.

On John Fleming's retiral in March 1929, at the age of 70, the local paper looked back over his career:

> Last Saturday Mr John Fleming, signalman at Broomlee, retired on reaching the age limit, after 41 years' service. He joined the staff of the NBR at Peebles in 1888 as a surfaceman, and two years later he was appointed to Broomlee as porter, and then on the erection of a fully-appointed signal cabin, he was put in charge. ... During the time of his appointment many changes have come over the conditions of railway service and working: in the earlier years his shift sometimes exceeded twelve hours daily. Incidentally, it may be noted that, despite the often praised superiority of present facilities for travel, there was then an infinitely superior train service to Edinburgh than that scheduled at this time. ...

His LNER colleagues presented him with an easy chair 'as a parting token of respect'.

In her *Scots Magazine* article, Jean Fleming recalled the staff:

> In the first decade of the present century my home station, Broomlee, was a very busy place, employing a stationmaster, signalman, two clerks, two porters, not to mention surfacemen working on the permanent way, plus two engine drivers, two firemen, and two guards.* Altogether, 26 people were employed full-time on the line, including a stationmistress for Macbiehill and Lamancha. During the First World War there was also a female porter at Broomlee – my cousin Annie Fleming.

Angling on the Lyne Water had long been an attraction of the area but, by the 1880s, West Linton was developing more generally as a peaceful, healthy, holiday retreat. Some families bought a holiday home in the village, or built their own – particularly after the improvement in the village water supply, completed in 1898. The *Peeblesshire Advertiser*'s review of 1899 referred to the villas erected during the year:

> The villas give the village a more aristocratic and important appearance, especially when nearing Broomlee on the railway ... We trust that those of the villas still for sale will find purchasers in the spring, and that builders prepared

---

* The train crews were based at Dolphinton.

to speculate in this respect will be encouraged once more to do so, so that parties desirous of establishing their health amid the beautiful scenery and the bracing air may have no difficulty in finding the necessary accommodation, which hitherto has been comparatively so limited.

To maintain its position as a health resort, the paper stressed the need for a bowling green and a public hall. Work was put in hand the following year to establish a bowling green, as West Linton catered for its visitors' recreation. The golf course had been laid out in 1890 under the guidance of William Millar, the village schoolmaster, and the bowling green and tennis courts under the guidance of his successor, James Halley.

Set against the backdrop of the Pentland Hills, West Linton was a favourite spot with the citizens of nearby Edinburgh, and many of them came by train. In 1890, quite apart from the large number of 'day trippers' on the Edinburgh September Monday holiday – 'probably the largest such number to date' – the village had been very busy throughout the summer months: 'The visitors comprised all classes of the community, including a goodly sprinkling of literary men, and men well known in the world of science and art, and all of them found methods of amusement and means of enjoyment suitable to their taste', according to the local paper. James Halley's 1912 *Guide to West Linton and District* listed 74 houses and other places with accommodation available for summer visitors, together with 'a description of walks, drives and cycle runs', and included the tariffs for golf, bowling, tennis, billiards and croquet (cost: one penny per mallet). As the village increased in popularity, so the NBR responded with additional services (described in Chapter Five), and publicized West

1912 *Guide to West Linton*: recreation charges.

T.C. Atkinson collection

Broomlee station circa 1908–1910 with station master Joss and other station staff and surfacemen. *Oakwood collection*

Linton's attractions: its 1898 *Golfers' Guide* included 'BROOMLEE, West Linton (Peeblesshire) golf course, about 12 minutes walk from Broomlee station [that was highly optimistic!], is of 9 holes …' , and *The Anglers' Guide to the best Fishing Streams and Lochs in Scotland reached by the North British Railway* included 'The Lyne. Capital trouting stream. Route – rail to Broomlee or Peebles stations.' On the Monday Spring holiday in 1920, 'Edinburgh excursionists to the number of between two or three hundred arrived in West Linton by morning and noon trains, in addition to a large number who were resident for the week-end. Cyclists, pedestrians and motor parties passed through the village. The weather was fine.'

In the late Victorian era, it was the fashion for middle-class families to move to their 'summer quarters', often for a month, with servants, pets, and mountains of luggage. The business – or, more particularly, the baggage – caused major headaches for the railways, particularly at the turn of the month. The NBR offered an advance delivery service, but it was insufficiently used and special restrictions had to be put in place in order to cope. Luggage was accepted on certain trains only, and had to be loaded on to through vans or trucks, with special trains being run from Edinburgh to the popular resorts, including the East Neuk, Lothian Coast and Peeblesshire. In 1899, for example, on the Saturday, Monday

Left: Joe Charters, booking clerk at Broomlee, 1933. He had formerly been stationed at Stobs and Leadburn. *Marion Moore collection*

Right: Broomlee signal box c.1933. Sandy Angus (*left*) and John Duncan, the last two signalmen at Broomlee. *Rae Montgomery collection*

Broomlee station looking towards Dolphinton in May 1936, after closure. A porch has been erected at the entrance to the general waiting room.
National Railway Museum / Science and Society Picture Library

and Tuesday, 29th and 31st July and 1st August, 1899, Dolphinton branch luggage was conveyed only by the 6.50 am, 10.40 am Special, 1.05 pm Special and 6.05 pm departures from Edinburgh (change at Leadburn). The 11.13 am branch train from Leadburn had to await the arrival of the 10.40 am Special, and both Specials had to have through luggage vans or trucks for Dolphinton. Similar arrangements applied in the opposite direction. While the family was on holiday, the breadwinner would travel daily to business in Edinburgh. The railway catered for the growing holiday traffic, and for these early commuters, as we shall see.

Special events such as the Agricultural Show at Broomlee Mains could transform the quiet rural station into a hive of activity, and the scheduled arrival of 14 trains of Territorials on one Sunday in July 1910, described later, was unprecedented.

'The Splash'

'The Splash' was the name given locally to the where the road forded the West Water, which in turn was crossed by the railway, half a mile southwest of Broomlee. After the line closed, the railway overbridge was removed, and the ford was replaced by a road bridge over the river.

'The Splash', in 1953, after the railway bridge had been removed. The ford was later replaced by a bridge over the river.
NRS/Department for Transport under Open Government Licence v3.0.

Broomlee Siding (2)

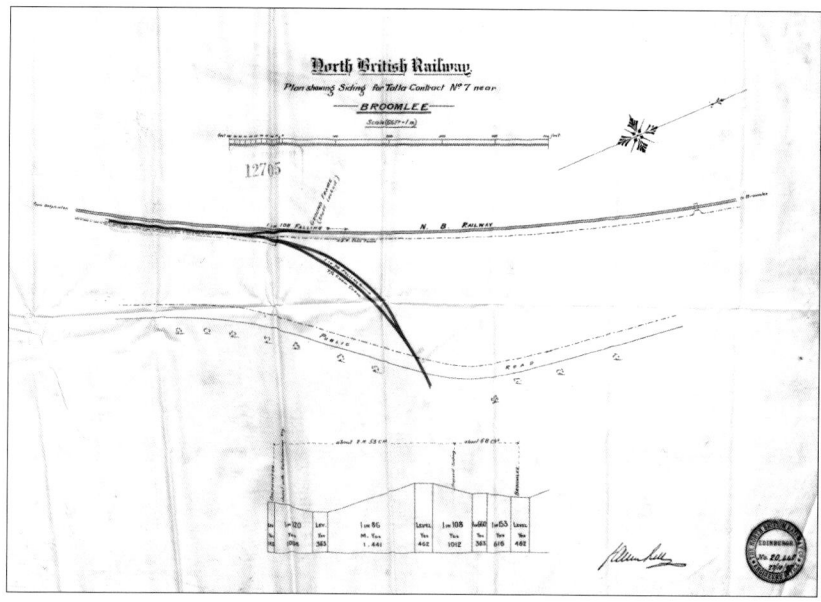

NBR October 1897 plan of the connection to McAlpine's standard gauge works railway, a little under a mile south-west of Broomlee station.
Reproduced by permission of the National Archives, Kew, Ref MT 8/805/12

Contract No. 7 of the Talla Waterworks Scheme, for the construction of an 'Aqueduct Between Broughton and Broomlee', was advertised in the Press on 16th June, 1897 and was let to Robert McAlpine & Sons. This section of aqueduct was to be about 10 miles in length, partly in tunnel and partly in cut and cover, and the finished size was to be 7 feet 6 inches high by 6 feet wide. At Broomlee, it would join up with Contract No. 2, the aqueduct between the Lyne and North Esk valleys.

In November 1897, the NBR sought approval from the Board of Trade to bring into use a siding which had been laid in just less than a mile (68 chains) south-west of Broomlee to serve Contract No 7; it consisted of a head-shunt, as entered in the direction of Dolphinton, on the south-east side of the line. A connection then reversed off towards the north-east, passing through the NBR's boundary gate and connecting with McAlpine's standard gauge works railway. The NBR plan shows a loop before the single line crosses the unclassified public road from West Linton to Romanno Bridge, near to the present-day entrance to the

White Moss garage. Colonel Yorke of the Railway Inspectorate reported on 28th November that the new connection was worked from a 2-lever ground frame, controlled by the key attached to the train staff. The line here was on a rising gradient of 1 in 108 towards Dolphinton, and so traffic in and out of the siding was to be worked only by trains having the locomotive at the northern (Broomlee) end, so as to prevent any runaways. The May 1901 *Appendix to the Working Time Tables* gave the usual strict instructions as to the working of the siding :

> 1. No shunting is to be done at Messrs R. M'Alpine & Sons' Siding, near Broomlee, unless the Engine is at the lower end of the Wagons.
> 2. The Station-master at Broomlee, as well as the District Inspectors, must satisfy themselves from time to time that these instructions are being strictly carried out, and it will be their duty to report every instance of failure to comply with them which may come under their notice.
> 3. The Engineer will fix a board at the Points leading to the Sidings, on which the foregoing instructions must be painted.

McAlpine's employed two 0-4-0 saddle tank locomotives on their works railway – Andrew Barclay Nos. 28 of 1864, and 731 of 1893; they were in use there from mid-1898 until around April 1900.* On 23rd February, 1899, a fireman was seriously injured when his engine derailed near Hamilton Hall, west of Romanno Bridge. The Penicuik 'ambulance wagon' was summoned and took the injured man to Edinburgh Royal Infirmary.

On 20th October, 1899, the Edinburgh and District Water Trustees paid an inspection visit to McAlpine's works. By then, these were nearing completion between Broomlee and Blyth Bridge. The party of about 20 arrived at Broomlee station by the 10.25 am from Waverley, and joined their waiting road carriages. After a pause at the old mill at Blyth Bridge for an explanation of the works, they continued for a further three miles to Stirkfield, to examine the work in progress. The *Scotsman* reported that 'On the return journey the party left the conveyances and travelled from Blyth Bridge over the service railway in a waggon, the rough and jolting journey being evidently a new and not very pleasant experience for the passengers'. Then it was back to their carriages for a drive through the estate of Sir James Fergusson (son of the late Sir William) to examine the 'handsome iron bridge which carries the two 33-inch pipes over the Lyne'. Dinner was served at the Gordon Arms (formerly the Hayston Arms) at West Linton.

---

* Information from *Contractors' Steam Locomotives of Scotland op cit.*

An Unofficial Stop?

The NBR Works Committee meeting on 17th January, 1895 authorized the erection of a gatekeeper's house at both Felton and Hyndfordwells [sic] level crossings, between Broomlee and Dolphinton, at a cost of £190 each, exclusive of land, and the company took powers in its 1896 Act to acquire land at the north-east corner of each of these ungated crossings over minor roads. No traces of such houses exist, nor is there a record in the staff register of gatekeepers being employed, and so it appears that the work was never undertaken. However, a lady from West Linton, now in her later years, was told some years ago by a Mrs Dickson, then a lady's maid at Bordlands House (near to Mountain Cross) that, when she was young, she and her sister (the Misses Wright) used to go Christmas shopping in Glasgow. They walked over the hill to join the Dolphinton branch train, which stopped at Hyndfordwell on request, although there is no mention of such an arrangement in the Working Time Tables! It is not known whether they travelled to Glasgow via Dolphinton, where the connections between the NBR and CR were infrequent, or via Leadburn and Edinburgh.

Dolphinton Station

Road access to the NBR station at Dolphinton was immediately south of the bridge which at that time carried the Edinburgh – Biggar (A702) road over the railway. The layout was very basic, with one platform line, extended to serve the goods yard, a run-round road parallel to it, and a line to the single road engine shed, with a short siding for a locomotive

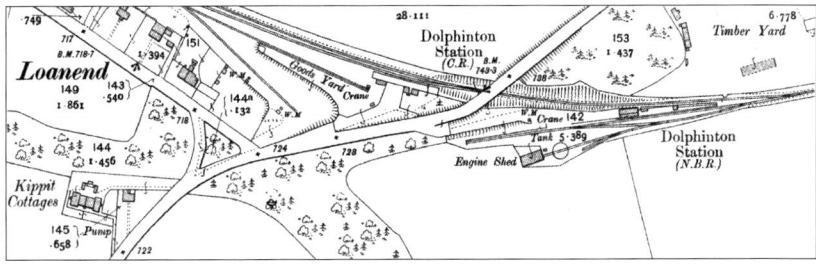

Ordnance Survey 25 inch map of Dolphinton published in 1908. The NBR and Caledonian stations were on opposite sides of the bridge which then carried the Biggar Road (now the A702) over the CR's connecting line.

Reproduced by permission of the National Library of Scotland

coal wagon. The engine shed, with a pit, was reached across the turntable and there was a small water tank at the entrance to the shed. There was a small goods shed and a 30 cwt. crane on the south side of the line. A single-line exchange siding, belonging to the Caledonian Railway, came from the Caley station, under the road bridge, and ran alongside the NBR goods yard and the rear of the station building, joining the NBR beyond the far end of the platform; the final 3 chains of the connecting line, and the junction itself, belonged to the NBR. When both stations were occupied, any traffic to be exchanged was left on the connecting line.

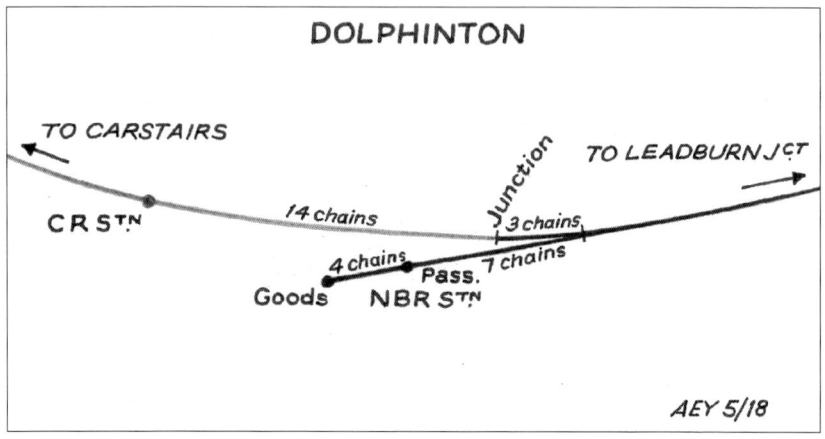

Diagram of the connection between the NBR and CR at Dolphinton.

The connecting line from the CR ran at the rear of the NBR station and formed a junction just beyond the platform end. The small goods transfer loading bank is beside the line in the foreground, and the heavy parcels transfer bank protrudes from the rear of the station building. *Lens of Sutton Association*

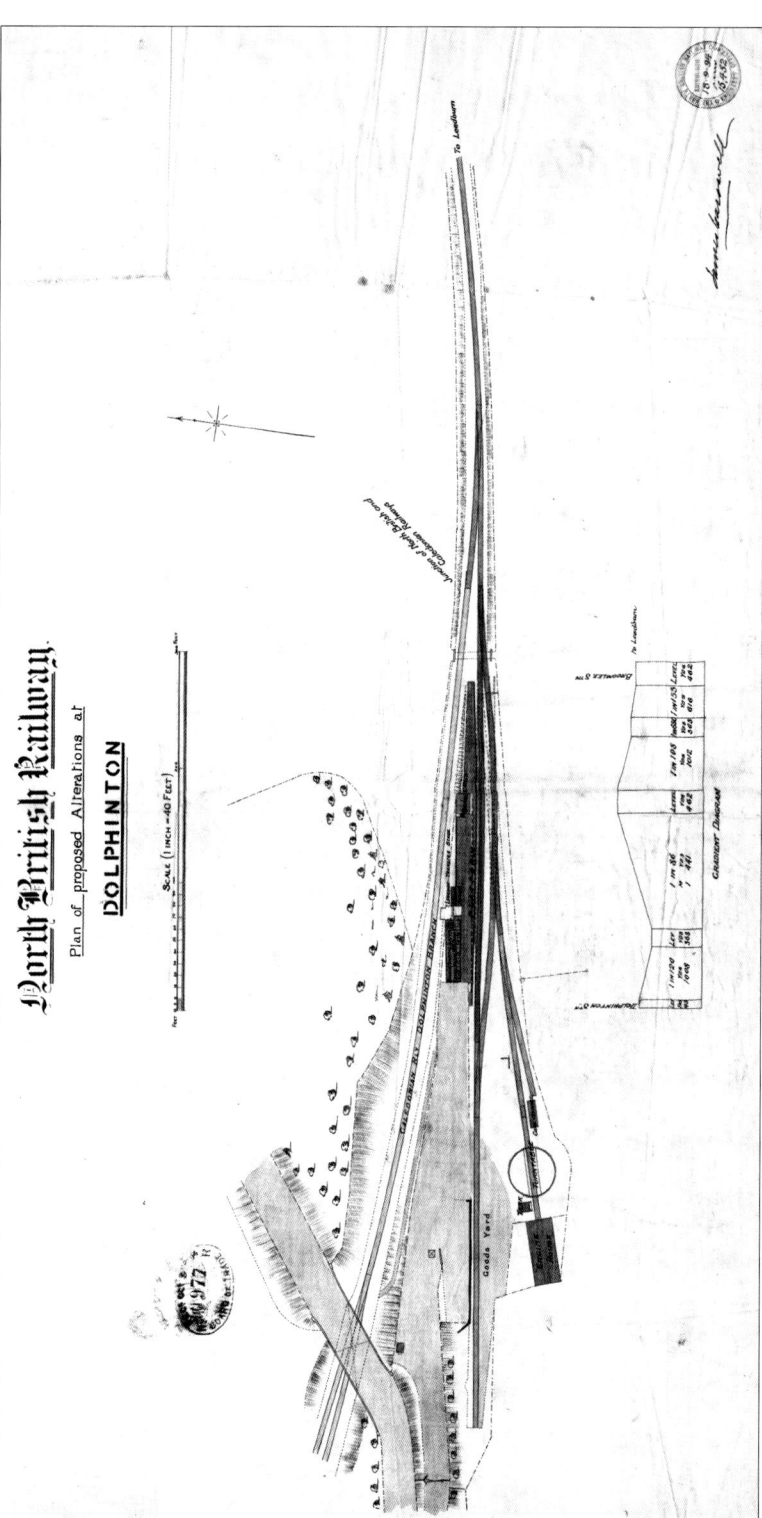

NBR September 1894 plan for the reconstruction of Dolphinton station, the extension of the platform, and adjustments to the trackwork. *Reproduced by permission of the National Archives, KewRef MT 6/718/1*

The revised 1858 6-inch OS map shows only one very small building on the platform, which accords with Major Marindin's description in 1893. The NBR's 1894 plan shows a completely rebuilt station in similar style to Broomlee, with booking office, general waiting room, ladies' room and WCs/urinals, and a separate lamp room. A full length canopy extended over the building. A full-size signal box, provided in the *circa* 1892 alterations, was sited at the Broomlee end of the platform. The 1898 Second Edition 25-inch OS map shows a weighing machine and a crane in the yard, where there was also a loading bank. A sketch plan of the station area, drawn in 1977 by Robert Brown, and representing the period 1920-1923 when he was a clerk at Dolphinton, shows a goods shed in the yard, and a small boiler house on the platform for heating the foot-warmer pans used prior to the introduction of steam train heating. His plan also shows a goods transfer loading bank where the CR exchange line passed alongside the NBR yard, a loading bank for the transfer of heavy parcels where it passed behind the NBR station building, and the 'disused signal box'.

The Dolphinton Creamery Company's premises were situated on the far side of the CR's connecting line at the rear of the NBR station. It commenced operations on 1st October, 1920, processing milk from local farmers and sending cheese and surplus milk by rail to dairymen in Edinburgh. On 16th February, 1922 it was advertising 'MILK delivered by Rail or Motor Daily to any district, Edinburgh and Leith'. After the railway closed, the milk was delivered by road to the Edinburgh dairies. The site has since been developed for housing.

Dolphinton Creamery *c.*1920s with Matt Scott and his sister Nan and the Creamery's ex-First World War lorry. *WLDHA collection*

An undated postcard of Dolphinton station. The signal box is in place, which dates the view to post-1892. The station master is either George Cruickshank (died December 1911) or his successor, Robert Wilson. The sign on the side of the building reads 'Post Office Dolphinton'.

NRS/Department for Transport under Open Government Licence v3.0.

Dolphinton NBR c.1910. The locomotive is thought to be NBR Drummond 4-4-0 tank No. 76. The signal box opened in 1892/93 but by March 1898 it had been downgraded to a lever frame for working the points, with no signals. Its size seems quite out of proportion to the number of train movements. *Lens of Sutton Association*

Dolphinton came second to Broomlee in terms of passenger numbers and coal and mineral traffic. In terms of livestock it lagged behind Macbie Hill: farmers in the area had the choice of sending their animals to market in Lanark by the Caledonian, or to Edinburgh* by the North British. Alison MacDonald** relates how lambs would be driven to Leadburn from all over the Moorfoots and rested overnight at the field known as Station Park before being transported to Lanark by rail.

For the year ended 31st July, 1874, it booked 5,673 passengers. Its best year was y.e. July 1901 when 9,104 passengers were booked, possibly in connection with the Blyth Bridge to Broughton section of McAlpine's aqueduct contract; in the last full year of operation, it booked 1,073.

As with Peebles, and other points on the system where the two companies' lines connected, Dolphinton was designated as the point of exchange for goods traffic between specified groups of CR stations and specified groups of NBR stations, as set out in the voluminous routing instructions issued by both companies, although it is unlikely that the flow of cross-company traffic here was great. It was also a point where the NBR could return empty coaching stock vehicles belonging to the Caledonian Railway, either by goods or passenger train. No record has been found of any passenger trains using the connecting line; if one did, then the passengers would have had to get out and walk between the two stations as the connection wasn't passed by the Board of Trade for their conveyance! There was a steady exchange of sheep and cattle, and horsebox traffic, a factor taken into consideration when the branch was proposed for closure (Chapter ten).

Jean Fleming's *Scots Magazine* article records that there were two engine drivers, two firemen and two guards on the branch in the first decade of the 20th century. The crews lived in Dolphinton, where the branch engine was stabled. The Caley had an engine shed at Dolphinton too, although it appears to have been out of use by the end of 1914.*** Together with the staff of both stations, that made for a fairly large railway community, and it is difficult to distinguish between NBR and CR staff in the Census and other records.

---

* or Peebles or Dalkeith.

** *op cit*

*** Harold Bowtell, in Caledonian Railway Association's Journal *The True Line* No 50, Summer 1995. *LMS Engine Sheds Volume 5, the Caledonian Railway* by Hawkins & Reeve (Wild Swan Publications, 1997) says that it closed on 31st December, 1915, with the final removal of the building and turntable being recorded in LMS Minutes of May 1933.

Dolphinton Shed, after closure. The rails have gone, but the turntable pit has not yet been filled in. The original roof vent is in place, as is the water tank.

Bill Lynn collection

Dolphinton LNER looking towards Leadburn on 11th February, 1969 and showing the engine shed in the foreground, the Dolphinton Creamery on the left, and the former station, centre. *J L Stevenson*

The NBR station staff at Dolphinton on 18th April, 1874 were the agent, signal porter, and the passenger guard, William Thomson who, in the 1871 Census, is shown as a railway porter there. In 1881, his son James is recorded as an engine stoker. There are eight different signal porters listed over a 30-month period between 1876 and 1878, none of whom stayed long, or even took up their appointment; perhaps lodgings were hard to find. On the transfer of the last incumbent on 6th October, 1879, the staff ledger records: 'Place not to be filled up'. The agent, George Cruickshank, born in Huntly on 24th August, 1849, received a slightly higher salary than other agents on the branch – £59 16s. p.a. – because no station house was provided. He married Martha Walker from Gladsmuir on 16th June, 1876, and in April 1881 they were living in one of the group of four Kippit Cottages in Dolphinton (Peeblesshire), situated just west of the little post office, with their daughters aged three and one, baby son aged two months, father-in-law and a servant. Ten years later, he was a widower, living with his two daughters and a son aged six. His baby son had died a month after the April 1881 Census, another son was born in September 1884, and his wife had died of blood poisoning on 5th April, 1887, one day after the death of her day-old child. The house at Kippit Cottages 'lately possessed by Mr Cruickshank, Stationmaster' was advertised for let in February 1888; it consisted of 'Kitchen, Pantry, Room and attics'. George married Annie Cattanach from Kingussie* in July 1891, and the April 1901 Census shows them still living in a Kippit Cottage with two sons and a daughter all aged four and under. George, now aged 51, is shown as 'Station Master and Post Master'. In April 1911, the family is recorded as living at the Post Office, and Mrs Cruickshank is 'Assistant Post Mistress'; four children are living at home.

Following a series of national agreements between the NBR and the CR in December 1907, George Cruickshank was additionally given charge of the Caledonian station at Dolphinton with effect from 11th March, 1908. The Caledonian Railway paid 51 per cent of the wages of the joint staff. He died on 2nd December, 1911, age 62, after at least 37 years in the same post. Mrs Cruickshank continued as sub-postmistress until April 1916, being replaced by William Brown, shoemaker and auxiliary postman, whose daughter later took on the role.

George Cruickshank was replaced in February 1912 by Robert Wilson, aged 31, formerly chief booking clerk at Portobello, initially on £85 but rising to £230 following the large cost of living increase on 1st August, 1919. In September 1915, on the occasion of his marriage, he was

---

* Possibly a distant relation of the author, whose family also comes from Kingussie.

Dolphinton LNER station c.1925/26. Standing (*l. to r.*) are Donald Tweedie, lad porter; Bob Fell, fireman; and Robert Brown, clerk. Seated are Jack Hutchison, guard; Peter Small, driver; Robert Wilson, fireman; and Bob Stobie, driver.

WLDHA collection

presented with a marble clock by Mr Ash, the local schoolmaster, 'on behalf of his fellow workmen and many friends ... whose respect he has won by his unfailing courtesy, his obliging manner, and his universal urbanity'. He transferred to Innerleithen on 1st June, 1921 (and thereafter to Ladybank, Cowdenbeath and Kittybrewster) and was succeeded by Neil Spiers, who had come from Uddingston West. He was noted for his height – 6 feet 6 inches. Like his NBR predecessor, Mr Spiers resided in one of the two Caledonian Railway cottages backing on to the CR station area – the one previously allocated to the CR station master. The staff ledger records 'Position Closed' as at 29th December, 1932, and Dolphinton, too, came under the supervision of Broomlee; Mr Spiers became station master of the LNER stations at Uddingston [East] and Uddingston West.

Peter Small was well remembered locally as one of the NBR drivers in the LNER era. In 1901, he was still resident in the Canongate district of Edinburgh, not far from St Margarets locomotive depot, but by 1911 he was living in East Lodge in Dolphinton, across the county boundary in Lanarkshire, as were his fireman, Bob Fell, boarding in 1911 at Beechwood Cottage, aged 25, and another NBR 'Stoker', William Bonnar, living at the Old Toll with his wife and two children. The other

NBR driver in 1911, Robert Stobie, lived in one of the four Kippit Cottages with his wife and six children. Peter Small retired on 6th March, 1928 at the age of 70 and died at Dolphinton on 29th November, 1929. Bob Stobie was still driving, and Bob Fell still firing, on the line's closure. The other driver at closure was John Dobson. Robert Wilson was another of the firemen in the last years of the line.

William Thomson is the first branch guard recorded in April 1874. He died in July 1899, aged 62, described as 'Retired Railway Guard and Coal Agent'. There is no record of an immediate replacement. A new post of porter/relief guard was filled in January 1900 by David Johnston; in 1901 he was one of three railwaymen boarding with William Thomson's widow, the other two being 'Railway Stokers'. Johnston became the branch guard the following year, transferring to Edinburgh in September 1906. He was replaced by Andrew Simpson, formerly a passenger shunter at Edinburgh. Simpson, another well-remembered character, was to remain in post until the branch closed. The porter/relief guard position changed to that of second passenger guard in April 1919 with the appointment of Jack (John) Hutchison, who would also see out the end of services on the branch. Brought up in Dolphinton, he transferred from the CR to the NBR in 1910 as a porter and relief guard and, after a short spell in Edinburgh from 1916 to 1919, returned to Dolphinton. 'Linden Cottage', for many years his property, still has, as its front porch, part of what appears to be a former NBR signal box, acquired possibly from either the Peebles or Dolphinton branch.

In April 1911, guard Andrew Simpson was living with his wife and two children in one of the two CR Railway Cottages and they had a boarder – 16-year-old Adam Somerville, appointed to a new post of temporary apprentice

Guard Andrew Simpson, photographed in the last week of the passenger train service.
Marion Moore collection

clerk in May 1909, and son of the Somervilles at Macbie Hill station. He transferred to Broomlee the following month. The post was later made permanent and the incumbent in 1914 was James Cruickshank, probably the son of the late station master – the name and age match. He transferred to Abbeyhill in 1916 and was replaced by a clerkess, Marion Simpson, who may well have been the daughter of Guard Simpson – name and age similarly match. Her services were dispensed with in 1919 to make way for an NBR employee returning from the First World War. There were two clerks at Dolphinton from 1920 – 1927, covering the two stations: Bob Stobie Junior, son of driver Bob Stobie, formerly at Broomlee, who transferred to Melrose in March 1927, and Robert Brown. At one time, no fewer than three porters were in post at Dolphinton for the two stations – appointed in 1916, 1917 and 1920. The reason is not apparent but may have been connected with wartime traffic. In 1921-1922, one post was dispensed with, and the other two were made 'Lad Porter' posts. These continued until August 1930, when one of the remaining posts was dispensed with, leaving only Donald Hutchison, the younger son of Jack. An earlier incumbent as lad porter was Charles Hutchison, the name of Jack's elder son. Nothing like keeping it in the family, particularly when wartime recruitment and accommodation would have been difficult in a rural location.

Andrew Simpson died at Kippit Cottages on 21st January, 1956. Alex Aitken remembered him as:

> the ideal type of public servant, calm and unruffled, always with a cheery word and a helping hand, yet firm withal. More years than I care to recollect, I, a small boy schoolwards bound, was placed in the care of 'Andrew the Guard', as were many others of my time. He remained our staunch friend for life. He was not afraid of an outspoken opinion and took a foremost part in the political arguments of the years before 1914. The then driver of the Dolphinton train was as staunch a Tory as the guard was Liberal, so that a Leadburn wit christened the train 'Tariff Reform in the front and the Budget in the back'. On a summer afternoon in 1916, while engaged in shunting at Broomlee, he suffered a severe accident due to the slipping of a pole. He made a good recovery and saw the end of the train service sixteen years later.

Mrs Margaret Thomson, widow of guard William Thomson (*above*), carried on his coal business from 1899 until about 1909 when the business was transferred to her youngest son George B. Thomson, although it still traded under his mother's name until sometime between 1915 and 1920. Mrs Thomson registered two 10-ton wagons with the Caledonian Railway in 1900 – Nos. 1 and 2 – but in the CR Traders' List of 1908 she is shown as having only one wagon, and that

Mrs Margaret Thomson's coal wagon No. 1. *Ed McKenna collection*

James Brown's coal wagon No. 21 at Dolphinton. *Ed McKenna collection*

had been dispensed with by 31st July, 1909. Also operating from the coal yard at the Caley's Dolphinton station was 'Coalie Brown' – James Brown – who was trading by 1881. He was later joined in the business by his eldest son Thomas. The business owned two 8-ton wagons, numbered 15 and 21, both of which were still running in April 1941. Although the wagons were lettered 'Dolphinton, C.R.', Brown is also listed in the NBR Traders' Wagons Register, and so presumably ran traffic over that line too.*

Accidents

In addition to the fatal accident at Tipperwell in October 1863, the line saw more than its fair share of mishaps over the years. By 24th August of that same year, the works were making good progress, with the contractor's engine running between Leadburn and Coalyburn. An Irish labourer who was working at the face of the ballast quarry at Cowdenburn was watching the engine shunting when there was a fall of earth which knocked him off his feet and on to the track. He was severely crushed between two trucks, and died shortly afterwards.

On 12th February, 1864, a labourer who was ballasting the new line near the West Water bridge at Bogsbank (about half a mile south-west of Broomlee) saw a horse and wagons approaching at speed. Thinking that the driver had lost control, he attempted to seize the reins, but fell in front of the wagons and was killed, 'not a syllable having escaped his lips to account for his attempt to stop the horse'.

On 31st May, 1864, some workmen were removing the beams from the bridge over the Black Burn at Medwyn Mains (east of Dolphinton) to substitute new girders, when one man fell 15 feet from the bridge and broke his neck, dying instantly. This appears to have happened in the course of remedying the defects identified by Captain Rich during his inspection of the new line on 21st May.

On 25th August, 1874, as the 5.08 pm train from Leadburn to Dolphinton was approaching Lamancha station, an axle on a mineral wagon broke. The rails were torn up and the carriages derailed, but there were no injuries.

The only accident resulting in the death of a passenger occurred at Broomlee station on 17th November, 1887. Mrs Christina Brown, a fishwife from Fisherrow, Musselburgh, had travelled to West Linton to

---

* Information from Ed McKenna.

sell fish and, when crossing behind the train with her creel, the train reversed and she was killed on the spot. The *Southern Reporter* of 24th November reported the details:

> Melancholy Accident at West Linton. On the afternoon of Thursday last a shadow of gloom overspread the district of West Linton on the announcement that a Mrs Brown, who was well known to the inhabitants, had been killed at Broomlee Station. Deceased, who was a fishwife, had just stepped from the afternoon train and got on her creel, and was passing the level-crossing when the carriages were shunted backwards, and she was knocked down, three of the carriages passing over her. When the body was got out it was found to be fearfully mangled, and was taken from the goods Shed to the Police Station. Investigation is being made into the matter, and the greatest sympathy is expressed for the husband and large family of little ones left to mourn Mrs Brown's unfortunate end.

The *Peeblesshire Advertiser* of 19th November had the less likely version that Mrs Brown had been 'knocked down by the engine, and run over by the carriages'. The circumstances of the accident are not clear. The NBR Accident Book simply records: 'Run over. Killed'. The afternoon train (2.20 pm from Edinburgh, 3.25 pm from Leadburn) was a mixed train, and so may well have shunted back across the level crossing into the goods yard after dropping its passengers at the platform. In that case, the crossing gates would have been closed against road traffic. Perhaps Mrs Brown avoided the closed gates by crossing the line elsewhere. If she had been walking into the village, as most of the other passengers would have been, she would not have needed to cross the track, and so was presumably heading first to Broomlee House or Broomlee Mains to sell her fish. The husband and four children of Mrs Brown sued the NBR for damages, alleging that the train was suddenly and without warning shunted backwards. At first, the NBR denied liability, blaming the deceased herself for crossing the line where she did, 'instead of at the level crossing'. It later agreed to settle the action in the sum of £250 for the husband and £250 for the children plus costs.

On the evening of Friday 25th October, 1894, William Pate, aged 62, farmer at Easter Deans, Newlands, was proceeding from the Caledonian to the North British station at Dolphinton when he fell over the parapet of the road bridge, having apparently been looking for a short cut. He died of his injuries on the Monday morning in Lamancha station house, to where he had presumably been taken by train.

On the morning of 9th June, 1920, Peter Edmonds, a quarryman, aged 60, of Upper Whitfield, was on his way to work and took a path which led across the railway near Macbie Hill station. He was hard of hearing, and so was unaware of the approach of a 'special train'. He was struck by the engine and died the following day in Edinburgh Royal Infirmary.

Overnight on Saturday/Sunday 26th/27th November, 1921, a large squad of workmen from Messrs P. & W. MacLellan was working on the Bogsbank iron girder bridge over the West Water ('The Splash'). About 5 am on the Sunday morning, a girder slid off the pier, taking with it a number of workmen. Seven sustained leg and other injuries. The local doctor, district nurse and other local inhabitants were soon at the scene and the men were carried on stretchers to Broomlee station, and then by special train to Waverley and so to the Royal Infirmary, where five were detained.

Mr Greig's notebook records that the level crossing gates at Broomlee were damaged by the noon goods on 15th August, 1923; they were damaged again on 16th November, 1926: the 9.16 am train from Dolphinton to Leadburn had just pulled into the station at Broomlee when a lorry belonging to the Dolphinton Creamery Company, probably delivering milk churns to the station, crashed into the closed southern gate, causing damage to the gates and to the lorry. Nobody was injured. Frost on the road was blamed for the accident.

In the early afternoon on 10th January, 1938, after the line had closed to passengers, a spectacular pile-up occurred. The Press report made a good story of it:

> There was considerable excitement in West Linton on Monday afternoon, when some railway trucks were seen racing down the steep incline towards Broomlee station, pursued by a powerful locomotive, screaming out a shrill warning to all and sundry who might by any mischance be in their path. It appears that the trucks, loaded with tar chips for the County Surveyor's department, had during shunting operations at Lamancha station got into motion before being properly coupled up, and, gaining momentum, dashed down the incline from Macbiehill towards Broomlee, where the metals now end. The Broomlee gates were reduced to matchwood, the trucks rending large splinters from the face of the platform and hurling them through the windows of the booking office and waiting rooms now used as a dwelling-house. The trucks and guard's van practically buried themselves in the one-time permanent way in front of the station, three of them coming to rest just short of the steep descent into the River Lyne, the bridge over which has already been removed by the railway company in the process of dismantling the Dolphinton branch. Fortunately, the public road, which at Broomlee station crosses the railway track, was clear of traffic and no one was injured.

By this date, the track had been lifted from Dolphinton, and beyond Broomlee station, to the goods yard. Other reports had the wagons demolishing the sleeper buffer, which would have been in place at the end of the line, before crashing through a fence, rather than through the former crossing gates. Nanny Hodge, employed by the Thompson (Ben Line) family, witnessed the event while out pushing a pram, and so had a narrow escape! The occupants of the former station house had an alarming experience when the wagons flashed past their windows! A statement issued the following day by the LNER said that three wagons loaded with road metal and with brake van attached ran away from Macbie Hill about 2.35 pm and became derailed beyond the public roadway at Broomlee, West Linton. Safety precautions laid down in great detail in the 1890s for shunting on the steep gradients at Lamancha and Macbie Hill (referred to in Chapter Eight) appear to have been ignored!

The branch features in several claims over the years for the value of lambs and sheep killed on the line (or, as some cynics used to say, dead animals strategically placed by farmers!). For example: 'Law and Claims Committee, 14th March, 1889. Lamb killed near Leadburn on 13th July, 1888. Settlement for 17s. less 7s. 4d. realized from sale of carcass. Claim by Mr Pate.'

Snow

Severe snowstorms in the 19th and early 20th centuries often brought the railways to a stop for several days at a time, and the Peebles and Dolphinton branches were frequently affected. The railways employed a large number of surfacemen and they, along with a squad of labourers, could quickly be gathered into a large gang and armed with shovels, to supplement the efforts of a snowplough propelled by two or more heavy locomotives. It was backbreaking work, which often had to be sustained in harsh conditions over many hours, in the efforts to reopen the line and get traffic moving with a minimum of delay. During periods when heavy snow threatened, a snowplough would patrol the line to Peebles, with occasional trips on the Dolphinton branch.

On Friday 1st January, 1875, for example, a snowstorm blocked both branches; passengers from Edinburgh to Peebles reached Leadburn, where many of them had to wait until the Sunday evening, others having set out on foot on the Saturday. Being of higher priority, the Peebles branch was allocated the majority of the resources but, after it had been reopened, a gang of 200 workmen finally cleared the cutting at White

Moss, south-west of the 'Splash', on the afternoon of Tuesday the 5th. At the end of February, and in March, the line was again blocked, the largest drift being at Lamancha. Lamancha and Macbiehill were frequently the sites of blockages caused by deep snowdrifts blown by strong winds. The line was blocked for two days in March 1876. March 1881 saw particularly severe conditions. A Peebles passenger train stuck in a cutting a mile south of Leadburn and the engine sent to its rescue couldn't get close. The 20 passengers were instead conveyed back north to Pomathorn on the rescue engine's tender, presumably in relays, and the Dolphinton train was sent out to take them on to Edinburgh, but it too became stuck; the hapless passengers had to trudge through drifting snow for half a mile to the Penicuik branch, which was still open, and a special train was arranged. The Dolphinton branch remained blocked for several more days, as the locomotive propelling the snowplough overturned, severely injuring one of the crew. In December 1882 the line was closed for four days. Between Lamancha and Macbie Hill the snowplough and its locomotives charged a 13 foot bank of snow; a surfaceman riding on the tender was pitched forward and crushed between the plough and the snow, escaping with a badly splintered ankle.

As explained in Chapter Eight, the single-line Dolphinton branch was worked by means of the Train Staff, and possession of the staff by the engine driver was an absolute requirement so as to prevent the risk of collision with another train on the line. On 20th February, 1888 the 8.00 am train from Dolphinton stuck fast at Medwyn Mains, probably in the same White Moss cutting mentioned previously, in drifts as high as the carriages. The snowplough couldn't come on to the branch without being in possession of the train staff for the Leadburn – Broomlee section, which would have been at Broomlee, and so a messenger had to take the staff (on horseback, or on foot?) through the snow to Leadburn. The following month, a snowplough preceding the 11.40 am train from Leadburn to Dolphinton itself stuck fast short of Lamancha. February 1900 saw the worst block since 1881, and the Dolphinton branch was the last to be reopened. Despite the efforts of a snow plough propelled by three locomotives, little progress was made, and operations had to be suspended until the following day.

The first decade of the 20th century saw many similar scenes, but being stuck in the snow could have its up side too. In his valediction to the line in the *Peeblesshire Advertiser* of 1st April, 1933, *A Linton Plooman* (Alex Aitken) recalled 'the adventures of the snow drifts, when prodigious breakfasts at Macbiehill put heart into stranded folk till the line could be cleared'.

Fire

Snow and ice were the hazards of winter. In the summer, sparks from passing locomotives could set ablaze the moorlands of Auchencorth Moss. As with snowdrifts, a large gang would be assembled to tackle the blaze and to dig trenches around it to halt its progress.

The *Scotsman* of 13th June, 1912 reported the results of a severe thunderstorm: 'At West Linton a bullock, the property of Mr John Ross, Hamilton Hall Farm, was struck down dead, and at Dolphinton station, on the North British Railway, the chimney was knocked off the engine shed and the roof set on fire.'

Bob Stobie, driver, with the station cat at Dolphinton LNER on 25th March, 1933. The Dolphinton Creamery buildings are in the background. *Marion Moore collection*

Chapter Five

Train Services

Passenger Services

The passenger timetable for the Dolphinton branch was, inevitably, governed by that for the more important Edinburgh to Galashiels via Peebles branch, with which it connected at Leadburn, and was compiled to provide convenient connections to and from the Capital; connections to and from the county town of Peebles were given only secondary consideration and so there could be long waits at Leadburn for the $9\frac{1}{2}$ mile journey. Unlike the Peebles branch, there were never regular Sunday services on the LL&DR, although there were special Sunday workings in July 1910, as described later.

The opening day press advertisement, for Monday 4th July, 1864, (*see page 61*) shows four passenger trains in each direction. The August timetable showed the branch connections to and from Edinburgh and Peebles, if a wait at Leadburn of 1 hour 18 minutes for travellers on the 6.00 pm train from Peebles could be called a connection! Similar examples abound. Linton people trying to get to Peebles and back in a day could face a rather tedious journey, with a wait at Leadburn either

AUGUST 1864		am	am	pm	pm
Dolphinton	dep	8.30	11.20	1.20	5.55
West Linton*	arr	8.40	11.30	1.30	6.05
Coalyburn	arr	8.46	11.36	1.36	6.11
Lamancha	arr	8.50	11.40	1.40	6.15
Leadburn	arr	9.03	11.50	1.50	6.25
Peebles	arr	*9.50*	*12.25*	--	*8.10*
Edinburgh	arr	*9.50*	--	*2.50*	*7.20*
		am	am	pm	pm
Edinburgh	dep	*8.20*	*11.5*	*4.23*	*6.50*
Peebles	dep	*8.45*	--	--	*6.00*
Leadburn	dep	9.22	12.00	5.02	7.44
Lamancha	arr	9.31	12.09	5.11	7.53
Coalyburn	arr	9.35	12.13	5.15	7.57
West Linton*	arr	9.42	12.20	5.22	8.04
Dolphinton	arr	9.52	12.30	5.32	8.14

* 'Broomlee for West Linton' from 23rd August, 1864.
All trains are mixed (i.e. passenger and goods)
(*Italics denote connections, not through carriages*)

going or coming, and sometimes both, so that many looked to Edinburgh for business and pleasure, and sent their children to schools in Edinburgh for secondary education.

The best trains to and from Edinburgh were the 8.30 am from Dolphinton (1 hour 20 minutes) and the 4.23 pm 'Fast' from Edinburgh (1 hour 9 minutes).

A connecting coach left Blyth Bridge for Broomlee station at 7.40 am in connection with the 8.40 am departure, returning from Broomlee on the arrival of the branch train at 5.22 pm.

Over the winter months, the service was reduced to three trains daily each way – at 8.10 am, 10.50 am and 6.40 pm from Dolphinton, and at 9.04 am, 5.10 pm and 7.17 pm from Leadburn, leaving most of the afternoon for the branch locomotive to attend to any goods workings. From May 1865, additional trains – 11.45 am from Leadburn [Edinburgh depart 10.50 am; Peebles depart 10.57 am] and 2.20 pm from Dolphinton [Edinburgh arrive 3.50 pm] – were added for the summer, and this pattern of three trains each way in winter, and four in summer, continued until 1872.

Beginning with the 1872-73 winter timetable, four trains ran each way throughout the year, with departures from Dolphinton at 8.12 am, 11.00 am, 2.05 pm and 6.40 pm, and from Leadburn at 9.03 am, 11.50 am, 5.08 pm and 7.17 pm. By 1877, the final return working of the day had become an hour or so later. June 1878 saw the first through service to Edinburgh – a chance for the branch train with its probably elderly locomotive and first, second and fourth class carriages to have a day out on the main line: on Summer Saturdays, the early afternoon departure from Dolphinton was advanced to 12.25 pm and the train ran through to Edinburgh Waverley, arriving there at 1.35 pm. It then worked a 2.00 pm service to Innerleithen, arriving at 3.22 pm, and a 3.45 pm service back to Leadburn, arriving at 4.25 pm in time for the next branch working – the 5.17 pm to its home station at Dolphinton. This summer Saturdays working – described in the timetable as 'Market Train' – continued until the summer of 1886, after which additional branch duties put an end to such main line jaunts.

July 1887 saw the introduction of a fifth, mid-afternoon, train throughout the year.

A six-week strike over the Christmas and New Year period in 1890-91 disrupted services. Train crews and signalmen employed by the North British, Caledonian and Glasgow & South Western Railway companies were protesting against the excessively long hours that they were expected to work. Passenger services on the Peebles and Dolphinton

JULY 1887

		am	am	pm	pm	pm
				Mixed		
Dolphinton	dep	8.00	10.15	2.35	4.15	7.25
Broomlee	arr	8.10	10.25	2.45	4.30	7.35
Macbie Hill	arr	8.16	10.31	2.51	4.40	7.41
Lamancha	arr	8.20	10.35	2.55	4.45	7.45
Leadburn	arr	8.30	10.48	3.10	4.55	8.00
Peebles	arr	– –	*11.58*	*3.39*	*5.34*	*9.07*
Edinburgh	arr	*9.14*	*11.53*	*4.05*	*6.50*	*8.55*

		am	am	pm	pm	pm
			Mixed			
Edinburgh	dep	*6.40*	*10.40*	*2.20*	*4.30*	*7.45*
Peebles	dep	*8.10*	*10.35*	*2.52*	– –	*7.45*
Leadburn	dep	8.40	11.40	3.25	5.15	8.50
Lamancha	arr	8.48	11.49	3.33	5.24	8.59
Macbie Hill	arr	8.52	11.53	3.40	5.28	9.03
Broomlee	arr	8.59	12.00	3.48	5.35	9.10
Dolphinton	arr	9.10	12.10	4.00	5.45	9.20

(*Italics denote connections, not through carriages*)

branches returned to near normal after a few days, but goods and mineral traffic – including household coal – continued to be badly affected.*

In the winter timetables from 1895-96,** and then throughout the year from July 1902, the last train in each direction became Saturdays Only (Mondays and Saturdays Only in the high summer).

Thereafter, the last departure from Leadburn on weekdays – previously as late as 9.15 pm (8.25 pm from Edinburgh) – was never later than 6.50 pm (6.05 pm from Edinburgh). 'A.V.' of West Linton wrote to the *Edinburgh Evening News* on 4th July, 1902. Referring to 'this most delightful country retreat (deservedly so popular with Edinburgh folk, and to which some from the West Coast also now come)' he complained that 'For many years in summer, when many visitors are here, there has been a late train to Edinburgh and a late mail. This year the train is withdrawn, and the last mail from Linton is about 4.30. The step is a

---

* See a series of six articles by the author in the *North British Railway Study Group Journal* (2004 – 2006).

** Apart from an experimental re-introduction in December 1898.

most ridiculous one to take, and should lead to the Caledonian Company being strongly invited to run through from Dolphinton to Edinburgh.' The lack of an evening connection to West Linton on weekdays became a perennial cause for complaint, with suggestions that West Linton folk couldn't be trusted to be out after dark!

The peak years for passenger traffic on the branch were from 1897 to 1905 as West Linton grew in popularity with summer visitors and 'residenters' alike, boosted by traffic for the ongoing works on the Talla aqueduct. In June 1898, the service was augmented on Summer Saturdays by an additional lunchtime train in each direction; there was now a Summer Saturdays service of six trains in each direction. The June 1898 timetable, as corrected for July, was:

JULY 1898				SO	SX	SO		
		am	am	pm	pm	pm	pm	pm
Dolphinton	dep	7.45	10.05	12.50	2.10	2.13	4.40	7.30
Broomlee	arr	7.53	10.13	12.58	2.18	2.21	4.48	7.38
Macbie Hill	arr	7.58	10.18	1.03	2.23	2.26	4.53	7.43
Lamancha	arr	8.02	10.22	1.07	2.27	2.30	4.57	7.47
Leadburn	arr	8.10	10.30	1.15	2.35	2.38	5.05	7.55
Peebles	arr	– –	*11.38***A**	*2.00*	*3.19*	*3.19*	*5.32*	*8.56*
Edinburgh	arr	*8.49*	*11.21*	– –	*3.28*	*3.28*	*6.19*	*8.53*

			SX Mixed	SO Mixed	SO			Mixed
		am	am	am	pm	pm	pm	pm
Edinburgh	dep	*6.50*	*10.25*	*10.40*	*1.05*	*2.10*	*4.30*	*7.45*
Peebles	dep	*7.57*	*10.16*	*10.16*	– –	*2.22*	– –	*7.42*
Leadburn	dep	8.20	11.25	11.40	1.44	3.07	5.18	8.43
Lamancha	arr	8.28	11.34	11.49	1.52	3.15	5.26	8.51
Macbie Hill	arr	8.32	11.41	11.56	1.56	3.19	5.30	8.55
Broomlee	arr	8.37	11.48	12.03	2.01	3.24	5.35	9.00
Dolphinton	arr	8.45	11.57	12.12	2.09	3.32	5.43	9.10

SO – Saturdays only; **SX** – Saturdays excepted; **A** – 11.53 on Saturdays
(*Italics denote connections, not through carriages*)

The 1.05 pm SO from Edinburgh to Dolphinton, with a change at Leadburn, popular with summer visitors, was now scheduled to take only 64 minutes; by the summer of 1904, the stops at Lamancha and Macbie Hill had been omitted, although the journey time was 65 minutes. For early morning travellers to Edinburgh, the time from Dolphinton to Edinburgh was down to 64 minutes, and the 4.30 pm return only 73 minutes. (The longer times for up (Edinburgh to Leadburn) journeys are explained by the continuous steep gradients.)

From 1902-1903, the winter service was reduced from five to four trains each way, with an additional train on Saturdays. That, and the withdrawal of the evening service already referred to, called for action! The *Edinburgh Evening News* of 24th November, 1902 reported that:

> Proprietors, residents and others interested in the prosperity of West Linton and neighbourhood have presented a requisition to the directors of the North British Railway Company with regard to the railway facilities. ... What is suggested is that at least two trains from both ends of the line be run through, one in the morning and another in the afternoon, and thus avoid the unnecessary long stop and change of carriages at Leadburn Station. Attention is also directed to the height at Leadburn Station, between the platform and the carriage, which is not altogether without danger. A morning train from Dolphinton to connect with the 8.50 train from Peebles is asked for, and it is requested that the 1 pm (Saturday) and the 6.5 pm trains ex Edinburgh be run from the first day of April, and that the late trains be run every day of the week in place of being limited to Monday and Saturday.

The names of the 148 signatories to the requisition, which included the eminent architect Hippolyte Jean Blanc RSA, reads like a 'Who's Who' of the County, but to no avail. The Minutes of the NBR's Traffic Committee, meeting on 29th January, 1903, record: 'West Linton. Train Service to Dolphinton. A Petition from Proprietors, Residenters and others interested in the prosperity of West Linton and neighbourhood, as to the train service on the Dolphinton branch, was submitted and declined.'

The *Edinburgh Evening Dispatch* poked fun at the people of West Linton and their railway:

> This is a sign of how things are moving along, even on the slopes of the Pentlands. The branch railway by Leadburn to Dolphinton used to be one of the wonders of the world. The people of West Linton were the last to discover it, because, until a few years ago, nobody in West Linton was ever pressed for time. When the people of West Linton had to come into Edinburgh by rail they took provisions with them and made a day of it. If they were in a hurry, they walked...

The 'requisitionists' were not prepared to accept defeat! The *Edinburgh Evening News* of 27th March, 1903:

> Dolphinton Branch Railway Facilities. Following upon the requisition that was laid before the directors of the North British Railway Company some time ago, a large and influential deputation waited yesterday, by appointment, upon a

committee of directors, and emphasised the grievances that exist in connection with the travelling facilities on this branch. The following gentlemen spoke on behalf of the deputation: Mr Wm. Garson WS, representing Mr John H Forbes of Medwyn; ex-Bailie Lewis, as representing the feuars; Sir Thomas D Gibson-Carmichael, Bart. of Castlecraig, as representing the general travelling public, and Mr Hippolyte J Blanc RSA, as a summer visitor. The directors, after a courteous hearing, intimated that the statements made would receive their careful consideration.

The timetables don't show any subsequent changes; most pleas by deputations for improvements to train services failed to move the NBR Board!

March 1912 saw a miners' strike and the curtailment of services on the branch to two trains per day each way; the full service was restored on 13th April. At the end of May, the NBR advertised a new named train – the *Peeblesshire Express* – to run from 1st June to 30th September. It promised 'Delightful Summer Holidays in Peeblesshire' under the banner 'Peebles for Pleesure'[sic], 'Angling and Sylvan Scenery' and 'West Linton – the Centre of a Pastoral Country for Pure Bracing Air'. Leaving Edinburgh Waverley at 1.33 pm on Saturdays, passengers on the *Peeblesshire Express* reached Broomlee at 2.26 pm, by through carriage detached from the Peebles train at Leadburn – a journey time of 53 minutes, whilst Dolphinton was reached 8 minutes later. On Mondays to Fridays, the through carriage off the 5.31 pm from Edinburgh arrived at Broomlee in 56 minutes, and Dolphinton 8 minutes later. The first train of the day from Leadburn now terminated at Broomlee at 8.37 am in time for an 8.50 am return working with the *Peeblesshire Express* through carriage, to be attached to the Peebles – Edinburgh train at Leadburn. Macbie Hill and Lamancha stops were omitted and Waverley was reached at 9.37 am – a 47 minute journey from West Linton. In addition to catering for tourists, these 'executive' expresses, which included the *Fifeshire Coast Express* and the *Lothian Coast Express*, enabled the male breadwinner to travel daily to his office in Edinburgh from his family's 'summer quarters', put in a good six hours of work, and be back home in time for dinner and perhaps a round of golf in the evening. That summer (1912), there were the usual five trains each way on weekdays; on Saturdays there were six from Dolphinton or Broomlee, and seven from Leadburn, the addition being a 9.15 am from Leadburn to Dolphinton.

For Summer 1913, an additional Mondays to Fridays train was provided from Leadburn to Broomlee giving a service of five down (to Edinburgh) and six up. The additional service was the 5.17 pm from Leadburn, restoring the weekdays connection off the 4.32 pm from Waverley, the

Delightful Summer Holidays in Peeblesshire.

BROOMLEE (West Linton), PEEBLES, Etc.

New Morning and Evening Express Trains.

The Peeblesshire Express now runs as follows :—

	Sats. only. p.m.	p.m.	Ex. Sat. p.m.			a.m.
EDINBURGH (Waverley) ... leave	1 33	4 32	5 31	PEEBLES ... ... leave	8 44
BROOMLEE (West Linton) arrive	2 26	5:30	6 27	BROOMLEE (West Linton) ,,	8 50
PEEBLES ... ... ,,	2 28	5 30	6 24	EDINBURGH (Waverley) arrive	9 37

† 5·34 p.m. on Saturdays.

"PEEBLES FOR PLEESURE."
ANGLING AND SYLVAN SCENERY.
West Linton—The Centre of a Pastoral Country for Pure Bracing Air.
CHEAP PERIODICAL TICKETS.

P   JULY 1913

NBR timetable advertisement for the *Peeblesshire Express*, July 1913.

long-standing afternoon 'Fast' to Peebles, which had become Saturdays Only in 1912. It, too, was advertised under the *Peeblesshire Express* banner, although there was no through coach for the Dolphinton branch.

These unbalanced Summer workings were a feature of the line for some years, and required the branch engine to run light, or the branch train to run empty, back to Leadburn for the next up (to Dolphinton) passenger working. From the information in the Working Time Tables the arrangement seems to have been that, on Saturdays, the branch train left its coaches at Leadburn at 1.55 pm then worked the through coach off the *Peeblesshire Express* to Dolphinton at 2.13, before returning, light engine, to Leadburn to pick up its coaches again for the 3.07 pm return working. On weekdays, the *Peeblesshire Express* being the final working of the day (Mondays excepted), the whole train worked back empty from Dolphinton, to pick up the through coach.

One sad cargo, in the days before motor transport became widespread, was that of the bodies of deceased persons being returned home for burial. Mourners would be advised to meet on the arrival of the train at the local station, from where the funeral cortège would proceed to the churchyard. Broomlee and West Linton witnessed several such occasions.

The *Peeblesshire Express* ran again in the summer of 1914 but, as the First World War progressed, the service shrank to three trains in each direction,

JULY 1913 MON – FRIDAY		PbXP	TC				ECS	MSO Mixed
		am	am	am	pm	pm	pm	pm
Dolphinton	dep	7.40	– –	10.05	1.55	4.40	– –	7.25
Broomlee	arr	7.50	8.50d	10.13	2.03	4.48	5.38d	7.33
Macbie Hill	arr	7.55	– –	10.18	2.08	4.53	– –	7.38
Lamancha	arr	7.59	– –	10.22	2.12	4.57	– –	7.42
Leadburn	arr	8.07	9.02	10.30	2.20	5.05	5.50	7.50
Peebles	arr	– –	– –	11.34	3.23	5.30	– –	9.39
Edinburgh	arr	*8.50*	9.37	11.17	3.11	6.20	– –	8.57

				Mixed		PbXP	PbXP TC	MSO
		am	am	am	pm	pm	pm	pm
Edinburgh	dep	*6.58*	6.58	10.32	2.17	*4.32*	5.31	8.35
Peebles	dep	*7.50*	*8.44*	10.17	2.05	– –	*5.12*	*7.52*
Leadburn	dep	8.20	9.15	11.18	3.07	5.17	6.10	9.20
Lamancha	arr	8.28	9.23	11.27	3.15	– –	6.18	9.29
Macbie Hill	arr	8.32	9.27	11.34	3.19	– –	6.22	9.36
Broomlee	arr	8.37	9.32	11.41	3.24	5.30	6.27	9.43
Dolphinton	arr	– –	9.40	11.50	3.32	– –	6.35	9.52

PbXP – Peeblesshire Express. **TC** – Through carriage to or from Edinburgh Waverley.
MSO – Mondays and Saturdays Only.
ECS – empty coaching stock: after working the 5.17 pm from Leadburn, the engine and carriages return immediately to Leadburn to work the 6.10 pm. d – depart
(*Italics denote connections, not through carriages*)

JULY 1913 SATURDAYS		PbXP	TC			LE		
		am	am	am	pm	pm	pm	pm
Dolphinton	dep	7.40	– –	10.05	1.30	LE	4.40	7.25
Broomlee	arr	7.50	8.50d	10.13	1.38	– –	4.48	7.33
Macbie Hill	arr	7.55	– –	10.18	1.43	– –	4.53	7.38
Lamancha	arr	7.59	– –	10.22	1.47	– –	4.57	7.42
Leadburn	arr	8.07	9.02	10.30	1.55	LE	5.05	7.50
Peebles	arr	– –	– –	11.34	2.28	– –	5.30	9.39
Edinburgh	arr	*8.50*	9.37	11.17	2.48	– –	6.20	8.34

				Mixed	PbXP TC		PbXP	Mixed
		am	am	am	pm	pm	pm	pm
Edinburgh	dep	*6.58*	6.58	10.32	1.33	2.17	*4.32*	8.35
Peebles	dep	*7.50*	*8.44*	10.17	1.46	1.46	– –	*7.52*
Leadburn	dep	8.20	9.15	11.18	2.13	3.07	5.17	9.20
Lamancha	arr	8.28	9.23	11.27	– –	3.15	5.25	9.29
Macbie Hill	arr	8.32	9.27	11.34	– –	3.19	5.29	9.36
Broomlee	arr	8.37	9.32	11.41	2.26	3.24	5.34	9.43
Dolphinton	arr	– –	9.40	11.50	2.34	3.32	5.42	9.52

PbXP – Peeblesshire Express. **TC** – Through carriage to or from Edinburgh Waverley.
LE – Light engine: after working the 2.13 pm from Leadburn to Dolphinton, the engine returns light to work the 3.07 pm from Leadburn. d – depart
(*Italics denote connections, not through carriages*)

with an occasional extra summer working in the form of an early afternoon train from Waverley to Peebles with a connection for Dolphinton. From March 1916, the early morning Tuesdays-only cattle train from Dolphinton was combined with the first passenger train, which then ran as a mixed train on Tuesdays. By June 1919, a full service was slowly being resumed. That summer, there were four trains from Broomlee or Dolphinton and five from Leadburn on weekdays, with two additional trains each way on Saturdays, and the *Peeblesshire Express* was back, the through carriage taking 54 minutes from Waverley to Broomlee on Saturdays (59 on weekdays) and 48 minutes from Broomlee back to Edinburgh. The journey to Broomlee by the 4.46 pm 'Fast', with a change at Leadburn, took 62 minutes (59 on weekdays). The winter service was now three trains each way with an additional one on Saturdays. A 10-day strike by railwaymen at the end of September 1919 against Government plans to reduce pay again disrupted traffic.

1920 saw an improvement in the *Peeblesshire Express* timings to 53 minutes up (to Broomlee) on Saturdays and 47 minutes down, and there was yet another additional Summer Saturdays train from 1st August, taking the total to eight. The Working Time Tables show two light engine movements to balance the workings.

JUNE 1920 SATURDAYS		am	PbXP am	am	pm	pm	pm	TC pm	pm
Dolphinton	dep	7.30	– –	10.40	1.20	**LE1**	4.35	– –	7.40
Broomlee	arr	7.45	8.50d	10.48	1.28	– –	4.43	**LE2**	7.48
Macbie Hill	arr	7.50	– –	10.53	1.33	– –	4.48	– –	7.53
Lamancha	arr	7.54	– –	10.57	1.37	– –	4.52	– –	7.57
Leadburn	arr	8.02	9.02	11.05	1.45	**LE1**	5.00	**LE2**	8.05
Peebles	arr	– –	– –	*11.39*	*2.21*	– –	*5.39*	– –	*9.07*
Edinburgh	arr	*8.55*	*9.37*	*11.57*	*2.40*	– –	*6.30*	– –	*8.55*

		am	am	am	PbXP pm	pm	pm	TC pm	pm
Edinburgh	dep	*6.57*	– –	*10.33*	*1.25*	*2.20*	*4.32*	– –	*8.02*
Peebles	dep	*7.49*	*8.44*	*10.54*	*1.34*	– –	– –	*5.17*	*7.50*
Leadburn	dep	8.21	9.15	11.30	2.05	3.07	5.19	6.04	8.52
Lamancha	arr	8.29	9.23	11.38	– –	3.15	5.27	6.12	9.00
Macbie Hill	arr	8.33	9.27	11.42	– –	3.19	5.31	6.16	9.04
Broomlee	arr	8.38	9.32	11.47	2.18	3.24	5.35	6.21	9.09
Dolphinton	arr	– –	9.40	11.55	2.26	3.32	– –	6.29	9.17

PbXP – Peeblesshire Express. **TC** – Through carriage to or from Edinburgh Waverley.
LE1 – Light engine: after working the 2.05 pm from Leadburn to Dolphinton, the engine returns light to work the 3.07 pm from Leadburn.
LE2 – Light engine: after working the 5.19 pm from Leadburn to Broomlee, the engine returns light to work the 6.04 pm from Leadburn. d – depart
(*Italics denote connections, not through carriages*)

Another miners' strike from April to June 1921 meant a restricted timetable and there was no longer a reference in the public timetables to a through carriage to and from Broomlee off the *Peeblesshire Express*. The *Peeblesshire Express* continues to appear in the Peebles branch timetables until the summer of 1929, running non-stop from Edinburgh to Leadburn in 36 minutes.

Following the grouping of the country's many independent railway companies into the 'Big Four' on 1st January, 1923, the North British became part of the London & North Eastern Railway, but there were few changes to the timetables. In the later 1920s, the summer pattern settled down to five services from Dolphinton on weekdays and six on Saturdays, with five from Leadburn on weekdays and seven on Saturdays, and this continued until the final summer timetable in 1932. The winter timetable was latterly four trains on weekdays and six on Saturdays in both directions.

JULY 1932					SO	SX	SO		SO
MON – SATURDAY		am	am	am	pm	pm		pm	pm
Dolphinton	dep	7.37A	9.25	10.33	1.25	1.57	LE	4.34	7.47
Broomlee	arr	7.44	9.32	10.40	1.32	2.04	– –	4.41	7.54
Macbie Hill	arr	7.49	9.37	10.45	1.37	2.09	– –	4.46	7.59
Lamancha	arr	7.53	9.41	10.49	1.41	2.13	– –	4.50	8.03
Leadburn	arr	7.59	9.47	10.55	1.47	2.19	LE	4.56	8.09
Peebles	arr	*8.30*	*10.09*	– –	*2.15*	*3.12*	– –	*5.55*	*9.31*
Edinburgh	arr	*8.49*	*11.35*	*11.35*	*2.37*	*3.02*	– –	*5.41*	*8.55*

JULY 1932					SO		Mixed +		SO
MON – SATURDAY		am	am	am	pm		pm	pm	pm
Edinburgh	dep	7.17	9.12	– –	*1.10*		2.09	5.04	8.25
Peebles	dep	7.45	– –	*10.39*	*1.34*		*2.00C*	4.46	7.54
Leadburn	dep	8.20B	9.57	11.07	2.05		2.56	5.44	9.17
Lamancha	arr	8.27	10.04	11.14	2.12		3.05	5.51	9.24
Macbie Hill	arr	8.31	10.08	11.18	2.16		3.11	5.55	9.28
Broomlee	arr	8.36	10.13	11.23	2.21		3.17	6.02	9.33
Dolphinton	arr	8.43	10.20	11.30	2.28		3.26	6.09	9.40

SO – Saturdays only. SX – Saturdays excepted. LE – Light Engine
A – 7.27 on Tuesdays and runs correspondingly earlier as a mixed train, arriving at Leadburn at 7.57.
B – When vehicles require to be lifted at Lamancha, Macbie Hill or Broomlee, five minutes extra will be allowed at each point.
C – 1.34 pm on Saturdays.
+ – conveys Dolphinton branch Road Van from Leadburn.
(*Italics denote connections, not through carriages*)

TRAIN SERVICES

The introduction of new bus services in 1925 would eventually spell the end for the passenger service on the branch. The final timetable, from September 1932, showed four trains each way on weekdays, the same as the first timetable in 1864, but journey times were now 22 or 23 minutes for the 9.75 miles as compared with 30 minutes. Six trains ran each way on Saturdays.

WINTER 1932-33				SO	SO	SX		SO
		am	am	am	pm	pm	pm	pm
Dolphinton	dep	7.37A	9.25	10.33	1.25	1.57	4.32	7.47
Broomlee	arr	7.44	9.32	10.40	1.32	2.04	4.39	7.54
Macbie Hill	arr	7.49	9.37	10.45	1.37	2.09	4.44	7.59
Lamancha	arr	7.53	9.41	10.49	1.41	2.13	4.48	8.03
Leadburn	arr	7.59	9.47	10.55	1.47	2.19	4.54	8.09
Peebles	arr	*8.32*	*10.11*	– –	*2.17*	*3.14*	*5.57*	*9.33*
Edinburgh	arr	*8.49*	*11.35*	*11.35*	*2.37*	*3.02*	*5.41*	*8.55*

				SO	SO	Mixed SX +		SO
		am	am	am	pm	pm	pm	pm
Edinburgh	dep	*7.17*	*9.12*	– –	*1.10*	*2.09*	*4.57*	*8.25*
Peebles	dep	*7.45*	– –	*10.39*	*1.34*	*2.00*	*4.44*	*7.54*
Leadburn	dep	8.20B	9.57	11.07	2.05	2.56	5.44	9.17
Lamancha	arr	8.27	10.04	11.14	2.12	3.05	5.54	9.27
Macbie Hill	arr	8.31	10.08	11.18	2.16	3.11	5.58	9.31
Broomlee	arr	8.36	10.13	11.23	2.21	3.17	6.05C	9.36
Dolphinton	arr	8.43	10.20	11.30	2.28	3.26	6.12	9.43

SO – Saturdays only. **SX** – Saturdays excepted.
A – 7.27 on Tuesdays and runs correspondingly earlier as a mixed train, arriving at Leadburn at 7.57.
B – When vehicles require to be lifted at Lamancha, Macbie Hill or Broomlee, five minutes extra will be allowed at each point.
C – Leaves Broomlee at 6.03 if ready.
+ – conveys Dolphinton branch Road Van from Leadburn.
(*Italics denote connections, not through carriages*)

Mixed Trains

The first separate entries for the Dolphinton branch appear in the NBR's Working Time Tables in February 1873; before that, only brief details were shown as part of the Peebles branch timetable. No separate goods or mineral workings are shown, but all four of the passenger trains in each direction are shown as 'Mixed' (i.e. a combination of passenger coaches and goods wagons). Wagons might be set down or picked up at the intermediate stations, and some shunting carried out, to the despair of the passengers, judging by the (somewhat exaggerated) description in the *Southern Reporter* of 28th May, 1885:

> Shunting is generally carried on at most of the stations, doubtless to save the expense of a goods service. When the train arrives at each station, the engine is disconnected, and making a 'spurt' on in front gets thrown on to another line of rails; then for five, ten or fifteen minutes it fetches waggons and trucks and brings them 'bang' up against the train. The engine has got no buffers [!], and those on the carriages can hardly be of an approved kind, as they seem to have no power to lessen the effect of the violent shocks which passengers receive during these shunting operations. But this is not all that travellers on this line have to endure. Bad carriages, slow and inconvenient travelling, and shocks during shunting operations would seem bad enough without adding any more to the list of indignities and discomforts. Not so, however. The train arrives at Broomlee for West Linton at such and such a time, say the timetables. But where do they arrive? Not at the station, but a good way out of it, where you are allowed the choice of two things – either to gather up your parcels, if you have any, and risk breaking your limbs in trying to reach the ground – at least about six feet below the level of the carriage floor – or, the only other alternative, sit still for often between a quarter of an hour or twenty minutes awaiting the Company's convenience to take you forward to the station, and suffer in the meanwhile a series of the shakings above referred to. Young folks generally adopt the first method, and can thus be in the village before the train is into the station, but old folks and children are compelled to undergo the sufferings of the latter alternative. The Company have indeed a way of their own of managing this line; it is open to question whether it conduces to their own interest, but it certainly does not tend either to the comfort or convenience of those who are under the necessity of travelling by it.

A correspondent to the paper the following week felt that he was speaking for 'a large portion of the community of Linton' when he agreed that 'the inconveniences dealt with have long been felt and often spoken of'.

In an attempt to improve the service for passengers, from July 1875 it was decreed that the 8.15 am from Dolphinton, connecting at Leadburn with the morning train to Edinburgh, 'Does not carry Intermediate Goods or Mineral Wagons, but takes Through Wagons from Dolphinton to Leadburn, and Live Stock Traffic only'. The same restriction applied to the 5.10 pm from Leadburn which connected with the late afternoon 'Fast' from Edinburgh to Peebles. In 1880, all trains from Leadburn were still mixed, as were all but one from Dolphinton, but from 1878 the restriction 'This Train does not convey Goods or Mineral Wagons to or

Macbie Hill station looking towards Leadburn post-closure in 1933 but before the loop was reinstated for wartime traffic. The original waiting shed and booking office are nearest the camera, with the extension housing the ladies waiting room and WCs etc. adjoining. Access to the station was by the steps from the road bridge. *Bill Lynn collection*

Macbie Hill Station House was on the opposite side of the line from the station buildings, beside the access road to the goods loading bank.
NRS/Department for Transport under Open Government Licence v3.0.

from Intermediate Stations on the Branch' now also applied to the morning and late afternoon trains; on Saturdays, the 12.25 pm from Dolphinton, running through to Edinburgh, carried no mineral traffic at all and the balancing 11.50 am from Leadburn carried none to intermediate stations. By January 1888, the position had further improved: only one train each way was mixed and the Working Time Tables carried the note 'N.B. – The Passenger Trains on the Dolphinton branch must not work Goods or Live Stock to or from Intermediate Stations, excepting No. 2 Up (11.40 ex Leadburn) and No. 7 Down (4.10 ex Dolphinton), but they may convey Through Wagons of such traffic between Leadburn and Dolphinton.'

The 1889 Regulation of Railways Act limited the ability of railway companies to run mixed trains (Chapter Eight). As a result, the 1896 Working Time Tables show no mixed trains from Dolphinton, and only two from Leadburn, one of which latterly ran on Saturdays only. By October 1913, there was only one up mixed train, running on Saturdays only, and by October 1916, only one such down train – the first train out of Dolphinton on Tuesdays only, incorporating the formerly separate cattle train. From 1927, the timetable for the first train in the morning from Leadburn to Dolphinton has the note: 'When vehicles require to be lifted at Lamancha, Macbie Hill or Broomlee, five minutes extra will be allowed at each point.' One can only hope for the sake of the passengers that this concession was rarely invoked. A mixed working was reintroduced in 1931 to convey the 'road van' from Leadburn – a railway van containing small shipments of goods sent to or from 'roadside' stations from or to a central goods depot.

Goods Services

The first notice of a scheduled goods train working on the branch appears in the company's timetables for April 1875. It was worked by the branch engine and guard, leaving Leadburn at 2.50 pm and returning from Dolphinton at 3.45 pm, and calling at all stations in both directions. The trip took 45 minutes each way. Staff were instructed that 'the intermediate Goods work must, as far as possible, be confined to this trip, in order to relieve the Passenger Trains' (and, presumably, the passengers). It was short-lived and had disappeared from the timetable three months later.

The January 1886 timetable made provision for an afternoon goods trip: 'The Dolphinton Branch Passenger Engine and Guard will, when required, make a Goods Trip from Leadburn to Lamancha, Broomlee, or Dolphinton and back, as may be necessary, leaving Leadburn about 3.30 pm'. (Macbie Hill wasn't mentioned.) July 1886 saw the first scheduled cattle train on the branch running from Dolphinton to Leadburn, if required, on Tuesdays only; the cattle were destined for the market in Edinburgh. At first it departed from Dolphinton for Leadburn at 7.05 am, then at 6.25 am and finally 5.50 am, to make way for successively earlier passenger workings; the engine, guard and van returned immediately to Dolphinton to work the first passenger train out. A second cattle train, for cattle off the Caledonian Railway, appeared in the September 1886 timetable amendments and was booked to leave Dolphinton for Leadburn at 12.15 pm on Mondays to Fridays, if required. It had no intermediate booked stops and did the trip in 25 minutes; the cattle were forwarded by goods train from Leadburn to Hardengreen. A balancing goods trip left Leadburn at 1.00 pm, when required, and called at all stations. A new afternoon return goods working in the early months of 1887 was replaced by a mixed working as the passenger service on the branch increased. By June 1897, the CR cattle train was replaced by a general daily goods working, running unconditionally in both directions. From this period also, until 1912, there was a note in the Working Time Tables in relation to the early evening passenger train arrival at Dolphinton: 'The engine of this train will make a goods trip from Dolphinton to Leadburn, calling at Broomlee only, and returning immediately to Dolphinton.'

Following the passing of the Regulation of Railways Act 1889, shunting of wagons at Lamancha and Macbie Hill was restricted to trains heading for Broomlee, when the locomotive would be at the lower end of the gradient and so prevent runaways.

From March 1898, the daily 10.50 am mineral (coal) train from Hardengreen to Leadburn was extended to run forward to Broomlee, calling at intermediate stations; it could be extended to Dolphinton if it was carrying perishable traffic or livestock. In consequence, the lunchtime goods service from Dolphinton to Leadburn, and return, was cut back to run between Dolphinton and Broomlee only; on Saturdays during the summer months, it was advanced to around 9.00 am from Dolphinton and 9.30 am from Broomlee to accommodate the additional lunchtime passenger service.

From July 1910, the Hardengreen 'Mineral' train ('Goods' from 1911) is shown as running on Summer Saturdays only, being replaced on weekdays by a branch goods working, and it was discontinued completely from September 1914 during the First World War, reappearing in June 1919. From then until the end of traffic on the branch in 1933 it is shown as running on Saturdays only throughout the year from Leadburn to Broomlee and return; the branch engine ran the goods service from Leadburn to Dolphinton and return on weekdays, and a connecting service between Broomlee and Dolphinton on Saturdays.

Additional goods trains would have been run as required when traffic offered. The logs collected from St Margarets (Edinburgh) drivers by Willie Hennigan record additional weekday goods workings on to the branch in the 1911-1913 period:

> Friday 13/1/1911: Loco No. 781, relieving turn at Broomlee. Monday 30/10/1911: Loco No. 781, Broomlee goods. Tuesday 31/10/1911: Loco No. 628, Broomlee goods. Wednesday 4/11/1911: Loco No. 791, Broomlee, Whitehill, South Leith. Monday 6/11/1911: Loco No. 691, relieving Broomlee goods. Thursday 9/10/1913: Loco No. 688, Broomlee goods. Saturday 22/11/1913: Loco No. 758, Leadburn & Portobello goods.

A number of other goods services appeared in the Working Time Tables for short periods before being discontinued.

There is a curious entry in Mr Greig's notebook dated 12th December, 1928: 'Bank engine rear Broomlee to Dolphinton irregularly' and referencing correspondence from the district superintendent. It is not clear which, if any, trains would have required banking assistance in the rear between these stations, where the ruling gradient was 1 in 108.

Broomlee Station House on Station Road, c.1930, somewhat overshadowed by the signal box and station building. *Marion Moore collection*

Chapter Six

Special Workings

The coming of local railways gave communities an opportunity that they had not previously enjoyed to travel to events beyond the immediate locality. On 16th August, 1864, six weeks after the opening of the line, return tickets to Peebles at single fares were offered for the Peeblesshire Cattle Show. On 23rd January, 1874, special trains were run to Edinburgh from across the NBR network, including Dolphinton, 'to enable the public to witness the Illumination of the City of Edinburgh' marking the marriage of the Duke of Edinburgh. The return train times 'have been fixed sufficiently late to give parties from the Country ample time to witness the Illumination and return home the same evening'. A new experience for the children (and adults too) was the Railway Trip. In Linton in the 1870s the Band of Hope's annual trip must have been the event of the year: on 24th June, 1876 a special train left Broomlee station at 10.45 am with 200 children and 100 adults to Portobello for the day, and the *Peeblesshire Advertiser* of 8th July had a graphic account of the happenings. The Wellington Reformatory Band saw the train off and, on arrival at Portobello at noon, lunch was provided at Portobello Town Hall. Then it was off to the Pier – designed by Thomas Bouch and opened in 1871 – followed by hymn singing in the Town Hall before getting the train home to Linton where they arrived at 9 pm to a welcome by the Linton Brass Band. In 1878, the trip was to Innerleithen. In 1880 and 1883, it was again Portobello. Trips came to Linton too: the Edinburgh Roperie workers and their families had a picnic on the Green in 1880.

The weekly Special Arrangements notices issued by the NBR, extant from 1889, detail a host of planned special workings. The following is a short selection:

The July 1910 Territorials Camp

Probably the busiest days in the history of the railway occurred in July 1910. The second half of July was when the Territorials across the country held their annual fortnight under canvas, and a Camp for the Lothians Brigade was set up on South Slipperfield farm at the foot of the Pentlands, adjacent to the golf course at West Linton. On this occasion, the 4,000 or so men were to be under canvas for one week only before leaving on a long overland trek to take part in combined naval and

A detachment of Territorials, led by the pipes and drums, marches through West Linton, probably on 17th July, 1910. *Oakwood collection*

military manoeuvres concentrated on the Forth during the second week. The *Scotsman* on Saturday 16th July reported that:

> For some days the village of West Linton has been the scene of great bustle and activity, caused by the arrival of materials for the completion of the Territorial camp, the entrance to which is some five hundred yards down from the entrance to the golf course. On Thursday the first of the advance parties arrived … and as advance parties continued to arrive with their belongings, the bustle increased at Broomlee Station, which has been a scene of great activity for some days. Today will be specially busy, and on Sunday the main body of the troops will arrive by special train.

Broomlee station's limited layout, without even a passing loop, wasn't designed to cope with more than an occasional extra train but, on Sunday 17th July, 14 specials, with their passenger coaches, horse boxes, baggage vans and open trucks for machine guns, were timed to arrive at Broomlee between 7.56 am and 5.05 pm – 10 from Edinburgh Waverley and Leith Central, and one each from Walkerburn, Roslin, Haddington and Maryhill, Glasgow. The branch engine and guard were to leave Dolphinton for Broomlee at 7.30 am and work there as required; a spare engine was to be provided at Broomlee from 7 am and at Waverley from 10 am. The line between Broomlee and Dolphinton was used for the storage of empty trains until they could be worked back. The scene at Broomlee station must have been in amazing contrast to that of even a normal operating day, far less a Scottish Sabbath when no trains normally ran on the branch, with two locomotives in steam and the special trains arriving and departing, to say nothing of the sight of the officers and men with their horses, guns and equipment marching through the village on their way to the camp. The following Saturday, a special train from Bellgrove (Glasgow) arrived at 1.40 pm with Royal Engineers and Field Ambulance personnel for the following week's exercizes. New colours were to be presented that afternoon to the 8th Battalion, Royal Scots, by the Secretary of State for War, watched by some three to four thousand spectators: a relief train left Waverley at 2.10 pm for Broomlee, running seven minutes ahead of the scheduled Galashiels service and arriving about 3.15 pm. It returned from Broomlee at 6.30 pm and, as soon as it cleared the branch, an empty train from Craigentinny worked up to Broomlee to form an all-stations back to Edinburgh in relief of the normal 7.27 pm from Dolphinton to Leadburn. The next morning, Sunday 24th July, a special from Edinburgh brought another 450 Territorials, arriving at noon, and there were two return military workings from Broomlee, one to Leith Central and one to Edinburgh Waverley. The Dolphinton branch engine and guard were again required for duty.

The West Linton Agricultural Show

The West Linton Agricultural Society's Show, billed as 'Scotland's Excelsior Show', was inaugurated in 1874. From 1893, it was held on alternate years at Linton and Peebles, usually on the first or second Saturday in August. In 1933, after the railway's closure, it was held at Robinsland, West Linton, before moving permanently to Peebles in 1934. Until then, the site at Linton was Broomlee Mains, adjoining the station, to which special trains brought the farmers, their families, workers, and animals, as well as the general public. It was a big day for West Linton, and a very busy day for the railway. At its peak of popularity, the advertisements for the Show promised reduced fares and special trains on the North British and reduced fares on the Caledonian; those for 1890 promised special trains by the Caledonian too – presumably only as far as Dolphinton CR with a connection from Dolphinton NBR. In 1894, for example, a special train left Edinburgh Waverley at 8.25 am and arrived at Broomlee at 9.40 am, returning from Broomlee at 6.00 pm. The coaches used had been 'borrowed' from the London & North Western Railway

Press advertisement for the West Linton Agricultural Society's 1898 Show.

and had formed an overnight special excursion from Liverpool and Manchester to Edinburgh. The scheduled trains on the Peebles branch were strengthened with extra carriages, as was the branch train, which had to be provided with a 'heavy engine' and to make additional trips from Dolphinton and Leadburn to Broomlee.

For the Show on 6th August, 1898, a special train left Edinburgh at 5.40 am, lifting livestock and horse box traffic at intermediate stations and arriving at Broomlee at 7.25 am; it returned from Broomlee at 6.30 pm. A Hawick train crew set off at 4 am to work a similar special from St Boswells, arriving at Broomlee at 7.50 am, and returning at 6.15 pm. A special working of the branch train with show stock off the Caledonian Railway was timed to leave Dolphinton for Broomlee about 8.50 am, returning immediately to Dolphinton; after the Show, the branch engine and crew came down from Dolphinton for the return working at 4.15 pm. All routine goods and mineral traffic was held back at Leadburn and Dolphinton from the Thursday evening until after the show. A special excursion left Edinburgh Waverley for Broomlee at 8.35 am, arriving at 9.50 am. It then worked empty to Peebles, to form a 1.20 pm special for excursionists from there to Leadburn, where they changed into the branch train. The now-empty special then followed the branch train to Broomlee, where it waited to form the 6.0 pm special back to Edinburgh; complicated, but it made sense from an operating perspective! The 10.40 am from Edinburgh to Galashiels via Peebles was to be strengthened, and provided with extra engine power, to cater for the additional traffic for Broomlee. Passengers on the 9.20 am from Galashiels with cheap return tickets for the Show, issued at Galashiels and intermediate stations, changed at Leadburn into a special 10.45 am working of the branch train, strengthened with additional carriages and a 'heavy engine', for the trip to Broomlee. The branch train then hurried back to Leadburn for its next ordinary working. Dolphinton patrons weren't forgotten, with the branch train making a special run at 9.20 am for the 10 minute journey to Broomlee, before returning empty for the next ordinary train at 10.05 am. As if that wasn't sufficient complication, another special train with 16 men and 16 horses of the Yeomanry left the Haymarket dock platform at 11.35 am, travelling via the Suburban line, and arrived at Broomlee 55 minutes later. Having presumably performed at the Show, they returned to Haymarket from Broomlee at 5.45 pm – the first of four departures at 15-minute intervals.

Jean Fleming remembered special trains bringing in a few animals a day or two before the show, and these being grazed overnight by farmers near the showground; and then, on the day of the Show, 'train after train bringing in sheep, cattle, horses and pigs of all sizes and breeds'. There was a sigh of relief when all the animals were safely loaded back into their trains at the end of the day. The final show at Broomlee, held in 1930, was the 50th, Peebles following on to host both the 1931 and 1932 events.

'A Sufferer" wrote to the local paper in August 1879 complaining that, on returning from the Show, he had been sold a ticket for $8\frac{1}{2}$ pence from Broomlee to Pomathorn by the 4.25 pm train. On changing at Leadburn, he was told that there wouldn't be a train to Pomathorn until after 8.00 pm and so he set out, 'not in very good humour', to walk the three miles home – only to be overtaken by a passenger train!

SATURDAY 6 AUG 1898		Branch	Cattle (CR)	Branch Sp		Branch	Sp Edin ECS	Branch ECS
		am	am	am		am	am	am
Dolphinton	dep	7.45	8.50	9.20		10.05		– –
Broomlee	arr	7.53	9.00	9.30		10.13	10.30d	11.10d@
Macbie Hill	arr	7.58				10.18		
Lamancha	arr	8.02				10.22		
Leadburn	arr	8.10				10.30		11.23@
Peebles	arr					11.53	11.10@	
Edinburgh	arr	8.49				11.21		

		Goods Edin	Goods St B	Branch	LE	Branch ECS	Sp Edin	Branch Sp	Branch	Yeom
		am	am	am	am	am	am	am	am	am
Haymarket										11.35
Edinburgh	dep	5.40		6.50			8.35		10.40	
St Boswells	dep		5.20							
Peebles	dep			7.57				10.16	10.16	
Leadburn	dep	7.05	7.30	8.20			9.35	10.45	11.40	12.15x
Lamancha	arr			8.28					11.49	
Macbie Hill	arr			8.32					11.56	
Broomlee	arr	7.25	7.50	8.37	9.05	9.35@	9.50	11.00	12.03	12.30
Dolphinton	arr			8.45	9.15	9.45@			12.12	

SATURDAY 6 AUG 1898		Branch	Branch	LE	Branch	Yeom	Sp Edin	Goods St B	Goods Edin	Branch
		pm	pm	pm	pm	pm	pm	pm	pm	pm
Dolphinton	dep	12.50	2.13	3.50	4.40					7.30
Broomlee	arr	12.58	2.21	3.58@	4.48	5.45d	6.00d	6.15d	6.30d	7.38
Macbie Hill	arr	1.03	2.26		4.53					7.43
Lamancha	arr	1.07	2.30		4.57					7.47
Leadburn	arr	1.15	2.38		5.05	6.00x	6.15	6.35d	6.50d	7.55
Peebles	arr	2.00	3.19		5.32			7.39		8.56
St Boswells	arr							9.25		
Edinburgh	arr		3.28		6.19		7.12		8.10	8.53
Haymarket	arr					6.40				

		Sp Peeb	Branch	Sp Peeb ECS	Branch	Cattle (CR)	Branch			Branch
		pm	pm	pm	pm	pm	pm			pm
Haymarket	dep									
Edinburgh	dep		1.05		2.10		4.30			7.45
Peebles	dep	1.20			2.22					7.42
Leadburn	dep	1.38	1.44	2.04@	3.07		5.18			8.43
Lamancha	arr		1.52		3.15		5.26			8.51
Macbie Hill	arr		1.56		3.19		5.30			8.55
Broomlee	arr		2.01	2.17@	3.24	4.15	5.35			9.00
Dolphinton	arr		2.08		3.32	4.25	5.43			9.10

d – depart x – pass @ – estimated
Branch – Branch train; **LE** – light engine; **Sp** – Special Passenger
Edin – Edinburgh; **Peeb** – Peebles; **St B** – St Boswells
Yeom – Yeomanry
(*Italics denote connections, not through carriages*)

When the Show was held at Peebles, as on 8th August, 1908, the branch train from Dolphinton would be strengthened, with excursionists travelling to Peebles by the ordinary trains, but with an additional service home from Leadburn at 6.47 pm to connect with a Special from Peebles to Edinburgh.

Other Excursions

From the end of the 18th century, the second Thursday in July was traditionally observed as a holiday in Linton. On that day, the procession of Whipmen* formerly took place, but the event had since died out (to be revived in 1931) and in its place were the Annual Sports and Games. In 1899, 'Early in the forenoon the Newtongrange Brass Band awakened the echoes of the valley by marching through the village, led as formerly by the old historic flag, and at one o'clock the [horse] trotting took place in the field at Robinsland, where there was assembled a large number of spectators. The various athletic sports took place as usual on the Lower Green, in the afternoon, when a lengthy programme was gone through, closing about seven o'clock …' As well as a number of races, there was a quoits competition, a tug-of-war and a handicap dog race; competitors paid an entry fee and there were cash prizes. The event attracted visitors from Edinburgh and elsewhere and, for the Games on 14th July, 1904, 'The trains to and from Broomlee are expected to be busy, and must be provided with ample carriage accommodation'; the 7.30 pm branch train (normally Mondays and Saturdays only) was run to Leadburn to take the visitors home, returning empty. The cheap return fare from Waverley to Broomlee was 1s. 6d. On 13th July, 1922, cheap one-day excursion tickets were issued from all stations between Edinburgh, Peebles and Walkerburn, the branch train depositing them at Broomlee just before noon, and returning them home by the 7.48 pm departure. The connecting trains on the main line had to be made up to a 'full single Engine load for "K" class Engine'. On 9th July, 1925, similar arrangements applied but, for the Games on 12th July, 1928, Mr Greig's notebook records 'No special arrangements granted'.

Some visitors came by special train, others in reserved carriages or compartments in service trains. On 2nd June, 1890, Professor Balfour of Edinburgh University brought his Botany Class of 50 to Dolphinton and, after botanical studies on the walk back, they returned home from Broomlee. On 7th June, 1890 a school party of 700 from Peebles was booked to arrive in a special train at Broomlee at 2.25 pm and return home at 8 pm. A Choir 'Pic Nic' party from Edinburgh came on Thursday 19th May, 1892. On 13th June, 1903, 500 employees of Scottish Vulcanite arrived from Edinburgh. An excursion party of 250 from John Aitchison & Co. arrived at Broomlee from Edinburgh at 9.52 am on Saturday 2nd July, 1904 and left again at 6.30 pm. An advance party of the Boys' Brigade arrived from Edinburgh to set up camp on 16th July, 1906, and three companies arrived by service train from Edinburgh on 25th July, 1925; they stayed for a week.

---

* An old Scots word meaning a carter, carrier or cadger (pedlar), all of whom depended on horses for their trades. The Whipman Play was, and is, the annual West Linton festival.

On Edinburgh holidays in particular, Broomlee was a popular destination. On Monday 20th April, 1891, 'seldom has there been such a large crowd at Broomlee Station' waiting for the 7.35 pm train. On Monday 24th April, 1911, an empty train left Portobello at 5 pm for Broomlee, departing from there at 7.50 pm, calling at Macbie Hill and Lamancha, to take the day and weekend visitors home. Similar arrangements were in place for the Edinburgh Autumn Holiday. Queen Victoria's birthday on 18th May and, later, King Edward VII's birthday on 24th May, were popular holidays, and saw heavy excursion traffic. In 1899, a 6.45 am train, acting as a relief as far as Leadburn – much too early for all but the most enthusiastic excursionists – ran on to Broomlee, where it lay over until 7.30 pm to return the visitors who had arrived via Leadburn by special or ordinary trains during the day, to their homes at Penicuik (Pomathorn), Hawthornden, Bonnyrigg or Edinburgh. Tuesday 23rd May, 1922 was the Victoria Day holiday, with many extra services from Edinburgh; Peebles and West Linton were popular destinations. On these occasions, the NBR would borrow carriages from the North Eastern and the Midland railway companies. On Sunday 17th April, 1904, the day before the Edinburgh Spring holiday, 100 carriages and 20 brake vans were handed over to the NBR at Berwick, and 50 carriages and 10 vans at Carlisle. Such arrangements were reciprocal.

On West Linton local holidays, the NBR might offer ticket concessions. For the 'Broomlee' [sic] holiday on 25th May, 1904, and again on 11th August, return tickets at single fares were available to all of the NBR's stations in Scotland, and to certain of those of other companies. The return journey could be made up to 1st June – provided the NBR's route was used on both legs of the journey, and the minimum third class fare paid was at least 2s. 6d. For the holiday on 24th May, 1911, the offer was a day excursion ticket to either Edinburgh at 1s. 6d. or Glasgow at 3s. 6d.; the branch train made a connection at Leadburn with the 8.35 pm Peebles train home from Edinburgh, normally available on Saturdays only. Thursday 8th June, 1922 was again a holiday in West Linton and 30 members of the West Linton United Free Church Choir left Broomlee at 7.35 am for North Berwick (change at Leadburn and Waverley) with reserved accommodation throughout; one-day excursion tickets were offered to the public generally to North Berwick for 4s. 6d. third class by the same train, and to Edinburgh for 2s. 8d. by the 9.00 am departure. Perhaps not many were expected to take up the Edinburgh offer, as only one additional, six-wheel, third class carriage was to be provided. Choir and excursionists all arrived back at Broomlee at 9.09 pm on a special working of the branch train. One-day excursion tickets were also issued for special events such as the Royal Caledonian Horticultural Show in the Waverley Market in September 1928 at 3s. from Dolphinton and 2s. 6d. from Broomlee. The same fares applied in the reverse direction on the Edinburgh Spring Holiday on 14th April, 1930, jointly marketed by the LNER and LMS.

Some excursions went further afield. On 25th July, 1890, a special train left Dolphinton at 6.15 am to connect at Leadburn with the annual Special Constables' Excursion of 600 from Peebles, bound for Stirling; in the evening, the last branch train of the day waited at Leadburn for the returning excursionists. These 'Specials' Specials' were open to all. In 1878 the trip had been to Dundee, across the newly-opened Tay Bridge and again in 1891 (accompanied by the Peebles Brass Band). On 22nd July, 1892 it went to Berwick via Niddrie West and came home via Duns. The branch train had to make an extra run from Dolphinton at 6.00 am, and another from Leadburn at 9.40 pm, returning to Dolphinton by 10.10 pm. In 1894, the destination was Perth, and the branch train again made a special journey from Dolphinton at 6.00 am to connect with the Peebles excursion, the passengers returning home in the evening by the regular 8.40 pm from Leadburn. Thursday 11th August, 1904 was a shopkeepers' holiday at West Linton and the Special Arrangements booklet gives details of an unusual working. The branch train was to leave Dolphinton for Leadburn at 3.30 am, running empty, for a passenger working from Leadburn at 4.00 am, arriving back at Dolphinton at 4.25 am. In the evening, it had to leave Dolphinton 'on the arrival of Caledonian Special' and reverse the process. It transpires that the 'Farmers and Merchants of the Upper Ward of Lanarkshire' were running an excursion from Dolphinton (CR) to Stranraer, and the NBR was providing a feeder service for the CR. Changed days! (There was a rival attraction in Edinburgh that day – Buffalo Bill's show.) A similar outing had been organized in August 1899 – a Caledonian excursion from Dolphinton (CR) to Aberdeen – and the local paper reported that a large number of the inhabitants of West Linton had taken advantage of the cheap fare. But first they had to get to the Caley station, 'making their own separate arrangements, and in the grey, misty morning finding their way to Dolphinton station by 5.30 am'. The journey to Aberdeen took seven hours, and the excursionists arrived back at Dolphinton just before 1 am the following morning. For those from West Linton, a weary road of four miles still lay ahead!

For the Hiring Fair at Peebles on 1st March, 1892, a special train left Dolphinton at 6.25 am to connect with the early Edinburgh – Peebles train. The train was mixed – with one or more vans – as the farm servants seeking new positions would all have their bags and portmanteaux. According to Press reports, the demand for females was great, but the supply limited!

Sunday School trips were a major traffic challenge for the NBR on Saturdays from late May to early July, with as many as 10,000 adults and children leaving Edinburgh in a single day for a variety of local destinations, including Broomlee and Dolphinton, and usually in the NBR's oldest carriages stored specially for the purpose, or those reserved for workmen's trains drafted in for the day. For example on Saturday 11th June, 1892, a party of 800 from Peebles Parish Church Sunday School set off in a special train for Dolphinton at 2.00 pm, returning home at 7.55 pm. They were back again, 700 strong, on 11th June, 1904, and again on 13th June, 1908, 750 strong. In other years, the destination was Broomlee, with sports on the village green; 200 adults and 450 juveniles arrived on 17th June, 1922 at 2.39 pm and departed at 8.10 pm. The three Peebles United Free Churches Sabbath School – 260 children and 200 adults – came by special train on 13th June, 1903. On Saturday 18th June, 1910, 75 adults and 200 children from Cockpen United Free Church left Bonnyrigg at 10.30 am for Broomlee, returning home at 6.30 pm; the following Saturday, a Walkerburn Sunday School party of 350 arrived at Broomlee at 2.47 pm and left at 8.00 pm for the 51 minute journey home. A party of 195 from Lasswade Parish Church Sunday School came to Broomlee by service train from Bonnyrigg on 13th June, 1925, and the following week a party of 200 from Penicuik North United Free Church arrived mid-afternoon for a short visit. On 27th June it was the turn of 200 adults and 100 juveniles from St Andrew's UF Church, travelling by special train from Peebles. For that short journey from Peebles to Broomlee, an empty train had to leave Edinburgh's Craigentinny carriage sidings at 11 am in time for a Peebles departure at 1.57 pm. The party left Broomlee for Peebles at 7.05 pm after which the train worked back empty back to Craigentinny. The *Peeblesshire Advertiser* considered West Linton an ideal destination 'for the public greens there, free to all, afford ample facilities for the enjoyment of everyone whether old or young'. The traffic wasn't all one way. On 18th June, 1904 a party of 170 from West Linton Parish Church Sunday School followed in the footsteps of the Band of Hope for an outing to Portobello, and we find them making the same journey on 18th June, 1910 and again on 17th June, 1911, when three reserved third class carriages were provided on service trains. On Saturday 1st July the same year a party of 12 adults and 60 children from Dolphinton Parish Church headed for Portobello on the 10.39 am, arriving home at 9.17 pm, the Peebles service making a special stop at Portobello in both directions.

On Saturday 26th August, 1899, a picnic under the auspices of Mid-Lothian Liberal Association was held at Castle Craig, seat of Sir Thomas D. Gibson Carmichael MP, the successor to Prime Minister William Gladstone as the Member for Midlothian. A special train left both Waverley [NBR] and Princes Street [CR] stations by their separate routes for Dolphinton – carrying some 600 from Waverley and 400 from Princes Street. The NBR train left Waverley at 1.47 pm and arrived at Dolphinton at 2.58 pm. From there the picnickers were taken by road to the nearby Castle, although Sir Thomas had to apologize for the 'somewhat defective' transport arrangements owing to the shortage of vehicles. The return NBR train left Dolphinton at 7.45 pm and was back at Waverley at 9.02 pm.

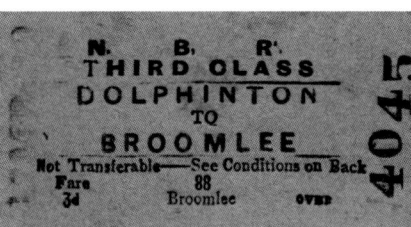
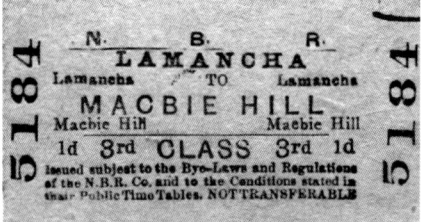
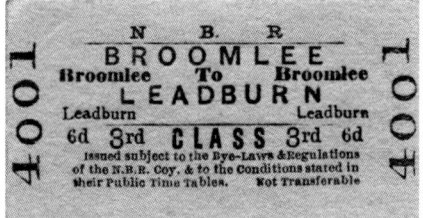
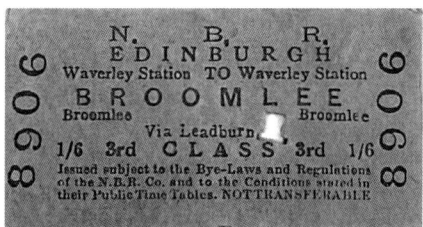

Selection of NBR tickets for the line.

TicketsNos. 4001, 4045 and 5184 courtesy of Michael Stewart
Ticket 8906 Rae Montgomery collection

NBR Hurst 0-4-2 well-tank locomotive No. 107 in the Dolphinton bay platform at Leadburn c.1878. The driver is James Scott and the fireman is William Davidson.
WLDHA collection

An unidentified sister engine of No. 107 outside St Margarets engine shed, Edinburgh.
NBR Study Group

Chapter Seven

Locomotives and Carriages

Under its working agreement with the LL&DR, the NBR provided the locomotives and rolling stock for the line. Being but a twig off the Peebles branch in the NBR's expanding empire, the LL&DR had to make do with 'hand-me-downs' in the way of locomotives and rolling stock. Full records of the regular locomotives and rolling stock used on the branch are no longer available, but some details are, and we can speculate as to others.

Locomotives

That great student of NBR locomotives and their crews, the late Willie Hennigan, whose father had been a driver at St Margarets locomotive depot in Edinburgh, wrote in November 1981 to Eddie Jefferies (who gathered much of the material on which this book is based): 'As a matter of fact, this branch appears to have been a sort of Cinderella, as far as St Margarets was concerned, over a long period and was worked by an odd assortment of engines – usually old tender engines. Thus, as far as we know, there was never any Drummond tank engine named *Dolphinton** and there seems to be no record of any regular tank engine … until 48 went on the job.'

In his extensive notes on the history of NBR locomotives, Edward Craven records that Hurst** 0-4-2 well-tank No. 107 was working the branch around 1878. This ties in with the photo of a Hurst tank in the Dolphinton branch bay platform at Leadburn, dated *circa* 1878. The *LNER Magazine* of June 1928 identifies it as No. 107, with driver James Scott and fireman William Davidson. These tanks were built specifically for work on the NBR's expanding branch line network in the 1860s, and Craven records that No. 107 was built at St Margarets in the first half of 1864. It is possible that it went new to the Dolphinton branch; it was withdrawn in 1886.

2-2-2 locomotive No. 227A was one of a batch built in 1847-48 by Sharp Brothers of Manchester for the Edinburgh & Glasgow Railway (E&GR), where it was No. 52, named *Isis*. Following amalgamation, it became NBR 227, then 227A in 1890, then 871 in 1895, before being

---

* It was the practice to name the regular locomotive after the branch during Dugald Drummond's time as locomotive superintendent (1875–1882).

** William Hurst, locomotive superintendent 1854-1867.

160 THE LEADBURN, LINTON AND DOLPHINTON RAILWAY

Ex-E&GR 2-2-2 locomotive NBR No. 227A, at one time the Dolphinton branch engine, on the South Leith to Portobello service c.1895. *WLDHA collection*

NBR Wheatley 2-4-0 locomotive No.63A, sister engine to No. 40A. No 40A was at one time the Dolphinton branch engine. *John Alsop collection*

LNER class 'D51' 4-4-0 tank locomotive No. 10467 (formerly NBR No. 77), sister engine of Dolphinton locomotive No. 76, at North Leith on 8th June, 1926.   *NBR Study Group*

withdrawn – the longest surviving member of its class – in November 1897. According to information from Willie Hennigan, it was at one time the Dolphinton branch locomotive.

A letter to the *Railway Magazine* of November 1920 from a former NBR railwayman reported that 2-4-0 locomotive No. 40A worked the branch at one time. Two old R. & W. Hawthorn locomotives, Nos. 40 and 63, were scrapped in 1873 and their replacements, built at Cowlairs the same year by Thomas Wheatley*, incorporated parts of the original locomotives. No. 40 was renumbered to 40A in 1890 and to 827 in 1895, suggesting that its service on the Dolphinton branch may have been between these dates. No 40A and (the renumbered) 63A eventually followed No. 227A to the South Leith branch, where both ended their days.

Drummond 4-4-0 tank No. 76 (later LNER class 'D51') was built in 1884 and lasted until after the Grouping of 1923, being withdrawn in 1924. The photograph on page 117 shows it at Dolphinton, date unknown, but after the erection of the signal box there *circa* 1893. It may have been a temporary stand-in, or the regular branch engine: there are examples of this class spending their entire working lives on a single branch line, such as sister engine No 79, which spent its working life on

---

* Thomas Wheatley, locomotive superintendent 1867-1875

NBR Wheatley 0-6-0 goods locomotive No. 400 (later LNER 10149 class 'J31') was on a goods working between Dolphinton and Macbie Hill on census date 20.10.1898.

NBR Study Group

the Galashiels – Selkirk line, and 76 may have been first assigned to the branch to replace Hurst well-tank No. 107 in the mid-1880s. Sister engine No. 77 is shown at North Leith on 8th June, 1926.

On Thursday 20th October, 1898 the NBR undertook a Census of all the goods trains running on that day, and the cost of the locomotive power. The record shows that Wheatley 0-6-0 goods engine No 400 was on a goods working on that date between Dolphinton and Macbie Hill and return. No 400 was built by Neilson & Company of Glasgow in 1869 and survived until 1925, becoming LNER No. 10149, class 'J31'.

No. 203, Hurst 0-6-0 goods engine, is seen at Broomlee, in the picture on page 105, sometime in the period 1908 – 1909. The photograph on the facing page shows the same locomotive at St Margarets, Edinburgh. It, and others of the same class, may have been temporary replacements for the Drummond 4-4-0 tank described above, or perhaps a permanent replacement if the Drummond tanks were re-allocated to work some of the light railways built around the turn of the century, such as Gifford, Lauder and Carmyllie. No. 203 was built by Dübs & Co of Glasgow in the 1865-67 period.

2-2-2 locomotive No 802 was apparently at one time the Dolphinton branch locomotive, probably in the early 1900s. It was built in June 1861 by Beyer, Peacock of Manchester for express passenger services on the E&GR, where it was No. 2; on the amalgamation of the E&GR

NBR Hurst 0-6-0 goods locomotive No. 203 at St Margarets engine shed, Edinburgh.
W. Hennigan collection per Bill Lynn

Ex-E&GR 2-2-2 locomotive NBR No. 802 photographed at the west end of Waverley station with a spectral Scott Monument in the background. Later, as No. 1002, it was the Dolphinton branch engine. *Rae Montgomery collection*

NBR Holmes 0-6-0 locomotive No. 781 (later LNER class 'J36') at Dolphinton c.1910. From the left are James Verth, porter/relief guard; Bob Fell, fireman; and Peter Small, driver. The wood in the background was cut down during the First World War.

WLDHA collection

and NBR on 1st August, 1865, it became NBR No. 212, and carried the name *Corstorphine* in Drummond's time, being rebuilt by him *circa* 1880-82. It was re-numbered as 802 in 1895, and 1002 in 1901, before being finally withdrawn in February 1910. Willie Hennigan recalls hearing from a St Margarets driver, George Bell, who had been a cleaner at Dolphinton and had lodged there with Mrs Small, wife of driver Peter Small, that there was a photo in the house of No 1002 at Dolphinton. Unfortunately, that photograph is now lost.

The photograph above shows Holmes* 0-6-0 goods engine No. 781 at Dolphinton around 1910. In Willie Hennigan's notes on this class, there is reference to the regular use of these locomotives (later LNER class 'J36') on branch goods workings. Hennigan quotes the logs compiled by St Margarets driver Bob Low, detailing several goods trips to Broomlee in the 1911-13 period. Built at the Cowlairs Works in 1900, No. 781 survived into British Railways (BR) days as BR No. 65333, being withdrawn in 1959.

The photo of the unidentified 0-4-2 locomotive reproduced on the facing page is of one of a batch of 18 0-4-2s built for the Edinburgh and Glasgow Railway in the period 1859-64, some in-house at Cowlairs and some by Beyer, Peacock. The photo shows the locomotive as rebuilt by Holmes in the 1890s. This particular variation of the class was withdrawn between 1911 and 1915, which dates the photo to the

---

* Matthew Holmes, locomotive superintendent 1882-1903

LOCOMOTIVES AND CARRIAGES

An unidentified ex-E&GR 0-4-2 locomotive, as rebuilt by Holmes, at Dolphinton in the period 1890 – 1915. The turntable is in the left foreground.
NRS/Department for Transport under Open Government Licence v3.0.

LNER class 'C15' 4-4-2T locomotive No. 9048 (formerly NBR No. 48) waiting to depart from Dolphinton LNER *c.*1925/26. The station buildings are obscured by the train. Between the station and the Dolphinton Creamery (*on the right*) was the connecting line from the Caledonian station. The goods yard is to the rear of the train and the siding to the left, off the run-round loop, leads to the one-road engine shed.
R Brown/WLDHA collection

period 1890–1915. A number of these locomotives were used on branch and suburban services around Edinburgh and three must have appeared on the Peebles line, as they were named in Drummond's time as No. 321, *St Ronans*; 323, *Cardrona*; 325, *Peebles*; but, as mentioned above, there was never a *Dolphinton*.

Of more recent memory are the two 'Yorkies', the last regular engines on the branch. These were 4-4-2 tank engines Nos. 43 and 48, part of a batch built for the NBR in April 1913 by the Yorkshire Engine Company in Sheffield to a design by the NBR locomotive superintendent, William P. Reid*. Both were allocated to St Margarets locomotive depot in Edinburgh. It is not recorded when they first appeared on the branch but it may have been soon after the Grouping, perhaps replacing the 'D51' referred to above, withdrawn in 1924. By then, Nos. 43 and 48 had become Nos. 9043 and 9048, class 'C15', in the LNER classification system. No. 9048 was the regular engine, but No. 9043 was to see out the last week of passenger service on the branch. Thereafter No. 9043 was transferred to Dundee in April 1937 and to Dunfermline in August 1946 and became BR No. 67469 post-Nationalization in 1948; it ended its days as a stationary boiler at Burntisland before being condemned in September 1954. Sister engine No. 9048 was transferred to Polmont in October 1934 and to Parkhead in December 1945; it appears never to have carried its British Railways number (67470) post-1948 and was in store before being withdrawn in December 1954.

Carriages

It is safe to assume that the regular coaching stock on the branch consisted of vehicles nearing the end of their working lives, and anywhere between 20 to 35 years old. The branch locomotive and passenger carriages were stabled at Dolphinton and so, once the carriages had been assigned there, there would have been little reason to change them, other than for maintenance or eventual replacement, with additional vehicles being supplied when trains required to be strengthened for the holiday season or for special workings.

In the early days of railways, travel was not for those who valued their comfort, and it was many years before all classes of passenger could expect to travel in comfortable, well-lit, and heated vehicles with lavatory facilities. Until the passing of the Railway Regulation Act in

---

* Reid was locomotive superintendent 1903-1919.

1844, the cheapest form of accommodation might consist of an open truck, without seats.* The 1844 Act provided that one train per day in each direction, travelling at an average speed of not less than 12 miles per hour (including stoppages), should call at all stations, that the fare should not exceed one penny per mile, and that these 'third-class passengers' should be provided with seats and be protected from the weather. They were often referred to as 'Parliamentary Trains'.

The coaching stock provided by the NBR to operate the service when the branch opened in 1864 would probably have consisted of its earliest 4-wheel carriages, built around the time of the opening of the Edinburgh – Berwick line in 1846 and by then 18 years old. The earliest NBR public timetable for the LL&DR, for August 1864, shows that first, second and third class accommodation was provided, the same as on the Peebles branch. From 1868, however, one train each way on both the Peebles and Dolphinton branches is shown as first, second and *fourth* class. From 1875 to 1878, *all* passenger trains on these lines are shown as first, second and fourth class. It follows that fourth class, where provided, must have satisfied the 'Parliamentary' standards required for third class passengers laid down in the 1844 Act. So why call it fourth class? Around 1870, new thirds from the Ashbury railway carriage company in Manchester were being delivered and, from *circa* 1875 onwards, new thirds to Drummond's design were being produced by the NBR's Cowlairs Works. As this newer stock was introduced, the NBR may have felt that it could charge higher 'third class' fares for it, with the older stock providing the 'Parliamentary' accommodation, and re-designated as 'fourth class'.

These older vehicles may well have been in use on the branch from its opening in 1864 and could have been 'Omnibus' type vehicles from the 1840s. Allan Rodgers suggests that 'fourth class' was used by the NBR to indicate carriages which provided some standing accommodation. The very early NBR thirds built for the opening of the Berwick line were designed to carry 32 passengers, 24 seated and 8 standing. They had a single door on each side with seats arranged around the sides of the vehicle, similar to that found in a horse-drawn omnibus of the period. The space in the centre of the carriage was left clear as a standing area.

---

* The Engineer of the Edinburgh & Glasgow Railway submitted a return to the Board of Trade in January 1842 describing the open carriages which it proposed to use for 3rd class passengers. Seating was to be provided in its 'slow' trains ($3\frac{1}{2}$ hours). For its 'quick' trains ($2\frac{1}{4}$ hours), 'stand up' carriages were to be provided, with four 'bodies' [compartments], each holding 12 passengers, or 15 in 'throng trains'. In his report prior to the opening of the line in February 1842, the Inspector General of Railways, General Pasley, commented that 'Persons in vigorous health will prefer the latter'!

This was contrary to the practice on most other British railway companies in the mid-1840s whose Parliamentary carriages (i.e. thirds) provided all-seated accommodation; those built using an omnibus layout (as opposed to compartments) had seating down the centre of the carriage. The NBR's approach was probably influenced by the practice on the Edinburgh & Glasgow Railway (opened in 1842) whose early carriage stock included some thirds which were 100 per cent stand-ups. Allan's research suggests that, as late as 1858, the E&GR ordered some six-wheel standing carriages for commuter services on the Glasgow, Dumbarton & Helensburgh Railway. They had four large compartments each holding 25 standing passengers. The NBR's thirds built in the 1840s for the main line and the Hawick branch were all of the omnibus layout and accommodated both seated and standing passengers. Some of the first examples with a single door each side were later altered to provide two doors per side; the illustrations below show an early third so altered and a later example of an omnibus third, built with two doors per side.

By the end of the 1870s, all third class vehicles were providing the same standard of accommodation and most of the older 'omnibus' vehicles had been withdrawn. First, second and fourth class continued to be offered until December 1878, when the NBR Board, after a successful trial, decided to abolish all third class fares that exceeded a penny per mile from 1st January, 1879 with one or two exceptions. Thereafter, the classes on the branch become first, second and third. From June 1879, second class provision disappeared from the branch. (The North British Railway Board agreed in December 1891 to follow the

Left: An early NBR 4-wheel third class carriage at the east end of Waverley c.1876.
Extract from Alexander Inglis image, Alan Brotchie collection

Right: A later example of an NBR 4-wheel omnibus third class carriage, built with two doors per side, at the east end of Waverley c.1876.
Extract from Alexander Inglis image, Alan Brotchie collection

Left: NBR first class coupé carriage with two standard compartments, and one half-coupé compartment at one end only, at east end of Waverley c.1869.
Extract from George Washington Wilson image ref F1449X, University of Aberdeen

Right: NBR 1846 4-wheel, three-compartment first at east end of Waverley c.1876.
Extract from Alexander Inglis image, Alan Brotchie collection

Caledonian Railway and abolish second class fares completely from 1st May, 1892, except to/from stations in England by the East Coast route.)

In the 1866 timetables, the ordinary (i.e. single) passenger fares between Edinburgh and Broomlee are shown as 3s. first class, 2s. second class, and 1s. 6d. Parliamentary. No third class fares are shown – presumably the Parliamentary fare was charged. Return tickets cost 4s. 6d. first class, or 3s. second class; no return Parliamentary fare was listed. The corresponding fares from Dolphinton were 4s., 3s. and 2s. single, and 6s. and 4s. 6d. return.

In July 1894, the third class single fare from Broomlee to Edinburgh was still 1s. 6d. and a return was double that amount; the first class single was still 3s. and a return 4s. 6d.

The second class carriages used in the early days of the branch were probably either 4-wheel all-seconds, or first and second class composites, built in the 1840s.

The 1878 photo at Leadburn on page 158 shows a mixed train at Leadburn with two open wagons behind the engine and what appears to be an old first class coupé carriage coupled to the second wagon. The vehicle has end windows and there are three lamps visible on the roof line. It could very well be an original NBR first class coupé carriage with just three compartments – two standard compartments plus one half coupé compartment at one end only; another example is in the picture *top left*. Depending on the demand for first class seating on the branch, 1846-built, four-wheel, three-compartment firsts may have been used; the picture above (*top right*) shows such a carriage in use at Waverley in about 1876. Older first/second class composite carriages were often

170   THE LEADBURN, LINTON AND DOLPHINTON RAILWAY

Top left: NBR 1846 4-wheel composite carriage at east end of Waverley *c*.1876. Note the rack on the roof for passengers' luggage.
Extract from Alexander Inglis image, Alan Brotchie collection

Top right: NBR 4-wheel Metropolitan first at east end of Waverley *c*.1876.
Extract from Alexander Inglis image, Alan Brotchie collection

Bottom left: NBR 4-wheel passenger brake at Waverley Bridge *c*.1877.
Extract from George Washington Wilson image ref E1295XB, University of Aberdeen

Bottom right: NBR 4-wheel brake composite at east end of Waverley *c*.1876.
Extract from Alexander Inglis image, Alan Brotchie collection

used on NBR branch services too; an example is shown *top left* above which shows an example of a *circa* 1846 vehicle at Waverley in 1876. (Note the railings on the roof, where passengers' luggage was stored.)

The picture below it on the left shows an NBR passenger brake van typical of those in regular service in the 1850-80 period, and one of this type may well have been used on the branch, or perhaps a brake composite, such as the *lower right* image above. The 1878 branch train pictured on page 158 may have consisted of: first coupé, composite, omnibus third, and passenger brake van.

The *Southern Reporter* article of 28th May, 1885 (*see page 142*) also had something to say about the carriages:

> The North British Railway Company ... would do well to turn their attention to the branch line from Leadburn to Dolphinton. The carriages, for example, on

this line have evidently been made in long bygone days, and were certainly constructed without much consideration for the personal comfort of passengers. It is no uncommon thing to hear them spoken of by the denizens of this stretch of country as well as visitors to the neighbourhood as 'no better than cattle trucks' …

As we have seen, winters on the Dolphinton branch could be severe, and it wasn't until the first decade of the 20th century that the use of steam heating in carriages became widespread on the NBR; a circular of October 1917 shows that most branch lines in the Edinburgh area still lacked such comfort, although the Dolphinton branch is no longer included. Before that, the best that could be hoped for was a foot-warmer. The earlier versions were simply tin or iron bottles filled with hot water, but later ones were permanently sealed and filled with a strong solution of sodium acetate and were immersed in boiling water at the terminal stations and placed on the floor of the carriage. They worked by a combination of heat from the solution inside the container (just like a hot water bottle) and then from a chemical reaction as the solution recrystallized (helped by an occasional vigorous shake!).* On some of the NBR's lines, foot-warmers were provided for both first and third classes, and this was the case on the Dolphinton branch according to the 1879 *General Supplement* (later 'Appendix') *to the Working Time Tables*; but, by the time of the 1901 *Appendix*, this privilege was restricted to first class passengers on the branch. Foot-warmers were provided both by Leadburn and Dolphinton stations. Detailed instructions were issued in respect of most aspects of railway operations, and foot-warmers were no exception:

> It will be the duty of the Station Masters at the Terminal Stations to supply the Carriages with Foot-Warmers, and to replace the cold pans with hot ones as often as may be necessary. The outside of the Foot-Warmers must be rubbed over with an oily cloth after they are taken from the boiler, and care must be taken that there is no leakage. The Foot-Warmers must not be placed before a fire at any time; and in removing them from the Carriages, they must not be thrown down upon the Platforms, but must be carefully laid aside until again required. The Guards must make a point of seeing that the Carriages of their Trains are supplied with Foot-Warmers, in terms of this order, and they will report in their Train Journals any failure to comply with its provisions.**

---

* Information from *The Railways* by Simon Bradley (Profile Books, 2016).

** *Appendix to the Working Time Tables*, 1st May 1901.

Left: NBR 4-wheel Metropolitan second at east end of Waverley c.1876.
Extract from Alexander Inglis image, Alan Brotchie collection

Right: NBR 4-wheel third at east end of Waverley c.1865 – 1877.
Extract from George Washington Wilson image ref F1449, University of Aberdeen

Early carriages were lit by oil lamps. These were pot lamps inserted through a hole cut in the carriage roof and a plug was inserted into the hole when the lamp was not in use. The fourth class omnibus carriages typically had just one lamp in the centre. Most thirds had two lamps as the carriages had low partitions separating each compartment. Seconds usually shared one lamp between two compartments and first class carriages always had one lamp per compartment. The carriages designed by Drummond (1875-1882) and continued by Holmes (1882-1903) were mostly gas lit, and passengers on the Dolphinton branch would have been treated to gas lighting when these four- and six-wheeled carriages were relegated to minor branch use from the early years of the 20th century. NBR carriages constructed in Reid's time (1903-1919) were mostly electrically lit; however, Dolphinton branch passengers probably never enjoyed electric lighting, as the final bogie brake composite carriage in use at the time of the branch closure to passengers was gas lit. The cylinders typically carried enough gas for about 16 hours using flat flame burners, or perhaps up to 40 hours if the carriage was equipped with incandescent mantles, and the branch carriages would probably have required a re-charge every couple of days or so in winter. The NBR manufactured its own gas for carriage lighting and it ran a small fleet of gas tank wagons to carry the gas to outlying depots. Perhaps the local goods from Edinburgh dropped off a full tank wagon at Leadburn and later picked it up empty or, as on the Jedburgh branch, a through carriage travelled from Edinburgh with a full tank and was coupled on to the branch train and the gas pressures equalized throughout.

From around 1875 to 1890, the very early stock would probably have been gradually replaced by carriages from the 1855-65 period. These replacements might have included carriages built in the mid-1850s for the Peebles line, such as the four-wheel four-compartment first/second composites, or some of the stock built in the mid-1860s by the Metropolitan company, such as the picture of a first on page 170 (*top right*) and a second (*facing page left*). By this time, all the NBR's omnibus thirds would have been scrapped and their replacements would likely have been five-compartment thirds built *circa* 1865 by the NBR and contractors (*facing page right*).

In the 1890-1905 period, replacement carriages would most likely have consisted of the stock built by Ashbury around 1870, such as firsts (*below top left*), composites (*below top right*) and thirds (*below bottom left*). Brake vehicles may have been either full brakes (*below bottom right*) or brake thirds (*page 174 top left*). All this stock would most likely have been four-wheelers. The 1905 – 1920 period would have seen the standard four-wheel stock built by Drummond and Holmes from around 1880 to 1895 now replacing life-expired stock on the branch. Possible examples

Top left: NBR 4-wheel Ashbury first at Banavie c.1900.   *North British Railway Study Group*

Top right: NBR 4-wheel Ashbury composite at east end of Waverley c.1877.
   Extract from George Washington Wilson image ref B1021 University of Aberdeen

Bottom left: NBR 4-wheel Ashbury third at east end of Waverley c.1876.
   Extract from Alexander Inglis image, Alan Brotchie collection

Bottom right: NBR 4-wheel Ashbury passenger brake at east end of Waverley c.1876.
   Extract from Alexander Inglis image, Alan Brotchie collection

Top left: NBR 4-wheel Ashbury brake third at east end of Waverley c.1876.
Extract from Alexander Inglis image, Alan Brotchie collection

Top right: NBR 4-wheel 4-compartment first in use as LNER Departmental vehicle No. 971521.
Allan Rodgers collection

Bottom left: NBR 4-wheel 5-compartment third No. 1072.
AG Ellis 37264

Bottom right: NBR 4-wheel 3-compartment brake third at Waverley on 14th February, 1906.
Extract from A.G. Ellis image 19120

include: firsts (*top right*), thirds (*bottom left*), brake thirds (*bottom right*) and full brakes (*facing page top left*). It is quite possible that some six-wheeled stock started to be introduced on the branch, particularly after the First World War.

The lower photograph on page 165, dated 1925-26, shows the branch train at Dolphinton. The lead vehicle appears to be a six-wheel brake third, followed by a four-wheel, four-compartment first, with what may be a four-wheel, five-compartment third at the rear. It is an interesting image as it confirms that four-wheel stock, by this time around 40 years old, was still to be seen on the branch.

The lower picture on the facing page shows the branch train approaching Broomlee from Dolphinton on the afternoon or early evening of Saturday 13th July, 1929. The carriages are all six-wheelers, the third vehicle from the locomotive almost certainly being an ex-NBR six-wheel passenger brake van of the type shown *top right* on the facing page. The vehicle next to the engine appears to have a guard's look-out (or 'ducket') near the end adjacent to the engine, and the window positions suggest that this is a brake third. The second vehicle is probably a six-wheel composite which would provide some first class compartments. The last vehicle is positioned after the full brake which suggests that it may be an additional vehicle attached for this Summer Saturday service. If the last vehicle is an additional one, the standard make-up of the branch train at this time may have consisted of just three six-wheeled vehicles – a brake third, a first/third composite, and a full brake.

Top left: NBR 4-wheel passenger brake van in use as a LNER Departmental vehicle.
W Hennigan collection per Bill Lynn

Top right: Ex-NBR 6-wheel full brake as LNER No. 3252.
W Hennigan collection per Bill Lynn

Above: The only known photograph of a passenger train in motion on the branch! A late afternoon working from Dolphinton to Leadburn on Saturday 13th July, 1929 is crossing the Bogsbank Bridge, nearing Broomlee, with a train of 6-wheelers, hauled by one of the two class 'C15' 4-4-2T branch locomotives.
NRS/Department for Transport under Open Government Licence v3.0.

Six-wheeled carriages are more evident in the 1920-1930 era, having replaced some, but not all, of the older four-wheelers during this last period of the branch's passenger operation. A report prepared in 1927 for the chief general accountant in relation to possible closure of the branch refers to the saving of one six-wheeled brake van, and one eight-wheeled brake composite coach, presumably all the stock then permanently allocated to the branch for off-season services. The six-wheeler may have been required to provide additional accommodation for parcels traffic at peak times.

The photograph below was taken at Dolphinton on 25th March, 1933 and shows that the branch train by this time, shortly before closure, consisted of just one bogie carriage. The vehicle is a brake composite coupé, one of six carriages built by Holmes in 1894 for the opening of the West Highland Railway. As viewed in this image, the internal layout was: third coupé compartment, lavatory, two thirds, brake compartment, one first, lavatory, first coupé. The carriage number is not discernible, and so the exact vehicle can't be identified. The carriage type was withdrawn by the LNER by 1939.

LNER brake composite coupé, one of six carriages built by Holmes in 1894 for the opening of the West Highland Railway, at Dolphinton on 25th March, 1933.

Marion Moore collection

Chapter Eight

Signalling and other Operational Matters

Operating the Single Line Branch

Prior to the opening of the Dolphinton branch, the Chairman and the Secretary of the North British Railway were required to certify under seal 'that the Line being a Single Line, is to be worked by "Train Staff" as described … in the circular on this subject issued by the Board of Trade and that at present there is no passing Station.'

Where a single line was worked by Train Staff, possession of the physical Train Staff, usually made of wood or metal and bearing the name of the section of line to which it applied, was an engine driver's authority to occupy that section – in this case the whole line between Leadburn and Dolphinton; as there was only one staff for each section, there could be no risk of another train being in the section at the same time. The Staff for the Dolphinton branch is described in the Working Time Tables for January 1865 as 'Colour of Train Staff and Train Ticket – Green', and 'No. of Train Staff 5'.* The tickets referred to were retained in a locked box in the signal cabin, opened by a key on the end of the Staff, and could be used where more than one train in succession was passing through a section of single line in the same direction: the signalman would display the staff to the driver of the first (and, if applicable, subsequent) train and issue a paper ticket to the engine driver, authorizing him to enter the single line section; the final train travelling in that direction would carry the staff. Not being a through line, and with only one locomotive timetabled to be in use on the branch at this era, tickets would have been used rarely; one example would be a snowplough preceding the branch passenger train. The *Appendix to the Working Time Tables* of 1st June, 1882 shows the Dolphinton branch as now being split into two separate sections, thus allowing one train to be in the section between Leadburn and Broomlee, and another between Broomlee and Dolphinton, at the same time. The latter section used Train Staff No. 3, with pink tickets.

The signalling principles and practice in operation in the early 1860s were still very much evolving, and a description is beyond the scope of

---

* The number related to the design of the staff, the idea being that staffs for adjacent sections were of different designs so as to avoid confusion (and would not open the wrong ticket box). For the same reason, the Staff, Tickets and Ticket Boxes for a particular section were all of the same colour. After a period of use, most staffs became the colour of dirty oil!

Webb & Thomson electric train staff for the Broomlee – Leadburn section of single line, introduced in 1898. The key at the end unlocked the ground frames at Lamancha and Macbie Hill.
Rae Montgomery

Annett's Key for Broomlee branch. This key token unlocked the points at Leadburn to give access to the truncated Leadburn – Broomlee branch post-1939.
Rae Montgomery

this book. In addition to Leadburn, only Broomlee and Dolphinton had a 'Signal Porter'* in post, according to the 1874 records, and the Dolphinton post was discontinued in December 1878. On the branch, the points controlling entry to and exit from a siding would initially have been operated by individual point levers and locks; the grouping of these into a ground frame (or 'signal lever frame'), unlocked and locked by the key on the end of the train staff, is a later development.**

Regulation of Railways Act 1889

In 1889, following the Armagh railway disaster on 12th June that year in which 80 people were killed, many of them children on a Sunday School excursion, Parliament passed an important piece of safety legislation, the Regulation of Railways Act, under which all companies had to implement a number of measures: (1) adoption of the 'block system' on all passenger-carrying lines, ensuring that only one train could be on one physical section (or 'block') of line at a time; (2) the interlocking of points and signals so that, for example, a signal could not show 'clear' while the points were set for a conflicting train movement; and (3) to

---

* '331. It shall be the duty of one Porter specially appointed by the station master at each Station to attend to Signals. He will be called the Signal Porter … He is required to have his Signal Lamps and Flags always at hand and ready for immediate use.' (NBR Rule Book 1866)

** The *Peeblesshire Advertiser* of 10th September, 1892 reported that 'Over all the sections interlocking frames will be substituted for the existing hand worked levers.

provide and use, on all passenger-carrying trains, continuous automatic brakes: i.e. instantaneous in action, and capable of being applied by the driver or guard; self-applying in the event of any failure (such as the train dividing in two); and capable of being applied to all the vehicles in the train whether or not carrying passengers. Companies were given time to implement the proposals, which involved extensive – and expensive – works on their part. They were allowed to raise additional debenture stock to the amount certified by the Board of Trade as having been expended on these measures – some £242,000 being claimed by the North British Railway. The meeting of shareholders in September 1894 was told that the work had now been completed throughout the system.

Under the block system, the line was divided into sections or 'blocks', with a signal box at either end, and signals controlling the entry to and exit from the section, usually with telegraphic instruments at either end to allow the signalmen to communicate with each other in regulating the traffic. Locations where signals and points were operated now generally required to have a signal box, with a frame for the signal and points levers, and a sometimes complicated series of rodding, wiring and links to operate the points and signals, interlocked to prevent them from being set to conflict with each other. Sidings at more isolated locations could be worked instead from a ground frame.

On most busy single lines, a 'tablet' or token in the form of a brass disc, authorizing a train to be in that block section, was issued by the signalman at one or other end of the section, and their electrically interlocked tablet instruments ensured that a second tablet for that section could not be withdrawn until the first one had been replaced in one or other of the machines. Later, other forms of token, particularly key-shaped ones, were introduced. The single line Peebles branch was equipped with the tablet system, and a new signal box was built at Leadburn, opened in 1892; it was in communication with the box at either end of the adjoining single line sections of the Peebles branch – Hawthornden to the north, and Peebles Engine Shed to the south. Broomlee and Dolphinton were also provided with new signal boxes around the same time but the lower volume of traffic did not justify installation of the tablet system. Instead, a combined system of block telegraph communication between the signalmen plus a single train staff was installed in place of the previous train staff only.* The system ensured that a train could be sent into the Leadburn – Broomlee section or the Broomlee – Dolphinton section only with the co-operation of the signalmen at either end. Problems could arise

---

* The 'Tyer's block and staff' system.

occasionally if the staff was at the 'wrong' end of the section for an approaching train, in which case the staff would have to be conveyed to the other end of the section on foot or perhaps on horseback! The cost of these new installations was £360 5s. 8d. for Leadburn to Broomlee, and £294 15s. 6d. for Broomlee to Dolphinton.

As part of his report on the condition of the stations (Chapter Four), Major Marindin carried out an inspection of the interlocking and other arrangements in May 1893. His comments were as follows:

> **Leadburn Junction** – There is a new signal cabin containing 36 working levers and 4 spare levers, and a subsidiary cabin [presumably for the level crossing] bolted from the station cabin, containing a 3 lever frame. Requirement. Nil.
> **La Mancha Station.** This is an intermediate station between two block stations [Leadburn and Broomlee] and there is a loop siding for goods traffic, but no passing loop and only one platform, altho' it is situated upon a steep gradient. The points and signals are worked from an outside panel. Requirements. A loop with second platform; covering to signal lever frame.
> **Macbie Hill Station.** The points and signals are worked from an outside frame containing 10 working and 4 spare levers. Requirements. A loop with second platform; covering to signal lever frame.
> **Broomlee Station.** There is a new signal cabin containing 15 working and 5 spare levers.
> **Dolphinton Station.** The new signal cabin contains 18 working and 4 spare levers. Requirements. Alteration of label on No 4 lever; distant signal to be made to apply to the platform line only.

The ground frames at Lamancha and Macbie Hill are recorded as each having 10 working levers and 4 spares.

The cost of interlocking the points and signals on the branch were certified by the NBR to the Board of Trade (after several revisions) as £1,862 2s. at Leadburn, £112 12s. at Lamancha, £106 16s. 6d. at Macbie Hill, £362 19s. 4d. at Broomlee and £244 6s. at Dolphinton.

Probably because of increasing traffic, the 'Block and Staff system' between Leadburn and Broomlee was replaced by March 1898 with the 'Electric Train Staff', while the section between Broomlee and Dolphinton reverted to the old train staff system with the use of tickets prohibited – i.e. 'One Engine in Steam'.

The Electric Train Staff system operated on the same principles as the tablet system referred to above. A number of train staffs were electrically locked inside the instruments at either end of the Leadburn to Broomlee block section. The signalman at the entry to the section, with the co-operation of the signalman at the other end of the section, would release a staff to be handed to the driver of an approaching train. When the train arrived at the other end of the section, the staff was replaced in the instrument there, so allowing a staff to be withdrawn for the next train, in whichever direction.* The end of the staff was in the shape of a key, and this enabled the train crew to unlock the ground frames controlling the points at the intermediate stations of Lamancha and Macbie Hill, and later the two Broomlee sidings in connection with the Talla aqueduct works, for shunting operations. The staff couldn't be withdrawn from the ground frame until the points had been restored to their normal position and the ground frame locked. Dolphinton-born David Newlands recalls driver Peter Small and fireman Bob Fell losing the staff one night – which caused considerable disruption!**

The large signal box at Dolphinton presumably then became a glorified ground frame, without signals. The 1901 *Appendix to the Working Time Tables* states that access to the sidings at Dolphinton (and also to the McAlpine & Sons siding near Broomlee) was controlled by the key fixed to the train staff 'which renders the provision of fixed signals unnecessary'. The October 1922 *Appendix* shows Leadburn Junction to Broomlee as being worked by Electric Train Staff No. 3, and Broomlee to Dolphinton worked by No. 3 Train Staff (One Engine in Steam). The signal box is shown as disused in the 1920-1923 plan by Robert Brown referred to on page 116, but its date of removal is not known; but it does not appear in a poor quality photo dated 1927-28. From 1st March, 1933, a month before closure, the whole branch reverted to being a single block section, with the Broomlee box downgraded simply to controlling the level crossing.

In September 1938, the LNER's Traffic Committee received a report from the Divisional General Manager (Scottish Area) that the Leadburn box required heavy repairs. The electric token instruments were located in the booking office and it was proposed to make economies by removing the signal box and locking frame, providing a new locking frame in a smaller lean-to structure, and removing the platform for the Dolphinton branch (by now closed to passengers). Consideration had been given to the abolition of Leadburn as a block post and passing loop, but owing to the distance on the single line between Hawthornden Junction and Peebles – 15 miles 55 chains – it was considered essential to retain it in order to provide sufficient line capacity. The start of the Second World War being but a year away, the work was not carried out, and it was 1st March,

---

* This enabled four trains in succession to depart from Broomlee for Leadburn on 6th August, 1898 at 15-minute intervals from 5.45 pm. See Chapter Six.

** Harold Bowtell, *op cit.*

1954 before the towering 1892 box was replaced by a smaller brick structure. This was done by constructing the new brickwork around the base of the existing wooden box (*see page 71*). The 1954 box closed with the Peebles branch on 5th February, 1962, the connection to Macbie Hill having been removed by 3rd June, 1961. It is not known when the Dolphinton platform face was removed but it had gone by June 1953.

Jean Fleming, in her *Scots Magazine* article, August 1988, recalled the Broomlee signal box in which her father worked:

> As a small child it was a great delight for me to climb the steep stairs to the signalbox to see my father. Of course there was a notice on the door which said 'No Admittance', but then I couldn't read. ... Then there was that great big wheel to open the gates on the level crossing. I thought it was wonderful that my father could open and shut the gates all by himself and stop the traffic on the road (not that there was much of that in those days).

The hours of attendance at the Broomlee box, as set out in the May 1901 *Appendix*, were from 6 am on Mondays and Tuesdays (to accommodate the goods and cattle trains on those days), and from 7.30 am on Wednesdays to Saturdays, until 9.40 pm. By March 1914, the box closed at 5.40 pm, Mondays to Fridays, and 9.40 pm on Saturdays. By June 1920, the hours were from 7.15 am to 6.00 pm Mondays to Fridays, and to 9.20 pm on Saturdays.

Shunting on Steep Gradients

Major Marindin was concerned about the working of goods traffic at Macbie Hill and Lamancha which were both situated on steep gradients running downhill towards Broomlee (*see gradient diagram page 49*). His 1893 report (*see page 180*) included a requirement for running loops and second platforms to be constructed at these stations, which puzzled the NBR, given that two trains could not be at the station at the same time; it was presumably intended that catch points be fitted to the rear of the Leadburn-bound platform lines to derail any runaway vehicles. After representations by the NBR, the Board of Trade accepted the compromise that shunting there would be carried out only by up goods trains (i.e. heading towards Dolphinton) when the locomotive would be at the lower (Broomlee) end of the train on the gradient and so prevent runaways. Various instructions to give effect to these requirements appear in the NBR's May 1901 *Appendix to the Working Time Tables*, and subsequently, and notice boards situated at the points leading to the sidings at Lamancha and Macbie Hill reminded train crews of the instructions.

In practice, this meant that while wagons coming *from* Leadburn could be left off at Lamancha and Macbie Hill, and wagons *from* those places bound for Dolphinton and the Caledonian could be picked up, those going *to* Leadburn from Lamancha and Macbie Hill would first have to be taken to Broomlee or Dolphinton before being returned to Leadburn by the next goods train; similarly, any wagons going *to* Macbie Hill and Lamancha from Dolphinton would first have to go to Leadburn and then be left off by the next Broomlee-bound goods. A later revision permitted Leadburn-bound goods trains – ascending the incline – to stop at the platform at Lamancha and Macbie Hill for the purpose of 'leaving or lifting Road Van Goods only', provided there was sufficient brake power at the rear of the train to hold it in the case of a break-away taking place.

So far as passenger trains were concerned, no Leadburn-bound train was allowed to stop at Macbie Hill or Lamancha unless the continuous automatic brake was working on the rear vehicle. Mixed passenger trains bound for Leadburn and requiring to shunt wagons at Lamancha and Macbie Hill could do so provided that the rear vehicle was fitted with the automatic brake in working order.

Station masters and district inspectors were required to satisfy themselves that these instructions were being carried out, 'and it will be their duty to report every instance of irregularity or failure to comply with these instructions which may come under their notice'.

Mixed Trains and Continuous Brakes

The requirement to have a continuous automatic brake on passenger trains would effectively have put an end to the running of mixed trains (passenger and goods vehicles), as many goods wagons were not so fitted. The NBR took advantage of a modification to the Order relating to continuous brakes under the 1899 Act:

> A limited number of mixed trains for the conveyance of goods and passengers in which the goods waggons are not required to have continuous brakes, may be run subject to the following conditions, namely –
> (a) That the engine tender and passenger vehicles of such mixed trains shall be provided with continuous brakes worked from the engine.
> (b) That the goods waggons shall be conveyed behind the passenger vehicles, with brake van or brake vans in the rear of the train in the proportion of one brake van for every ten waggons or fractional part of ten waggons.

(c) That the total number of vehicles of all descriptions on any such mixed train shall not exceed 25.
(d) That the maximum average speed of such train throughout the journey between stations shall not exceed 25 miles an hour; and
(e) That all such trains shall stop at all stations, or at intervals not exceeding 10 miles, or in the case of stations more than 10 miles apart, at each of such stations.

The precise number of mixed trains was subject to the approval of the Board of Trade. The NBR asked for all of its trains on the LL&DR to be so exempted, but the Board of Trade allowed only two each way – one in the morning and one in the afternoon. As we saw in Chapter Five, the number of mixed trains on the branch declined substantially over the following years.

Other Operational Matters

Among other information to be gleaned from the *Appendices to the Working Time Tables*, we learn
- that the Level Crossing at Broomlee was protected by signals, and the crossing gates were normally maintained across the railway;
- that the towing of railway vehicles with a rope or chain attached to a locomotive moving on an adjacent line was prohibited by the NBR unless specially authorized; Macbie Hill, Broomlee and Dolphinton were so authorized; and
- that both horses and [road] carriages could be unloaded at Leadburn, Broomlee and Dolphinton, and horses only at Lamancha and Macbie Hill.

Also included are details of the whistle signals that drivers were expected to give when approaching Leadburn Junction, to indicate their intended route to the signalman:

Route	Number of Whistles
Main Line (Up or Down)	1
To or from Branch Line	2
Branch Line to Dock Platform, or vice versa	3
To or from Up Line Sidings	4
To or from Shed Siding	5
To or From Branch Sidings	6

Leadburn was hardly the busiest or most complicated of junctions, and the use of these signals was perhaps of doubtful benefit!

Chapter Nine

The Caledonian Railway's Dolphinton Branch, and the proposed Douglas & Dolphinton Railway

The Caledonian's Dolphinton Branch

Having unsuccessfully tried to woo the LL&DR, the Caledonian set about promoting its own line. Plans and Sections of its proposed Carstairs and Dolphinton Branch Railway were deposited, as required, with the Principal Sheriff Clerks of Peeblesshire and Lanarkshire, and with the Clerk of the Parliaments, on 26th November, 1862 – the same date on which it was reported to the LL&DR Directors that John Waddell had commenced construction of their branch. The CR line was to run from the main line at Carstairs (Dolphinton Junction), with intermediate stations at Bankhead, Newbigging and Dunsyre and a separate passenger terminus at Dolphinton, with a connecting line extending to the NBR's Dolphinton branch.

Dolphinton CR station. The official route from the NBR station, seen through the road bridge, was up the NBR access road to the road bridge, then across to the CR wicket gate. The shortcut along the track was probably frequently used instead. The goods transfer bank can be seen beyond the bridge on the right, where the CR exchange line passed alongside the NBR yard. *John Paton collection*

The *Peeblesshire Advertiser* of 22nd November, 1862 saw a bright future for the latter: 'The junction will at all events crown with success the line contracted for from Leadburn to Dolphinton, the promoters of which may be congratulated on having adopted a route that has so significantly proved to be the best. ... So far as the Peebles Railway is concerned, the benefit will be very considerable, for the line must inevitably enjoy the traffic opened out between Dalkeith and Glasgow'. Although the Caley's Bill was entitled 'An Act to enable the Caledonian Railway Company to make a Branch Railway from Carstairs to join the Leadburn Linton and Dolphinton Railway', there was to be no through route between Peeblesshire and Lanarkshire for passengers. The Caledonian line was as much about blocking any encroachment by the NBR as it was about providing a service to the stations on the new line. Thomas Salkeld, Chairman of the Caledonian Railway, addressing the shareholders on 7th April, 1863, told them that 'if they did not make it, the line would inevitably be made by other parties; and whilst in the hands of the Caledonian it would be a valuable feeder to the main line, in the hands of others it would be just the reverse'.

The Caledonian Railway (Dolphinton Branch) Bill received the Royal Assent on 11th May, 1863, but the Caley was in no great hurry to start construction. It was 30th August, 1864 before the contract was awarded – again to John Waddell – for the sum of £44,570 7s. 7d., and 1st March, 1867 before the line opened.

Captain Rich RE inspected the line on 20th February, 1867 and passed it for passenger use, subject to some minor improvements, including the provision of a distant signal on the CR's connecting line to the NBR, worked from the NBR station, 'to prevent waggons coming from the Caledonian Stn approaching the North British branch without the permission of the signalman of the latter Co.'.

The junction with the North British was stated to be 'constructed only for minerals and goods' and so was not passed by the Board of Trade for passenger use, and no subsequent approval, or any use by a passenger train, has been uncovered. At 10 miles and 59 chains [72 chains per the inspection report, and 11 miles to the junction with the LL&DR according to the deposited plans], it was a mile or so longer than the NBR's branch of 9 miles and 70 chains. Land was taken, and overbridges constructed, to accommodate a double line of rails, but it was built as – and remained – a single line of railway. A turntable was provided at Dolphinton, and there was one at Carstairs. No agreement having been reached for a joint station at Dolphinton despite the approaches by the LL&DR, each company provided its own terminal

THE CALEDONIAN RAILWAY'S DOLPHINTON BRANCH 187

An early 20th century view of the CR station at Dolphinton from the bridge over the railway. *Lens of Sutton Association*

There was a joint staff for the two Dolphinton stations from March 1908. Robert Brown, clerk, and Donald Tweedie, lad porter, pose for the camera in the mid-1920s at the CR station, on a bench with an elaborate CR cast-iron seat end. *WLDHA collection*

station complete with all facilities: platform, station buildings, loop lines and sidings, turntable, goods shed, crane and water supply, although latterly they shared a station master and staff.

For a village the size of Dolphinton, the population of the majority (Lanarkshire) portion of which was 260 in 1861, it was a curious arrangement, to say the least. Between the two stations, one on each side of the Biggar road, was the short connecting line for the exchange of wagons. Passengers had to climb up to and over the road to get from one platform to the other, although no doubt some took a shortcut alongside the track and under the road bridge. But they could be in for a long wait!

The *Aberdeen Journal* of 1st September, 1880 described how 'with characteristic perversity, the two rival Companies, the Caledonian and the North British, have stations situated within a few hundred yards of each other, but connected only by a siding for the transfer of waggons, and where the passenger trains are most ingeniously disconnected in their hours of arrival and departure.' 'Most ingeniously disconnected' wasn't entirely fair. As with the Caledonian and North British stations on either side of the Tweed at Peebles, each company scheduled its branch trains to connect with its main line trains, rather than to provide

Dolphinton station (LMS) on Saturday afternoon 10th September 1932, the final day of operation before the first closure of the former CR line to passenger traffic. The guard is not the LMS train guard, but Jack Hutchison, LNER. The locomotive is Carstairs-based LMS 4-4-0 class '4P' 'Compound' No. 917, ex-Midland Railway. *Marion Moore collection*

through connections between the two companies, and the Caledonian's Dolphinton branch passenger trains numbered only three per day, as compared to the NBR's five or six; but better connections could no doubt have been provided had the will been there. There were, however, some opportunities for passengers from the NBR branch to travel on to Glasgow (Central) or Edinburgh (Princes Street) on Caledonian metals, and vice versa.

CONNECTIONS AT DOLPHINTON

		am	pm	pm	pm
NOV 1889					
NBR	arr	9.00		3.53	
CR	dep	9.15		4.05	
CR	arr	9.05	12.35		6.16
NBR	dep	10.15	2.35		7.25
JULY 1910		am	pm	pm	
NBR	arr	8.45	3.32		
CR	dep	9.05	3.55		
CR	arr	8.51	3.47	6.00	
NBR	dep	10.05	4.40	6.15**SX**	
SEPT 1924		am	pm	pm	
NBR	arr	8.47	3.30**SX**		
CR	dep	9.15	3.45		
CR	arr	8.57	3.26	6.20	
NBR	dep	9.16	4.50	7.40**SO**	

SO – Saturdays only; **SX** – Saturdays excepted.

Harold Bowtell* relates a story from his friend David Newlands:

Although the branches were connected, and came under the same station master, at Dolphinton, they were quite independent of one another. ... I was on the platform of the CR station one day in 1923, and there was a train just about ready to go. The station master was there too, probably with his watch in his hand. Just then a train arrived in the NB station. Some seconds later, looking back under the bridge that carried the A702 over the railway, I saw some people, obviously off the NBR train and striving to catch the Caley one. Unfortunately for them, the station master was looking the wrong way, and gave the Caley driver the right away while the unfortunate NB folks were maybe only about 300 yards away. How they would finish their journey I can't imagine, for there were no buses then.

But surely the joint station master for the two stations would have known the arrival and departure times on both branches?

---

* *op cit*

Nevertheless, the Linton farmers gained a link with the important markets at Lanark, and in time a fair amount of trade in sheep and lambs and horses developed between Lanark and the stations on the LL&DR. The report of 5th November, 1927 in relation to possible closure of the LNER branch (Chapter Ten) stated that in the previous year 123 loaded horse boxes had been exchanged to the LMS at Dolphinton, and 74 received.

The former Caledonian branch closed to passengers on and from 12th September, 1932 – six months before the closure of the NBR's Dolphinton branch – but reopened with a restricted service on 17th July, 1933, after complaints were received from farmers and traders in the area. Finally, it closed to passengers on and from 4th June, 1945. Freight services continued until 31st October, 1950, closing the following day.

The Douglas & Dolphinton Railway

There was nearly a third railway line and a third railway company at Dolphinton. In the run-up to the major Scottish railway amalgamations in 1865 (Caledonian with Scottish Central; North British with Edinburgh & Glasgow), Richard Hodgson of the NBR called a meeting in Edinburgh with the E&GR and the Glasgow & South Western Railway (G&SWR) on 24th October, 1864. Looking to the 'wholesale and indiscriminate projection of new schemes' by the Caledonian and Scottish Central, 'calculated to attack the independence and prosperity of all the Companies represented', he proposed joint action and agreement to protect themselves against the 'threatened aggression' by the Caledonian and to 'promote freedom and interchange of traffic between their respective systems'. A joint 'Parliamentary Committee of the North British and Edinburgh and Glasgow and Glasgow and South Western Railway Companies' was formed to co-ordinate the response.

The Caledonian had opened its branch from Lanark to Douglas on 1st April, 1864 and was now seeking to extend to Muirkirk, and from there (via a client company) to build a new line to Ayr – right through the heart of G&SWR territory. The latter countered with a number of schemes, including building its own line between Muirkirk and the Caledonian branch at Douglas where they invited the NBR to meet them with a line – through Caledonian territory – from Dolphinton. A difficulty was that the NBR didn't yet own or lease the newly-opened LL&DR, it simply worked it, and so its preference was for the G&SWR itself to build the line to Dolphinton where the North British, by leasing

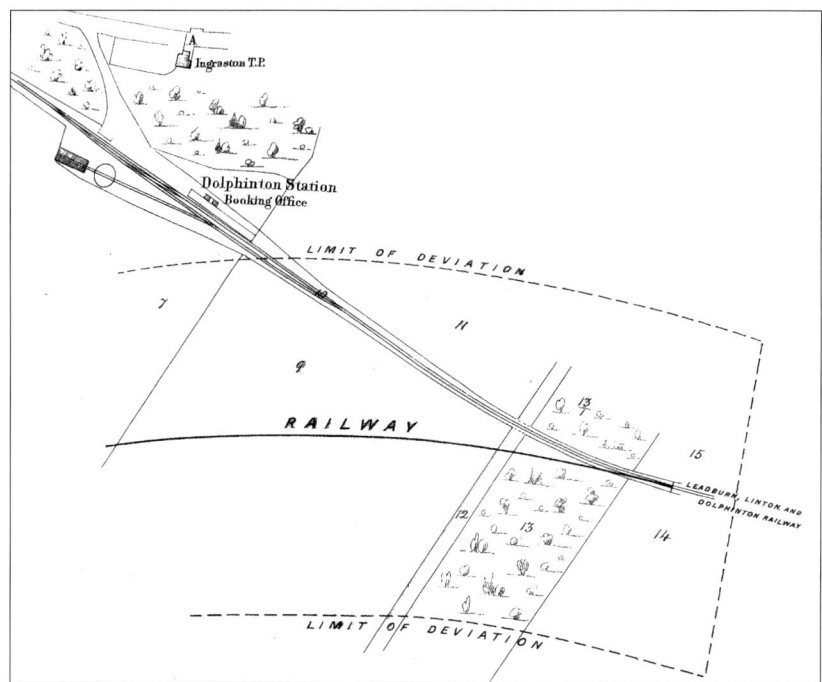

Proposed Douglas & Dolphinton Railway: Parliamentary plan showing the connection between the D&DR and the NBR some 330 yards north-east of the latter's Dolphinton station. *Author's collection*

the LL&DR, would meet it and receive it with every facility. Hodgson explained a number of proposed schemes to the E&GR representatives for the amalgamated NBR/E&GR, including 'the lease of the LL&DR at a rent not exceeding 3 per cent on the capital of £40,000 …if such a lease can be obtained'. As explained in Chapter One, Hodgson had promised the LL&DR 4 per cent in 1861.

In the end, the Douglas & Dolphinton was promoted by a nominally independent Company, but backed by the NBR and G&SWR. In November 1864 it deposited its plans in Parliament for a 20-mile line 'commencing at or near a point 50 yards or thereabouts to the north-westward of the Passenger Booking Office of the Caledonian Railway Company, at the Happendon [Douglas] Station of their Douglas Branch Railway and terminating by a Junction with the Leadburn, Linton and Dolphinton Railway, at or near a point thereon, 330 yards or thereby to the north-eastward of [their] Passenger Booking Office … at their Dolphinton Station'. It would have crossed the Caledonian main line at

Thankerton, and formed a junction with it there. The NBR and G&SWR were to have powers to raise money for, and hold shares in, the company, and to make agreements to work the railway. The Engineer was Ronald Johnstone CE. The line would have created a direct link between allies the NBR and G&SWR, and posed a threat to the traffic of their common enemy – the Caley! The Bill was read a second time in the House of Commons on 15th February, 1865, but withdrawn eight days later. Common sense had eventually broken out, with an agreement, signed in March 1865, between the G&SWR and the Caledonian to modify their proposed adversarial schemes. The Caledonian dropped its proposal for the line to Ayr, and the G&SWR withdrew its proposal for a Muirkirk to Douglas branch. A line from Ayr to Edinburgh and the East Coast, via Dolphinton, West Linton and Leadburn remains but an interesting thought!

Broomlee station and staff c.1908 – 1910. Left to right are Joe Joss, station master; Tom Cowe, clerk; Bob Miller, signalman, and John Fleming, signalman. Milk churns are much in evidence. The signal lamp has been wound down on the windlass to ground level.

Lens of Sutton Association

Chapter Ten

The LNER Era, and Closure

The Threat of Closure

Prior to 1914, the railway system of Great Britain was made up of a large number of independent companies. As in the case of the North British and Caledonian, this had often given rise to wasteful competition, although that diminished latterly, as instanced by the 1907 agreement between the NBR and CR which led, amongst other things, to a joint station staff for the two Dolphinton stations. The companies were brought under State control for the duration of the First World War, control lasting until August 1921. By the end of the War, the companies were on their knees as a result of the demands and privations of wartime, and the consequent lack of maintenance and renewals, and they faced a huge capital expenditure. In 1921, 'With a view to the reorganization and more efficient and economical working of the railway system of Great Britain', but stopping short of full Nationalization (which would come on 1st January, 1948 under the Transport Act of 1947), Parliament passed the Railways Act which led to the 'Grouping': with effect from 1st January, 1923, the companies would be grouped into the 'Big Four' – the London and North Eastern Railway (LNER), the London, Midland and Scottish Railway (LMS), the Great Western Railway (GWR), and the Southern Railway (SR). The five main Scottish companies were divided between the LNER and the LMS, with the North British and Great North of Scotland being constituents of the LNER, and the Caledonian, Glasgow & South Western, and Highland becoming part of the LMS. Dolphinton continued to be a frontier – now between LNER and LMS.

Initially, there were few changes in day-to-day operations and the timetable on the LL&DR continued much as before. But the world was changing. The end of the First World War in 1918 had seen large numbers of Army surplus vehicles released on to the market, together with the demobilization of men who had learned how to maintain them. The result was the growth of the road transport industry with the formation of many bus companies and haulage contractors. Branch lines were coming under threat, particularly in rural areas where door-to-door road transport of goods and people could replace inconvenient journeys to and from the nearest railway station, often several miles away. The writing was on the wall when Andrew Harper's royal blue and cream-liveried buses started running from Biggar to Edinburgh via

Harper's Motors timetable commencing 4th October, 1927.
courtesy Andrew Harper

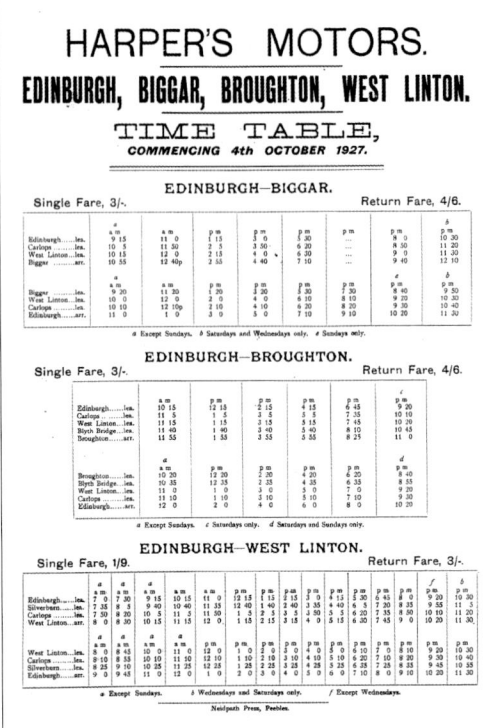

Harper's Dennis bus DS1235 at West Linton in 1927, with driver B. Lowrie.
courtesy Andrew Harper

West Linton on 16th March, 1925, and from West Linton to Peebles in May 1925. Services between West Linton and Broughton followed in October 1927, with a West Linton, Peebles and Penicuik service two months later.* Despite maintaining service levels and offering fare concessions, the railway was losing the battle. Total booked passenger journeys on the NBR branch had peaked at over 38,000 in 1898-99 but were down to just over 10,000 for 1927-1928. It was difficult to see what else the railway could do, although advice from the *Peeblesshire Advertiser* was not lacking:

> A board advertising the activities of the LNER has recently been erected in the village, apparently a local manifestation of the present railway offensive in the transport war. We cannot help thinking, however, that the Company's chances of success in this quarter would be more improved were a better and more reasonable passenger service afforded. The afternoon train takes 1 hour and 27 minutes to reach Edinburgh, and the last train home leaves town at least three hours too early at night. No matter what fare concessions are given – and of late these have been considerable – they are almost completely nullified by the lack of an evening return service, in which respect this district is actually worse off than it was fifty years ago! (31st August, 1928).

On 9th July, 1932, the Scottish Motor Traction Company (SMT) began a bus service from Edinburgh to Lanark via Penicuik, Carlops, West Linton and Dolphinton. By 1933, buses provided a service, at least hourly, from Edinburgh to West Linton and Dolphinton departing as late as 9.30 pm on weekdays and 10.40 pm on Saturdays, with similar timings in the opposite direction. By contrast, the last train out of Broomlee on weekdays was at 4.39 pm and from Edinburgh at 4.57 pm.

The 10-day railway strike at the end of September 1919 is said to have been the first nail in the coffin for rural branch services, but the writing was on the wall before that. The *Scotsman* of 28th March, 1912 reported that one effect of the then-current coal strike was 'to introduce to the notice of the numerous commercial and industrial firms the advantages of mechanical road transport ... who, but for the compulsion of the strike, might not have been convinced for some time to come'. The General Strike of May 1926 that lasted on the railway from 4th to 12th May, 1926, and the summer-long Miners' Strike that followed, accelerated the diversion of freight traffic from rail to road. Before the strike, 13 dairies had sent a consignment of milk daily to Edinburgh or Fife from Broomlee, with two van loads daily from the Dolphinton branch; after it, only five dairies, and these five gradually

---

* Harper's Motors was sold to the Caledonian Omnibus Company Ltd in January 1932.

went over to road transport. Farmers found that motors could carry their livestock and dairy produce from door to door with greater speed and efficiency, and the railway never regained the business.

The LNER nationally was facing a difficult commercial environment and needed to make economies. By the end of 1925, the chief accountant at LNER Headquarters, King's Cross, was collecting data on branch lines from the divisional accountant in Edinburgh. On 21st January, 1927 he wrote seeking more detailed information about the Dolphinton branch, under the heading 'Economies – Closing of Branch Lines'. It had been calculated that the branch was losing £2,942 per annum, and a detailed report dated 5th November, 1927 to the General Manager (Scotland) by his senior officers discussed some options:

- the use of a Sentinel-Cammell steam railcar had been considered, but trials made in the area showed that because of the steep gradients it would be able to haul only one vehicle. On 38 occasions in the previous year, the branch train had conveyed more than one horse box, or similar vehicle.*
- a more intensive passenger service had also been considered; but as the district was sparsely populated and the principal station (Broomlee) was 'one mile distant' from West Linton, giving buses a distinct advantage, it was unlikely to be remunerative, particularly as additional connections at Leadburn would be required. A 50 per cent increase over 1924 traffic levels would be required to cover the loss, and the prospect of achieving this was remote.

In considering goods traffic, Lamancha and Macbie Hill were left out of account, their traffic being minimal, but the officers noted that there was currently a fair volume of traffic passing to Broomlee in connection with the new Baddinsgill reservoir then being constructed,** and it was expected that this would continue for another 12 – 18 months. It also noted that there was a heavy milk traffic from Dolphinton and Broomlee to stations in Fife. The officers' conclusion was that the branch should be closed to passenger traffic but retained meantime for goods. In the past year, 123 loaded horse boxes (which ran as passenger traffic) had been exchanged to the LMS at Dolphinton, and 74 received. Some of these could instead be

---

* A Sentinel railcar was used on the Penicuik branch from time to time. They were painted green and white, which apparently led some locals to believe that the LNER had been taken over by the similarly liveried SMT bus company!

** Opened in 1930. Mr Greig's notebook records the arrival at Broomlee of 930 tons of pipes in June and July 1929.

Harper's Albion bus reg. no. DS1304 at West Linton, driver Hugh Harper.
courtesy Andrew Harper

Caledonian Omnibus Company bus timetable for West Linton, Dolphinton and Biggar, 31st March, 1933.

exchanged at Peebles (another 'frontier' town, where both the LMS and LNER had connected stations).

The withdrawal of the branch passenger locomotive and men would result in a saving of £2,048, net of the cost of a main line goods engine to provide the proposed daily goods-only service on the branch. The class 'C15' branch locomotive could be disposed of, and one six-wheeled brake van, and one eight-wheeled brake composite coach (i.e. containing both first and third class accommodation, as well as a brake compartment for the guard) would be allocated elsewhere. With only one service per day for goods traffic, the existing method of signalling – Electric Train Staff between Leadburn Junction and Broomlee, and No. 3 Train Staff between Broomlee and Dolphinton – could be replaced by the standard arrangement for such branches of 'One Engine in Steam'.

By the end of the decade, in the era of the Great Depression, many unremunerative LNER branches were being closed; seven closed on a single day on 22nd September, 1930. The Dolphinton branch was reprieved – for the time being.

The Decision to Close

At its meeting on 5th January, 1933, the LNER Traffic Committee received the following report recommending closure from the General Manager (Scotland):

CLOSING OF BRANCH LINES:- DOLPHINTON BRANCH (SOUTHERN SCOTTISH AREA)
Submitted Memorandum, dated 23rd December, 1932, by the General Manager (Scotland) reporting that the economic position on the Dolphinton Branch, which has not been good for some time, has in recent years been aggravated by road competition and bad trade, and as traffic could not be encouraged to such an extent as to make revenue cover expenditure, the continuance of Passenger and/or Goods train services can no longer be justified.

The branch consists of about ten miles of single track, extending from Leadburn Junction, on the Edinburgh and Galashiels Line via Peebles, to its junction with the L. M. & S. Railway at Dolphinton, and serves an agricultural community by Stations located at Lamancha, Macbie Hill, Broomlee and Dolphinton.

For twelve months ended 30th June, 1932, the Branch Receipts amounted to £1,118, while the gross Contributory Revenue was £2,358, but if the line were closed the loss of revenue would be considerably more than offset by reductions in expenditure.

London and North Eastern Railway.
(SCOTTISH AREA.)

JOINT CIRCULAR. 30th March 1933.

To Station-masters, Parcel Agents and Others concerned.

Closing of Dolphinton Branch.

With reference to General Manager's (Scotland) Circular G.M. 248, of 26th January, 1933; on and from Saturday, 1st April, 1933, passengers must not be booked to Dolphinton, Broomlee (for West Linton), Macbiehill or Lamancha, and the Station names and fares must be neatly struck out of the fare books and the list of fares exhibited to the public. All series of printed tickets must be withdrawn and sent to the Divisional Accountant, Edinburgh, accompanied by the usual list.

Road services operated by The Scottish Motor Traction Company, Limited, between Edinburgh, Penicuik, West Linton and Dolphinton, and by The Scottish Motor Traction Company, Limited, and The Caledonian Omnibus Company, Limited, jointly, between Edinburgh, Penicuik and Lamancha, are available, and passengers for places on the Dolphinton Branch should be advised accordingly.

Parcels and Miscellaneous (Guard's Van) traffic by Passenger train should be accepted for Dolphinton, Broomlee (West Linton), Macbiehill and Lamancha, and charges thereon should be based on the present throughout mileage to these Stations. Such traffic should be forwarded by Passenger train to **Penicuik**, from which point it will be conveyed to destination by L.N.E.R. Road Motor Lorry; and, in the reverse direction, traffic from these places will be conveyed to Penicuik by road for despatch by Passenger train to destination. Parcels traffic should continue to be stamped as hitherto, but in dealing with "waybilled" traffic, the following instructions must be adhered to :—

Station.	Waybills to be headed.	Rates to be applied.	Waybills to be abstracted.	
			Local.	Foreign.
Dolphinton	Penicuik for Dolphinton	Dolphinton	Penicuik for Dolphinton	Penicuik for Dolphinton
Broomlee	Penicuik for Broomlee	Broomlee	Penicuik ...	Penicuik for Broomlee
Macbiehill	Penicuik for Macbiehill	Macbiehill	Penicuik ...	Penicuik for Macbiehill
Lamancha	Penicuik for Lamancha	Lamancha	Penicuik ...	Penicuik for Lamancha

Transfer Vouchers should be declared to Penicuik, and all communications relating to traffic for, or from, the places served by the motor lorry should be similarly addressed.

All concerned to give these instructions careful attention and acknowledge receipt.

G. S. BEGG,
Passenger Manager,
Southern Scottish Area.
(G.C. 30/1784.)

W. PHILIP,
Divisional Accountant,
Scottish Area.
(D.A. 553.)

J. G. SINGER,
Traffic Superintendent,
Northern Scottish Area.
(P.R. 33/874.)

LNER Circular to station masters and others re closure of branch, 30th March, 1933.
Rae Montgomery collection

It is accordingly proposed that the Passenger and Goods Services on the Branch be withdrawn as from 1st April, 1933.

The closing of the branch will permit of a net saving estimated at £1,315 per annum being effected, as under:-

	Per Annum £	Per Annum £
SAVINGS		
Maintenance of Way and Works	748	
Maintenance & Renewal of Rolling Stock	122	
Locomotive Department	2,313	
Traffic Department	1,319	
Miscellaneous	41	**4,543**
LOSS IN REVENUE		
Passengers	1,366	
Parcels	177	
Goods	1,663	
Miscellaneous	22	**3,228**
Net Saving		**1,315**

There is no legal objection to the withdrawal of the trains and as an adequate service of road omnibuses is provided in the district by the Scottish Motor Traction Company Limited and the Caledonian Omnibus Company Limited, it is not anticipated that any serious complaints will arise so far as Passenger traffic is concerned. Several operators provide Goods road services in the district and the Freight train traffic meantime carried will be transferred to road, but in order to maintain contact with farmers and traders it is proposed to establish an experimental rail-head distribution service from Penicuik.

The Committee recommended that in order to effect economy the passenger and goods services on the Dolphinton branch be withdrawn as from 1st April, 1933, the question of abandoning the works to be dealt with at a later date. The LNER Board agreed and the fate of the branch was sealed. The *Scotsman* of 20th January, 1933 carried the announcement:

LNER Stations Closing. The London and North Eastern Railway Company announce that the passenger and goods train service operating between Leadburn and Dolphinton will be withdrawn on and from 1st April, 1933 and in consequence Lamancha, Macbiehill, Broomlee for West Linton and Dolphinton stations will be closed. A service of Scottish Motor Traction Company's omnibuses is available at Leadburn, Broomlee and Dolphinton for the conveyance of passengers.

The bus services operated by the SMT and by the Caledonian Omnibus Company between Edinburgh, West Linton and Dolphinton, and between Edinburgh, Penicuik and Lamancha, would serve three of the four branch stations; there was to be no replacement bus service for the more remote Macbie Hill station..

Special provision was to be made for the carriage of a quantity of road metal to Dolphinton for the County Council Roads Department, but when that job was finished the railway would be completely closed. At its peak, as many as 26 men and women had been directly employed on the railway and, although staff would be transferred elsewhere, their jobs would be lost to the local area. Meanwhile, it was announced on 15th March that the LNER branch to Gifford was also to be closed to passengers on and from Monday 3rd April, the last trains running on Saturday 1st April, one day later than to Dolphinton; it would retain a goods service, but there was to be no such reprieve for the Dolphinton branch.

The Last Train

The *Edinburgh Evening Dispatch* of Friday 7th April recorded the administration of the last rites:

> When the last train passed over the line on Friday night, the occasion was made somewhat notable. The engine carried many decorations and at each station the villagers turned out to see the last of the 'iron horse' especially at Broomlee. A few photographs were taken of the water tank engine [sic] with its crew and station staff and a few passengers amongst them on this route. In future, all passenger traffic to West Linton and the vicinity will be by bus. The Edinburgh route lies over the 'High Road to Linton' a thoroughfare famous in song as it is in history books. The people of the district witnessed the closing down of the branch line with not a little regret, but diminishing business left the railway company with no alternative.

Alex Aitken, then aged 27, was a passenger on the last train:

> And so to the end. I have been a daily traveller on the branch for eight out of the last twenty years, and have numbered all its servants in that period among my acquaintances and friends. I determined to be a passenger on the last train, and to preserve, against the vigilance of all officials, my ticket as a memento of the enterprise.
>
> If you think that the last trip was undertaken in a saddened mood, you make a mistake, for the passengers saw to it that there was a flag at the mast-head, so to speak, and there was a detonator from somewhere to give us a hearty send-off from Leadburn. The sky was grey, but if there was a twinge at the heart at the

Shift change at Dolphinton on the final Saturday of operation 25th March, 1933. From left to right are Bob Fell, fireman (with the station cat); Andrew Simpson, guard; Bob Stobie, driver; John Dobson, driver; relief fireman; and Jack Hutchison, guard. LNER class 'C15' 4-4-2T locomotive No. 9043 (ex-NBR No. 43) is coupled to the branch brake composite coupé, one of six carriages built in 1894 for the opening of the West Highland Railway.
Marion Moore collection

Waiting for the final branch train at Leadburn: not an exploding balloon, but a fault with Alex Aitken's camera! From left to right are Rev. Mr Nicolson; Mr Brown, Wayside; Ellen Lawson; Jean Fleming; (unidentified); Ella Niddrie; Mrs Fleming; and David Greig.
Marion Moore collection

Smile please! The last train at Broomlee. From left to right are Bobby Smith, Frank Greig (station master's son), Donald Angus (son of signalman), William Scott, (unidentified), Ella Niddrie, Ellen Lawson, Jock Smith, Ann Taylor, Willie Robb (carter), Mrs Rose Angus with young Willie Lawson, George Greig (station master – obscured), Jack Hutchison (guard), Bob Stobie (driver) with Patrick Angus, Robert Brown (clerk, Dolphinton), John Dobson (driver), Sandy Angus (signalman – holding the train staff), Bob Fell (fireman – behind), Joe Charters (clerk, Broomlee), relief fireman (?) – behind, Dolphinton porter (?), and William Rae.

Marion Moore collection

The group is joined by Alex Aitken, who had been taking the photographs. He is standing on the step board of the coach (right). *Marion Moore collection*

All change! New faces in this group include Jean Fleming (between Ella Niddrie and Ellen Lawson) and, to their left, David Greig, Adeline Mather and Olive Mather. Guard Andrew Simpson is at the back, right of centre.   *Marion Moore collection*

The same group as above, with Andrew Simpson waving his flag. A union flag and a golliwog are at the masthead!   *Marion Moore Collection*

thought of so violent a change in the habits of a lifetime, it was hidden beneath a smile and a joke, such as have lightened many an earlier journey.

And so, the mails and parcels duly stowed in the van, 'Andrew', for Guard Simpson was far too coldly official for so loyal a servant and obliging a man, waved his flag, and we left Leadburn to the accompaniment of cheers and fog signals – the ancient honours for honeymoon parties. As the travellers dropped off at the wayside stations, there was a handshake and a word of good wishes for success in their new spheres of labour, combined, shall we say, with thanks for countless safe and happy journeys these long eventful years.

At Broomlee was Mr. James Lockie*, waiting to see the last, as he had seen the first train to Linton. It was the work of a moment to take a photo, and then another wave of Andrew's flag and the Dolphinton train passed on.

To those who manned it, good luck in their new jobs, and thanks for their years of ungrudging service on the branch.

Jean Fleming was also there: 'I travelled on the last passenger train from Leadburn to Dolphinton on 31st March, 1933. We school travellers made a large golliwog which we attached to the tender of the engine, and it remained there as it travelled to St Margarets engine depot in Edinburgh next day. The age of the train was over for us.'

Fifty years later, in the *Peeblesshire News* of 25th March, 1983, Eddie Jefferies commemorated that last journey:

The date was Friday the 31st March, 1933. The 5.44 pm train consisting of locomotive No 9043 and one coach left Leadburn Junction for Linton and Dolphinton with rather more than the usual handful of passengers – the few commuters from Edinburgh and the scholars coming from Peebles High School were joined by a number of enthusiastic train lovers determined to be on the last train. The solitary coach held them all. At Broomlee, the station for West Linton, a crowd of well-wishers waited and Alex Aitken was there to photograph the arrival of the train before it left almost empty for the remaining $3\frac{1}{2}$ miles to Dolphinton.

The Railway Company had announced a few weeks previously that the branch line was to be closed for all traffic from the 1st April 1933. Most of the travellers to and from West Linton scarcely noticed the event because by that date there was an excellent hourly bus service to Edinburgh. Only the few regular train-users were inconvenienced, particularly the High School pupils. Despite the Railway Company's notice of closure, it was to be the 18th of April before the County Council's replacement service for the children began; Mr Lithgow's motor took them to Leadburn in the morning and brought them back in the afternoon. They were given season tickets for the train between Leadburn and Peebles.

As well as the three High School pupils, Mr Lithgow conveyed the two children from Lamancha who attended Primary school in West Linton.

---

* Retired mason, James Lockie (1850 – 1938), who lived in Woodbine Cottage, West Linton.

The morning after! Signalman Sandy Angus, station master George Greig and clerk Joe Charters on 1st April, 1933, the morning after closure. *Marion Moore collection*

At the end of summer 1933, the direct weekday bus service between West Linton and the county town was withdrawn, necessitating a lengthened and roundabout route, a change of bus, and inflated fares, either by Broughton or Penicuik. It was now cheaper to travel to Edinburgh than to Peebles. Alex Aitken wrote that 'if a Linton man or woman is summoned to take part in jury service at 10 am he or she must hire a private car to be at court in time'. On the other hand, it was pointed out that, previously, it was necessary to post a letter at West Linton by one o'clock in order to secure first delivery in London the next day, but that now letters posted by 6.10 pm would be delivered by the first post*.

The public timetables for May to September 1933 carried a notice that 'parcels and miscellaneous passenger train traffic will continue to be accepted'. Presumably this related to the experimental motor lorry distribution service from Penicuik referred to above, and aimed at traders, but given that there were no staff left on the branch after Mr Greig transferred to Scotland Street on 8th May, it is unclear who would have accepted parcels etc. for dispatch from the former stations. It is not clear how long the motor lorry service lasted.

---

* Possibly because the mail now went by road to Carstairs to be loaded direct on to the 'West Coast Postal' mail train, rather than going via Edinburgh.

Demolition Begins

For a few weeks after the official closure date, Messrs Roxburgh & Forrest brought in road material to Dolphinton for Peeblesshire County Council but, at its meeting on 27th September, 1934, the LNER Traffic Committee approved a recommendation by the Divisional General Manager (Scotland) [the new designation of that post] 'that the time has now arrived when the rails should be uplifted and the signalling etc removed'. The cost of removing the permanent way, signalling and telegraphs would be £1,277 but the value of recoverable material was estimated at £4,654. It was also reported that: 'The question of the conversion of the station buildings into hostels for holidaymakers is under consideration and an endeavour will be made to find tenants for lettable ground and property within the fences'. Plans were drawn up in February 1935 for the conversion into hostels of the Broomlee and Lamancha station buildings, but that seems to have been the end of the matter.

All hopes of the line being re-opened were dashed when lifting of the track from Dolphinton began in the Spring of 1936. By September the bridge over the West Water, some 700 yards south-west of Broomlee at

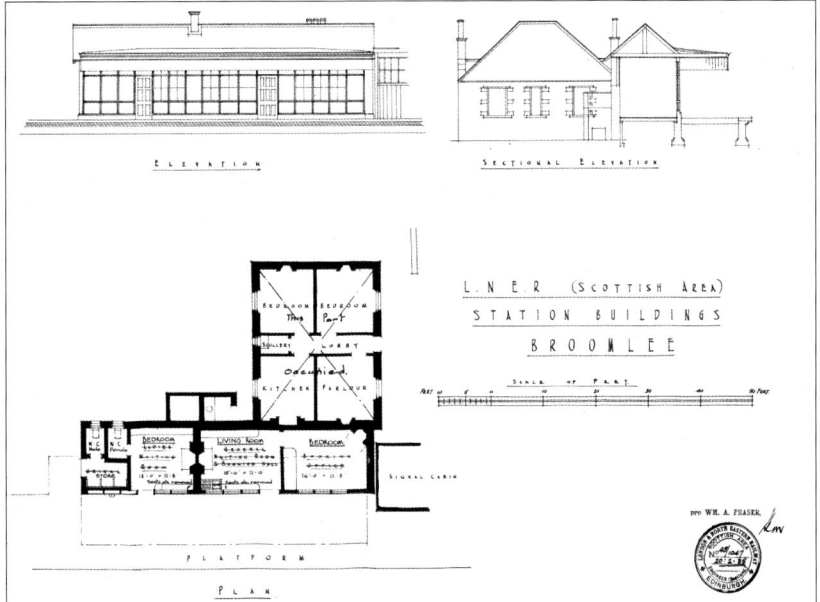

LNER February 1935 plan to convert Broomlee station into a hostel for holidaymakers.
NRS/Department for Transport under Open Government Licence v3.0.

'The Splash', was partly dismantled; in due course, the County Council erected a bridge in place of the ford and 'The Splash', too, was no more. The bridge that spanned the Lyne, immediately west of Broomlee station, had gone by the beginning of November. However, only the Dolphinton to Linton section was lifted, with the line now terminating in the Broomlee goods yard, and some traffic continued to use the northern end of the line, as evidenced by the spectacular breakaway in January 1938, described earlier, during shunting operations at Macbie Hill.

Harold Bowtell* remembers the exchange line from the LMS to the LNER at Dolphinton still being *in situ* on 25th November, 1942.

Physical Remains

In August 1935, the LNER Factor at 47 Leith Street, Edinburgh, was advertising 'Station Buildings at Lamancha, Macbiehill, and Broomlee, for storage or business purposes.' The *Edinburgh Evening Dispatch* of 27th December that year reported that: 'To date the station master's house [at Broomlee] is still standing as it is, as well as the porter's cottage now enlarged and used as a farmhouse annexe; and the [goods] shed taken over as a storage for farm implements etc; and its coal depot used for various purposes and a dwelling house styled as a bungalow.' The following October, the LNER Minutes recorded the lease to Mr J.S. Barnford of the station buildings at Broomlee, to be used as a dwelling house; the rent was £12 per annum. The station house and buildings were advertised for sale by the British Transport Commission in August 1949 and were bought by the Findlay family from Edinburgh in August 1958 for £450. Christine Findlay (McGregor) recalls that initially there was no running water and no electricity. Water was hand pumped to a tank from a natural spring at the bottom of the garden and lighting was supplied by Tilley lamps. The ladies' waiting room became her bedroom, en suite with the toilet and its penny-in-the-slot lock. Electricity was in due course installed, and with it an electric motor for the water pump; when the property was re-sold in 1968, the former station and station house combined now formed a 'des res' with 'open outlook over surrounding countryside, large lounge with French windows to sun terrace, living room, 3 bedrooms ...' etc.

In 1938, the LNER Factor advertised the 'Disused Engine Shed, 54 ft x 20 ft 5 in., at Dolphinton Station to let from 28th May, 1938.' In July 1947

---

* *op cit*

Broomlee station in its converted condition on 18th May, 1963.   *J L. Stevenson*

the Minutes record the sale to David Gilchrist of the former Dolphinton station buildings (including the engine shed) and 1.03 acres of land for the sum of £500.

Today, the station houses at Leadburn, Lamancha, Macbie Hill and Broomlee remain, all in private ownership. Nothing remains of the station buildings at Leadburn; the station site was transformed by the local authority into a picnic area in the 1980s – sadly now closed off and neglected – with the down platform and cut-back up platform of the Peebles line still prominent. No station buildings remain at Lamancha or Macbie Hill although the remnants of the platforms and loading banks are partly visible. At Broomlee, the station building is incorporated into the station house; the stone goods shed has been imaginatively transformed into a private house, misleadingly named 'The Engine Shed'. At Dolphinton, which didn't have a station house, the station buildings are still recognizable and have been converted for use as a pleasant and comfortable home; some traces of the platform and loading bank remain. The single-road engine shed still stands, re-roofed without its former single vent, providing useful storage space. It should be noted that all these buildings are on private property, with no public access. Only one of the four main railway bridges remains in use, the overbridge at the former Macbie Hill station. Parts of the line of the railway can still be traced, and the Leadburn end of both the Dolphinton and Peebles lines lie within Leadburn Community Woodland, established in 2005, with walking and cycling paths.

Looking towards Broomlee from Macbie Hill in 2017, with Mendick Hill to the right of centre. It appears as if the long-lifted sleepers have only recently been removed.

Author

The former Dolphinton engine shed in 2016. *Author*

In Retrospect

To D.J. McArthur, writing in the *Edinburgh Evening Dispatch* on 23rd March, 1933 a week before closure, the four stations on the branch were 'Four Old Friends of the Hillman':

> The news of the closing down of these four delightful stations …will be heard with regret by many trampers and anglers of the older school. The only real drawback which the farthest-flung Pentland Hills and the Moorfoots presents to trampers is the journey to and fro ere the actual hill-tramps begin, and one must humbly admit that the tiny waiting-rooms of these four old railway stations were far more comfortable than waiting on the roadside for a modern motor-bus will be in the future.

To the elegant prose of Alex Aitken, friend and observer of the Leadburn, Linton and Dolphinton Railway, should be entrusted the last word. Writing in the *South Midlothian Advertiser* on 14th April, 1933, two weeks after the closure of the line, he reflected on the life and times of the railway:

> As you contemplate the view from the sun-drenched slopes, above the romantically named La Mancha, you will be viewing the remaining earthworks of a local enterprise which served the people of its day very modestly but which takes its place as a monument to a transport system following on from the Roman roads and turnpikes which preceded it.
>
> The hopes of industrial development did not materialise. The quarries steadily declined until in our own day they are wholly derelict. The Macbiehill coal mine supplied local needs in the way of boiler coal, but it too has been closed down these few years back. When the railway was opened the population of the parishes it served was at its maximum, and since then there has been a steady fall. Doomed thus to serve a population dwindling in numbers and a district static and latterly declining in economic resources, and the advent in recent years of lively competition from road services, finally sealed its fate.
>
> The improvement in railway rolling stock and the acceleration of speeds is shown by the fact that whereas the first train took 30 minutes to travel the $9^3/_4$ miles of the branch, the last train was timed to do the journey in twenty-three. But as between the number of trains per day there was no change as between first and last, though in the palmy days there were more than the four trips per day.
>
> The name and outward appearance of the rolling stock has also changed, as well as its comfort and facilities. Warming pans have given place to steam heating; oil lights to gas; cushions have appeared on the seats, while of late years lavatory and wash hand basin accommodation have also been provided. Naturally, there have been changes in personnel; nevertheless, the staff which

operated the last day's trains had among them 186 years of railway service, including individual records of 48, 43 & 33 years.

Vaster changes have come over the countryside the railway served. On the credit side, the standard of living has greatly advanced. Wages are better, houses immensely improved, hours and conditions of labour are better, facilities for education, recreation and travel, and the opportunities for enjoying their benefits, greatly increased. Against that there must be set the continued de-population of the rural parts, the contraction, now becoming serious, of agriculture, the disappearance of its ancillary pursuits and trades, the complete closing down of those mineral workings on which, as has been shown, the promoters of the railway set so great a store.

The social conditions have changed out of all recognition: whether for good or ill is not for me to say. Of the estates whose proprietors took part in the forming of the company, only one remains in the same family hands. There are still Mackenzies of Dolphinton, but Gordon of Halmyre, Fergusson of Spittlehaugh, Forbes of Medwyn, Beresford of Macbiehill, Woddrop of Garvald, Mackintosh of Lamancha, have gone, and the estates they controlled have been broken up and have passed into other hands.

That change has amounted to a social revolution, and has been completed in our own day. In a way undreamt of by the late John Ord Mackenzie when he spoke the words at the first meeting, Linton has become a suburb of Edinburgh. If that gentleman had lived to see it, I doubt if he would have approved of the change, which has been accentuated by the closing of the branch. We have all lost the protective leadership which these houses exercised, and in their going has disappeared much of the labour that helped to lend prosperity to the countryside.

The Education committee have solved their problem by arranging for transport to Leadburn to connect with the morning and afternoon trains, so that their pupils may reach the place of their studies. It is interesting to notice that this also is a reversion to former practice, for, in pre railway days, Mr. Robert Watson ran a coach from Linton to Leadburn to connect with the Peebles railway, which was opened nine years before the local line came into being.

And so the Leadburn, Linton and Dolphinton Railway passed into history – or so it seemed!

It is not clear whether the railway ever formally closed at the end of the 1930s. The LNER's Chief General Manager had reported to his Traffic Committee in March 1937 'that during 1933 and 1934 the Dolphinton Branch was closed completely', but January 1938 saw the runaway wagons, described on page 127. By that time, preparations for war with Germany – less than two years away – were in hand, and these were to see the railway serving a naval armaments base at Leadburn.

Chapter Eleven

Wartime Renaissance and Final Closure

RNAD Leadburn

Britain declared war on Germany on 3rd September, 1939. A year later, a Minute of the Emergency Board of the LNER, meeting at York on 24th October, 1940, records: 'Dolphinton Branch. Provision of loops, etc. for the Admiralty as shewn on plans Nos 69/66 A, B, C and D. Estimated cost £1,639 (Engineer) to be borne by the Admiralty.' Plans 69/66A – D have not been traced, but a Plan 69/66E, drawn in the LNER Engineer's Office in Edinburgh, and dated 8th July, 1940, shows proposed loops, subsequently installed, at Lamancha and Macbie Hill, and also at Mitchell Hill – the summit of the line approximately 1.5 miles from Leadburn Junction.

The reason for this activity was the evacuation from Chatham Royal Naval Depot of large quantities of armaments to what became 'Royal Naval Armaments Depot, Leadburn'. Eddie Jefferies, writing in the *Peeblesshire News* in April 1979, recalled that:

> … in 1939 we learnt that the railway line was to become a Royal Naval armaments depot. The ammunition depot at Chatham was evacuated to our

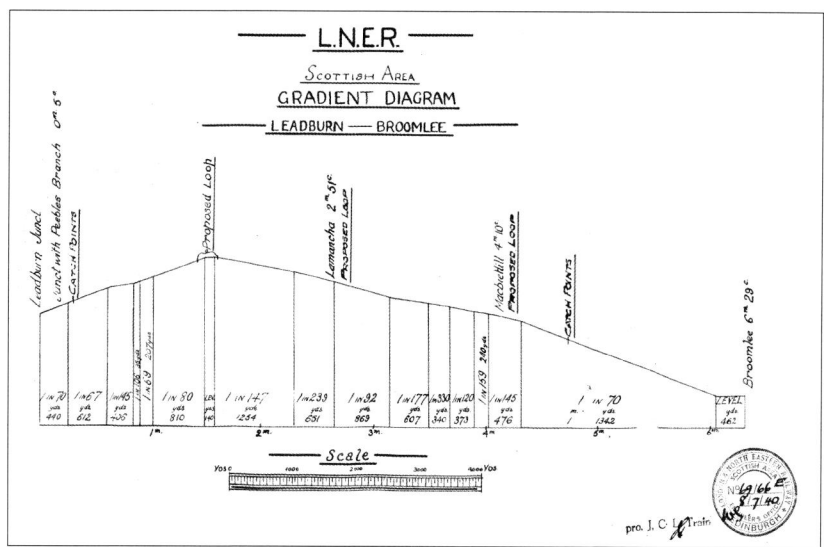

Leadburn – Broomlee gradient diagram drawn on 8th July, 1940 showing an additional loop to be installed at the summit, Mitchell Hill, and the reinstatement of the loops at Lamancha and Macbie Hill. The gradients differ slightly from those shown on the NBR's diagram of 1899 (*see page 49*).   *NRS/Department for Transport under Open Government Licence v3.0.*

branch line at the beginning of the war. I remember seeing train load after train load of naval armaments in covered vans being shunted on to the branch at Leadburn and left strung out along the railway until huts were put up to take the contents of the vans.

The vans had been labelled 'Dolphinton Branch' but, as the NBR Dolphinton branch had closed in 1933, the only one in the route book was Dolphinton (CR), which is where they went! Of course there were no longer any rails from Dolphinton to Broomlee, and so every van had to be hauled back round the country by Carstairs, Symington, across the junction at Peebles between the LMS and LNER and finally to Leadburn! Writing privately in October 1979, he dates that event to 1940, when he was working at Peebles NBR goods office. Once at their intended destination, the covered wagons were strung out along the line so as to minimize the risk of an explosion in one wagon triggering a chain reaction.

The ordnance remained in the vans until huts were put up to store the contents. The late Mr Frank Retson, who later owned part of the land on

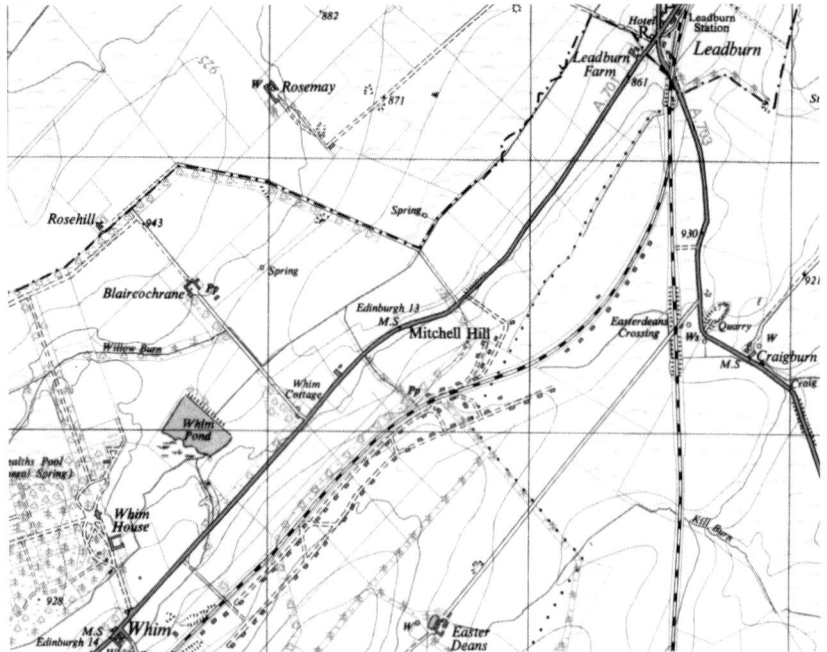

OS 1:25,000 map NT25 published in 1955 showing the main concentration of huts between Leadburn and Lamancha, and the entrance to the site off the A701.

Reproduced by permission of the National Library of Scotland

which the depot was built, remembered being told about '13 double decker buses with labourers' from the contractor, Carmichael, arriving to build the huts. Mr Retson continued, 'they hired a horse and cart ... one maybe from each farmer if they could get it, just to cart the stuff to the site from the railway, once they got the roads built.' These small roads connecting the huts were made from loads of ashes brought in by the railway. He also remembered security at Leadburn being very tight. The whole depot was surrounded by a large barbed wire fence, and anyone approaching on the A701 would be stopped by armed naval sentries, who were on guard 24 hours a day, and would have to produce a pass. In fact Mr Pate, who owned Easter Deans Farm at the time, needed a pass to tend his sheep!* After the war, Eric Stevenson worked for a time with a firm that was dismantling the huts for sale to farmers and others. He remembers the high quality of the timber of the wooden frame and floor, reportedly imported from Canada. The outer walls and roof were made of corrugated asbestos, and the inner wall of smooth asbestos**.

The site of the depot was extensive, as can be seen from the 1:25,000 OS map published in 1955, available to view on the maps website of the National Library of Scotland. There were over 100 huts, with a connecting road network, located at several sites along the railway. The main concentration was between Leadburn and Lamancha stations, with an access road off the A701 at map reference NT228545; other sites were between Lamancha and Macbie Hill, and immediately west of Macbie Hill station. Three accommodation blocks are believed to have been built – at Leadburn, Lamancha and Macbiehill – with Macbiehill having an entertainments hut for concerts and the like. The whole site was connected by telephone, running from HQ at Leadburn.

Until the accommodation blocks were built, the officers were billeted at Deanfoot Farm, and the other ranks in railway carriages on the branch nearby. Ron Glendinning recalls that there was a tin house on the bank on the east side of the Peebles road at Leadburn, between the cross-roads and the railway bridge, and that it was used by the naval sentries. Alison MacDonald records that 'there were huts around the station [at Leadburn] for the men and a row of showers and a high water tower with a boiler below to heat water for the washrooms. The Depot Manager lived and ran his office in the house on the bank overlooking the crossroads.' Also, that part of the huts 'later became a well-frequented bowling hall. Teams from all over the Borders would take

---

* Information from West Linton Historical Association's document archive.

** A number of the huts remain on site, in use by farmers.

RNAD Leadburn. An aerial view showing the junction of the Peebles and Dolphinton branches (*lower left*) with a train, or wagons, in view on the branch. The huts of the armaments depot are strung out alongside the railway line. There was an access road to the depot off the A701 road (*right*) just before the first belt of trees. Photo dated 1948/49.
Hampshire Record Office: 109M91/PH65

part in tournaments there. Trays of drinks being carried across from the pub would have been a common sight – and hazard – to passing motorists'.* A local resident recalled that the huts for the armaments were built by a squad of workers from London, who arrived in open top buses with rope starters, and that they worked from Monday to Thursday and spent Friday in the pub!

There was a decoy site at Auchencorth Moss, between Leadburn and Carlops (NT201565), intended to attract any attacking aircraft.** Three high explosive land mines were dropped in the area in March 1945 – one at Portmore, on the side of the Peebles Road, and two on the moor at Nether Falla, a little further north – possibly intended for nearby RNAD Leadburn.

---

* *Stories from the History of Howgate: Leadburn* by Alison MacDonald (Howgate Village Historical Society, 2010).

** See *Fields of Deception* by Colin Dobinson (Methuen, 2000).

WARTIME RENAISSANCE AND FINAL CLOSURE 217

RNAD Leadburn: 'Main Entrance 26.4.1949'. The location of the main entrance has not been definitely established, but may have been the access road off the A701 near Mitchell Hill, between Leadburn and Lamancha. *Hampshire Record Office: 109M91/PH133*

RNAD Leadburn: 'General View 26.4.1949'. The location appears to be Mitchell Hill, between Leadburn and Lamancha stations. Five railway vans are on the line.
Hampshire Record Office: 109M91/PH133

RNAD Leadburn: 'No. 25 Magazine 26.4.1949'. These appear to be bales of cordite.
Hampshire Record Office: 109M91/PH133

RNAD Leadburn: Ammunition storage boxes stacked against the wall of one of the former storage buildings near Whim Farm.
James T.M. Towill/Creative Commons licence CC BY-SA 2.0

Few details have been uncovered as to the activities carried out at RNAD Leadburn and, in particular, whether it was used simply for storage of ordnance produced elsewhere, or for its manufacture or assembly. There is no evidence of factory-sized buildings, or of civilian workers being bussed in, which suggests that any production was on a small scale. There have been suggestions that it produced cordite, the propellant for shells used in large calibre naval guns, as well as in .303 ammunition. Ron Glendinning, a former Royal Marine, remembers being told that the Depot manufactured naval mines, and that the site was initially guarded by Royal Marines. The huts were well spaced out and each one was surrounded by an earth embankment, designed to limit the effect of any explosion; the area of peat on which they were built would have aided this further. To tackle any fires, trailer pumps were housed in pump houses across the site, each with an adjacent brick-built static water tank. From the large number of ammunition boxes found at the site after the war, Leadburn appears also to have been used for the storage of rifle ammunition.

Local men were employed to load wagons during the day. According to a document in the West Linton and District Historical Association's archives, the trains travelled at night for security to Leith Docks, although this destination is doubtful; local historian Douglas Veitch writing in the *Peeblesshire News* of 26th May, 1989 says that they travelled to Rosyth Dockyard, and records compiled by Willie Hennigan of his father's trips include a train for Faslane (Military Port No. 1). These records, which detail the class of locomotive (eg 'J36') and its number, include the following:

Wednesday 7/1/1942 'Ammo Train to Macbie Hill J36 9713'
Thursday 26/3/1942 'Hardengreen Pilot. Ammunition Special to Leadburn J36 9782'
Saturday 29/8/1942 'Ammo Special Hardengreen – Macbie Hill J36 9753 (Hardengreen Pilot)'
Thursday 12/11/1942 'Ammo Special Macbie Hill to Hardengreen J38 1414 (St Margarets)'
Monday 16/10/1944 'Ammo Special to Macbie Hill J37 9429'
Wednesday 14/3/1945 'Van train Macbie Hill to Faslane 12.01 pm Special worked to Gorgie (changeover) J37 9105'

Macbie Hill station cottage was extended as office accommodation for the Admiralty administration, and the railway administration for the Admiralty traffic and accounts was handled at the Lamancha station office (*see page 81*).

One Edinburgh family had a holiday home in West Linton, on the Edinburgh road, overlooking Robinsland and the railway line to Macbie Hill. Speaking to the author, the daughter recalled how her father had thought that the family would be safer in West Linton and so they moved there, only to discover that the house was overlooking an ammunition dump! She remembers seeing a line of wooden trucks (possibly wagons awaiting repair) from the house. The family was advized to build a turf wall at the bottom of the garden, some six or seven feet high, in case the Germans bombed the depot. The wall would have provided some protection from the blast for the house and for its air raid shelter in the cellar. As children, they were told that spies might find out about the depot, and so all strangers to the village were regarded with great suspicion!

Leadburn continued 'in use' as a Royal Naval depot, a sub-base of RNAD Crombie in Fife, until at least 20th December, 1946 according to a written Parliamentary Answer given on 21st January, 1947 and listing naval establishments in Scotland as at the former date. Later, some of the huts were used by the Board of Trade, which was responsible during and after the Second World War for the production and distribution of commodities other than food for the civilian population. It appears that they were used to store merino wool and bales of rubber, being served by

RNAD Leadburn: 'Trailer Pump House and Static Water Tank 26.4.1949'. The railway track is just visible at the bottom right. *Hampshire Record Office: 109M91/PH133*

rail throughout the 1950s. A file in the National Archives at Kew describes an accident that occurred at the Leadburn Depot on 30th May, 1960 when an employee sustained a fractured ankle. Large bales of rubber stored inside one of the huts were being 'unstacked' by the simple method of two men climbing on top of the stack of bales, some 10 feet high, and pushing them over. They were then taken outside and craned on to a lorry for removal. According to an Edinburgh solicitor's whimsical report for the Board of Trade, the workers were experienced, and anticipated the bales bouncing around, but 'this bale bounced off one of the lower rows and stotted [*Scots*: bounced or rebounded] with unusual velocity toward the door. W___ saw it coming, and ran down the ramp to get away from it. The bale appears to have followed him in an extraordinary manner, rather like a homing guided missile. At the foot of the ramp, it caught him on the back of the leg, as he was still running away, and immediately fractured his ankle.' A financial settlement was duly reached between the parties.

Superannuated Trucks

During the war, a shortage of resources meant that many damaged and disabled wagons requiring repair – both railway and ex-Private Owner Wagons ['POWs'] – couldn't be dealt with, and they were stored at various locations; one was at the Broomlee end of the truncated branch line. According to Bill Lynn, the ammunition special recorded on 26th March, 1942 (*above*) then made a trip to Lamancha to pick up two private-owner wagons belonging to the Edinburgh Collieries Company. There were lots of wagons there after the war. In *Random Reflections of a Roving Railwayman*, John Bennett – then a district inspector (freight trains) with the LNER – describes how it was decided to remove some of them elsewhere one Sunday in May 1946:

> A start was due at 9 a.m. and the time estimated for the job was 12/14 hours. Inspector Kerr was allocated early turn and I had to relieve him in the afternoon.
>
> Lift after lift was taken out and the POWs which were to be returned left off at intervening station sidings or shunted back on [the] Main Line to Peebles. Progress was made but time ran on all too quickly. Our heavy shunting engines (J39) had to make occasional runs to Hardengreen Yard to fill tanks with water. At length the last train of 'Railway' repairs was despatched, and we were left with 79 wagons on the Peebles Line which had to be worked down the old Branch. The lift was easily hauled forward over the points, but I thought we were never going to get it moving back into the Branch. Success at last. The plan was I would ride in the leading wagon of lift with a hand signal lamp to

Lamancha station looking towards Dolphinton on 19th February, 1961. The wagons at the loading bank are waiting to be loaded with recovered rails. As can be seen, the loop had been reinstated for wartime traffic. *Rae Montgomery*

The remains of a trailer pump house, with the static water tank in front, in 2016. *Author*

guide the drivers to the wagons already stowed away. Alas when only half-way in my lamp became extinguished and I could not light it and what with the long train, overhead bridges and numerous curves it was a nightmarish journey. However daylight was beginning to break and the wagons were safely disposed of. Thence back to the Main Line and cleared at 6.30 a.m. just in time for commencement of traffic on the Peebles Line. On return to lodgings my landlady laughed at my appearance – bowler hat and black face, a proper goon. All District Inspectors wore bowler hats on duty.

A contemporary newspaper report talks of 'a seemingly endless line of superannuated trucks'. According to Bill Lynn, there were still some there on 28th February, 1948: 'J37' No. 4566 was sent to Leadburn to pick up some vans but, as they weren't there, the loco continued on to Macbie Hill to pick them up.

After a Century, the End

Eddie Jefferies records that the line continued in use to the level crossing gates at Broomlee until the Spring of 1948 and it appears that coal trains may have continued to serve West Linton until then – some apparently carrying unauthorized passengers! A resident of West Linton recalls the time in the winter of 1947 when he and his mother came by bus from Edinburgh to Penicuik to take supplies to his father who was renovating a farmhouse near West Linton. They knew that if they reached Penicuik they could hitch a lift by train to Broomlee. He says that they had a 10 shilling note to slip into the appropriate palm! The early months of 1947 saw one of the most severe winters of the 20th century. The line was blocked by snow and the train did not run. Many roads, too, were blocked that winter and they ended up walking the rest of the journey. While some of the details are lost in the mists of time, our informant seems certain that the coal train was a locally recognized, if unauthorized, handy means of transport at that time.

According to local sources, the track was lifted from Broomlee back to the overbridge half a mile west of Macbie Hill station during 1957 or 1958; a terminal buffer stop was in place by October 1958 at the overbridge – or at least it was until 'J35' locomotive No. 64532, which had been working as Hardengreen Pilot, collided with and demolished it, damaging its front buffer beam and cylinder cover. Rae Montgomery's diary records it as lying 'dead' at the Leadburn up line siding on 26th October, 1958; it was lifted for repairs from Leadburn by steam crane on 13th November. Rae's diary for 18th September, 1960 records that he saw 20 vehicles ('vanfits')

The line was lifted between Broomlee and the overbridge half a mile west of Macbie Hill station in 1957 or 1958 and a buffer stop was in place – until demolished by class 'J35' 0-6-0 64532 in October 1958. The debris was still there when photographed on 2nd January, 1959.
Rae Montgomery

at Mitchell Hill which had been placed there by the Hardengreen Pilot on 14th September, the first train on the branch since the 'J35' was removed in October 1958. Another note in his diary records that 14th November, 1960 was the last day that traffic was worked off the Dolphinton branch. The track from the Macbie Hill buffer stop to the junction at Leadburn was lifted between January and March 1961. The BR notice of Signalling and Permanent Way Alterations of 3rd June, 1961 records: 'Leadburn – The connection to the Macbiehill branch, together with the two-lever ground frame, has been removed.' It was 99 years and 10 months since that first 'meeting of Gentlemen friendly to the promotion of a Line of Railway through the Upper District of Peeblesshire'.

And so, almost exactly a century after these landowning gentlemen had met with the object of introducing a modern means of transport for the benefit of the local population and exploiting the natural and agricultural resources of their district – an aim never realized – the grandly entitled Leadburn, Linton and Dolphinton Railway finally slipped away, as unobtrusively as it had existed, into the pages of history.

Hardengreen Pilot class 'J36' 0-6-0 locomotive No. 65329 at Whim, on the bridge over the Shiplaw road, working a demolition train on 27th February, 1961. Driver Ian Turnbull; fireman Tom Hamilton.
Rae Montgomery

No. 65329 and its demolition train, and a platelayers' trolley, between Lamancha and the Shiplaw Road on 27th February, 1961. Whim Farm is in the background.
Rae Montgomery

Class 'J37' 0-6-0 locomotive No. 64599 on a demolition train, looking to Macbie Hill from Lamancha in February 1961. *Bob Flockhart/Rae Montgomery*

A view from the tender of No. 64599 taken at the summit of the line at Mitchell Hill, looking towards Lamancha, in February 1961. Former RNAD ordnance storage huts are on the left.
Bob Flockhart/Rae Montgomery

Appendix One

Inspections

Report of Inspection carried out on 21st May, 1864 by Captain Rich, RE

The New Line commences at Leadburn station, on the North British Railway, and extends thence to Dolphinton, a distance of 9m 68chs. The intermediate Stations are Lamancha Coalyburn and Linton. It is single throughout, with sidings. The Gauge is 4 ft $8\frac{1}{2}$ in. The rail is single headed, in lengths of 24 ft and weighs 65 lbs per lineal yd.

It is fished and fixed with wooden keys in chairs which weigh $19\frac{1}{2}$ lbs each. The chairs are spiked to transverse sleepers laid at an average distance of 3ft apart. Those next the joints of the rails are about 2ft apart. The sleepers are larch and baltic, semicircular, 9ft long 9in. x $4\frac{1}{2}$ in. some 10in. x 5in. The Ballast consists of gravel and broken stone, laid about 9in. deep.

Engine turntables have been erected at the terminal stations. It is proposed to deposit the passengers at the outer side of the passenger platform at Leadburn, so as not to form a junction for passengers with the main line. There are 8 Over Bridges built of Stone with brick arches. Two under Bridges have Wr[ought] Iron Girders (the spans are 45 & 50ft) and ten others have Cast Iron Girders – the Viaduct of 50ft span has Wr Iron Girders and two others have Cast Iron Girders. The whole of these have stone abutments.

The Masonry appears substantially executed and the Girders and superstructure of the bridges and Viaducts, appear sufficiently strong as regards the deflections and according to my calculations but only one engine was provided to load them. I cannot pronounce definitively on the merits of the three bridges of 50 and 45 ft spans until they are altered and two engines are placed on them. The cover[?] plates to [word illegible – 'lower'?] flanges are only 1 ft long – they are cut diagonally to correspond with the joints of the plates. The Girders do not stand vertically on the Abutments. The lower flanges have apparently been pressed outwards by the deflections of the 9 in timber cross beams and the tops of the girders have been drawn inwards. Wr iron transverse girders with vertical angle pieces will be required to stay them and keep them in their places, when put back in their proper positions. The Bridge rail is laid and bolted to the [word illegible] on the 9 in. cross timbers. A longitudinal sleeper 12" x 6" with proper transoms should be laid on the cross timbers, to distribute the weight and carry the rail which now lifts considerably at and near the joints as the Engine passes over the Bridge. This should also be done where the rail is similarly carried on the Cast Iron Bridges and if the bolts are put thro' the joints of the timbers and are caught by a longitudinal bar of iron underneath, it will prevent the jumping and stiffen the whole platform of the Bridges.

As regards the Cast Iron Girders they have all been cast bottom upwards, and though most of the castings look good and give small deflections such casting is very objectionable as the bottom flange is liable to be defective and the faults cannot be detected. Two [?] of the Cast Iron Girders appear honey combed in the bottom flanges and several others shew that the box in which they were cast was too short and was indifferently lengthened. I have suggested that one of the most defective [?] looking of the Cast Iron Girders be taken out and broken when the line is next inspected and that according as the fractured parts shew the casting to be good or otherwise, so shall the others be refused or rejected.

Four of the bed stones under one of the Cast Iron Girders shewed signs of splitting, these should be examined and new stones substituted if the splitting extends far inwards.

None of the signals was complete, as regards the fixing of the Lamps, and the Distant Signal from Leadburn, which was arranged to work in conjunction with the safety[?]

siding points, would not act properly, owing to the very temporary framing to which the gear attached to the points was fastened.

Some indicators and stop blocks to[?] sidings had not yet been fixed. A pair of facing points at Linton should be taken out and clocks are required at the Stations.

There is a pubic level crossing near Linton Station, where it is necessary to provide a house, for the man in charge to live in, as the station affords no such accommodation.

Lamancha station is placed on an incline of 1 in 92. There is a piece of level about two chains nearer Leadburn and the gradient shown in the parliamentary section from the road at the station to this piece of level line is 1 in 239 but it has been increased to 1 in 92 which is not safe for a Stn. I submit therefore that it should be altered to 1 in 300 or at least to 1 in 250 for a space of 100 yards. The line falls from this station continuously for about 3 miles, the Gradient for the most part being 1 in 70. Coalyburn Station is on 1 in 121 about halfway down this incline – by prolonging the gradient of 1 in 70, the Gradient on which Coalyburn stands may be altered to the same as Lamancha, and I submit that this alteration is necessary to secure the safety of the passengers. Linton Stn is on a Gradient of 1 in 173 which was quite unnecessary, as the sidings adjacent are on the level, but as it is close to the bottom of the incline it is not necessary that it should be altered, though a level space for the platform would have been desirable for trains stopping.

The chairs used are very light and I cannot consider them sufficiently large or strong to secure the safety of the permanent way. They are only $19\,{}^{1}/_{2}$ lbs and measure 10" x 4" in their bed. I submit that two larger and heavier chairs should be inserted next to every joint and if one was inserted in the centre of each length or rail it would be desirable. There is a deviation from the Parly limits about 20 chains from Lamancha Station, for which the landowner's authority is attached.

I have not yet received the undertaking as to the proposed mode of working, but I submit that the Leadburn, Linton and Dolphinton Railway cannot be opened for passenger traffic without danger to the public using the same by reason of the incompleteness of the works.

Report of Re-inspection carried out on 30th June, 1864 by Captain Rich, RE

The additions to the Wr[ought] iron bridges have been made. The Gradients at the stations have been altered and the signals completed.

The Chairs have not been altered but the Engineer stated that on weighing them, they appear to be somewhat over rather than under 20 lbs. They are too light but, as the line is not a main line, and will not be worked at high speed, I submit that they may be admitted, the Chairman having undertaken to have all renewals made with a heavier one. The points of the cross over road to North British main line at Leadburn should be always kept locked except when in use for the transfer of goods and carriages.

The cast iron trough girder that was broken was not a good casting but the Engineer has undertaken to have 10 in. beams added to all the small cattle creeps &c which are crossed with cast iron trough girders and that this work shall be completed before the line is opened on Monday next. I beg therefore to submit that the Leadburn Linton & Dolphinton Railway may be opened for passenger traffic without danger to the public using the same.

I enclose an undertaking as to the proposed mode of working signed by the Chairman and Secretary which appears satisfactory.

Appendix Two

Passenger and Goods Statistics

Passenger Numbers

Records of the number of passengers booked at stations exist from the year ended 31st July, 1874. In that year, Broomlee booked 12,205 passengers, Dolphinton 5,673, Macbie Hill 3,001, and Lamancha 2,412. On the basis of a six-day week over 52 weeks, that equated to an average daily total of 39, 18, 10 and 8 – spread over the service of four trains each way per day.

The peak year for bookings made at each of the stations was: Broomlee, year ended July 1899 (20,001); Dolphinton, July 1901 (9,104); Macbie Hill, July 1899 (6,227); and Lamancha, July 1898 (3,703). The best six years for Broomlee were year ended July 1898 -1904 inclusive; for Dolphinton, July 1895 and 1899, July 1902-1904, and July 1920; for Macbie Hill, July 1897-1901, and July 1903; and for Lamancha, July 1878 and 1879, and July 1897-1900. The lowest yearly number of passengers recorded was: Broomlee, year ended June 1929 (3,354); Dolphinton, June 1930 (1,059); Macbie Hill, June 1931 (1,039); Lamancha, June 1931 (1,122). As explained earlier, passenger numbers for the branch stations were boosted during the construction of the aqueduct in connection with the Talla Waterworks Scheme, principally in the period 1897 to 1901.

Table 1: Passengers booked at LL&DR Stations

Table 1a: 5-year periods for which figures are available

5 years to:	Lamancha	Macbie Hill	Broomlee	Dolphinton	Total
July 1880	14,162	11,999	65,614	26,421	118,196
July 1885	11,778	10,913	61,220	27,890	111,801
July 1890	13,340	9,720	59,298	29,798	112,156
July 1895	13,556	11,055	63,290	35,503	123,404
July 1900	17,039	24,164	86,099	40,020	167,322
July 1905	14,262	18,731	83,714	41,905	158,612
July 1910	12,991	11,902	75,661	34,853	135,407
June 1915	12,548	11,611	69,676	32,304	126,139
June 1920	11,419	10,902	57,435	29,737	109,493
June 1925	11,050	12,312	62,401	29,373	115,136
June 1930	8,253	8,311	25,491	9,635	51,690

Table 1b: First and last full year for which figures are available

Year to:	Lamancha	Macbie Hill	Broomlee	Dolphinton	Total
July 1874	2,412	3,001	12,205	5,673	23,291
June 1932	1,456	1,156	4,091	1,073	7,776

Goods Traffic

Records of Goods traffic also exist from the year ended 31st July, 1874. These cover 'Merchandise and Live Stock Forwarded and Received', but no distinction is made between traffic forwarded and that received. The statistics were recorded under the categories Goods (tons), Minerals (tons), Coals (tons), and – from July 1900 – also Cattle (Head), Sheep (Head) and Pigs (Head).

Table 2: Merchandise and Livestock Forwarded and Received

Note: the records do not distinguish between Merchandise and Livestock forwarded, and that received. Livestock records are only available from July 1900.

Table 2a: Coals (Tons)

5 years to:	Lamancha	Macbie Hill	Broomlee	Dolphinton	Total
July 1880	2,671	5,260	12,451	1,539	21,921
July 1885	2,700	5,972	12,194	2,043	22,909
July 1890	1,827	5,653	11,926	2,929	22,335
July 1895	1,522	1,473	11,043	3,754	17,792
July 1900	1,816	7,979	12,648	4,473	26,916
July 1905	1,024	4,736	9,945	4,039	19,744
July 1910	758	857	10,690	3,888	16,193
June 1915	625	975	9,702	2,574	13,876
June 1920	764	585	9,789	4,813	15,951
June 1925	440	443	10,307	5,287	16,477
June 1930	164	1,560	14,909	3,214	19,847

Table 2b: Minerals (Tons)

5 years to:	Lamancha	Macbie Hill	Broomlee	Dolphinton	Total
July 1880	613	12,463	1,544	5,386	20,006
July 1885	752	6,975	2,550	3,021	13,298
July 1890	478	6,613	1,929	1,954	10,974
July 1895	953	6,766	2,071	2,937	12,727
July 1900	1,509	10,309	6,973	1,153	19,944
July 1905	283	12,979	4,385	3,925	21,572
July 1910	588	14,073	2,921	1,648	19,230
June 1915	581	9,253	1,784	1,876	13,494
June 1920	669	3,048	1,745	3,097	8,559
June 1925	2,177	6,412	8,317	3,140	20,046
June 1930	3,629	6,736	16,375	3,788	30,528

PASSENGER AND GOODS STATISTICS

Table 2c: Goods (Tons)

	Lamancha	Macbie Hill	Broomlee	Dolphinton	Total
5 years to:					
July 1880	3,226	1,113	13,129	5,618	23,086
July 1885	2,944	420	11,718	4,047	19,129
July 1890	3,127	2,077	11,796	5,887	22,887
July 1895	2,708	562	12,816	4,425	20,511
July 1900	1,943	11,761	25,605	7,451	46,760
July 1905	1,696	4,671	14,088	5,649	26,104
July 1910	1,766	1,798	12,056	4,702	20,322
June 1915	2,423	1,127	14,087	6,143	23,780
June 1920	2,531	3,692	24,932	15,093	46,248
June 1925	776	1,902	7,482	9,186	19,346
June 1930	335	1,308	8,726	5,101	15,470

Table 2d: Livestock (Head)

	Lamancha	Macbie Hill	Broomlee	Dolphinton	Total
5 years to:					
July 1905	665	4,264	16,614	3,261	24,804
July 1910	1,284	8,157	14,808	4,416	28,665
June 1915	1,952	8,777	22,587	7,922	41,238
June 1920	1,295	9,754	24,971	5,876	41,896
June 1925	3,845	6,110	27,603	6,485	44,043
June 1930	3,256	6,854	24,150	5,836	40,096

Table 3: Cash forwarded to Bank (£)

	Lamancha	Macbie Hill	Broomlee	Dolphinton	Total
5 years to:					
July 1880	1,296	568	3,502	1,024	6,390
July 1885	1,042	574	3,995	844	6,455
July 1890	1,084	569	4,685	941	7,279
July 1895	876	312	3,735	1,257	6,180
July 1900	505	293	2,998	1,031	4,827
July 1905	325	595	2,942	805	4,667
July 1910	395	637	2,622	844	4,498
June 1915	362	638	2,320	1,182	4,502
June 1920	499	299	4,467	1,675	6,940
June 1925	386	1,213	4,937	2,184	8,720
June 1930	163	829	1,770	968	3,730

Source: NRS/BR/NBR/4/133-135, 239, and 274-281

Index

Accidents, Snow and Fire, 125-130
Aitken, Alex (A Linton Plooman), 74, 91, 103, 123, 129, 201-203, 205, 206, 211.
Aiton, Rev Dr, 9, 17, 31, 37, 38
Alexander, Archibald, 35, 36, 38
Alexander, Charles, 31, 38
Angus, Sandy & family, 10, 109, 203, 206
Bathgate, James D, 47, 58, 59, 64
Bathgate, John, 9, 10, 13, 17, 19, 27, 30, 31, 35-38, 43, 47, 52, 58
Beresford, George R, 18, 31, 35, 37, 38, 61, 212
Biggar, 11, 12, 18, 19, 21-24, 65, 66, 113, 188, 193, 197
Blyth Bridge, Blyth, 20, 22, 25, 56, 112, 118, 132
Bouch, Thomas, 10, 17, 27, 35, 39-41, 43, 47, 52, 53, 57, 60, 147
Broomlee, 2, 8, 9, 17, 20, 43, 47, 56, 57, Chapters 4, 5, 6 *passim*, 162, 164, 169, 174, 175, 177-184, 192, 195, 196, 198, 200, 201, 203, 205, 207-210, 213, 214, 221, 223, 224, App 2.
Broughton, 18, 19, 24-26, 94, 99, 111, 118, 195, 206
Brown, Robert, 4, 116, 121, 123, 181, 187, 203
Caledonian and Peebles Junction Railway, 17-20
Caledonian Railway, 11-13, 15, 16, 18, 19, 23, 27, 28, 29, 35-37, 39, 41, 57, 58, 61, 62, 64, 94, 113, 114, 116, 118, 120-123, 125, 126, 132, 134, 145, 149, 150, 155, 157, 165, 169, 183, 185-193, 214
Carline, John, 43, 60
Carlops, 12, 20-22, 24, 25, 65, 89, 92, 195, 216
Carnwath, 11, 13, 15, 16
Carnwath and West Linton Railway, 13-16
Carstairs, 9, 13, 15, 17-20, 23, 35-37, 57, 61, 185, 186, 188, 206, 214
Chambers, William, 26, 29, 30, 35
Croall, John, 23-25
Cruickshank, George & family, 117, 120, 123
Dolphinton, 1, 4, 9-12, 15, 17, 18, 20, 24-29, 34, 35, 37, 38, 41, 43, 47, 48, 52, 53, 57, 58, 60, 61, 62, 64, Chapters 4, 5, 6 *passim*, 158-167, 169-172, 174-184, Chapter 9 *passim*, 193, 195, 196-198, 200-203, 205, 207-210, 212-214, 216, 222, 224, App 1, 2.
Douglas & Dolphinton Railway, 190-192
Durrant, George, 105, 106
Edinburgh & Peebles Railway, 13-16
Fell, Bob, 105, 121, 122, 164, 181, 202, 203
Fergusson, William, 18, 35, 37, 38, 61, 112, 212
Fleming, Jean, 87, 95, 99, 104, 106, 118, 151, 182, 202, 204, 205
Fleming, John, 4, 99, 100, 104-106, 192
Forbes, William, 9, 17, 18, 27, 30, 31, 35, 36, 38, 42, 56, 62, 63, 136, 212
Forrester, John, 31, 38, 56, 64
Glasgow and Berwick Iron Railway, 11
Gordon, Richard, 9, 27, 31, 35-38, 61, 212
Greig, George, 72, 83, 90, 91, 102, 103, 106, 127, 146, 153, 196, 203, 206
Headridge, Andrew and Jane, 101, 102
Hodgson, Richard, 9, 27, 29, 36, 37, 56, 64, 190, 191
Hope, William, 24, 25
Howgate, 22, 23, 51, 65, 70, 72, 74-76, 216
Hutchison, Jack & family, 121-123, 188, 202, 203
Ingraston, 12, 20, 21, 28, 34, 66
Joss, Joseph, 100, 102, 105, 108, 192
Lamancha (Cowdenburn), 18, 20, 26, 28, 30, 31, 34, 35, 43, 56-59, Chapters 4, 5, 6 *passim*, 178, 180-184, 196, 198, 200, 201, 205, 207-209, 211-215, 217, 219, 221, 222, 225, 226, App 1, 2.

Lawson, Charles, 17, 35, 57, 87, 99
Lawson, John, 4, 102
Leadburn, 1, 9, 13, 15-17, 19, 20, 22-26, 28, 34, 36, 43, 47-53, 55, 58-61, Chapters 4, 5, 6 *passim*, 158, 159, 169-172, 175, 177-184, 186, 192, 196, 198, 200-202, 205, 209, 212-221, 223, 224, App1, 2
Lyne Valley Railway, 17
Macbie Hill (Coalyburn), 17, 18, 26, 28, 31, 34, 35, 43, 53, 56-59, Chapters 4, 5, 6 *passim*, 162, 178, 180-184, 196, 198, 200, 201, 208-213, 215, 219, 220, 223, 224, 226, App1, 2.
Mackenzie, John Ord, 9, 10, 15, 18, 27, 29, 31, 35-38, 40, 53, 56-58, 60, 63, 64, 177, 212
MacKinnon, Louisa, 82, 83
Mackintosh, James, 18, 30, 31, 35-38, 43, 56, 58, 78, 81, 212
Mitchell Hill, 65, 91, 213, 217, 224, 226
Mounsey, Andrew & family, 90, 105
North British Railway, *passim*
Peebles, 9, 11, 12, 17-19, 22-24, 26, 27, 29, 30, 31, 34, 35, 37, 42, 47, 61, 99, 105, 106, 108, 118, Chapters 5, 6 *passim*, 188, 195, 198, 205, 206, 214. See also Peebles Railway and Edinburgh & Peebles Railway.
Peebles Railway, Peebles Branch, 9, 16-19, 24-26, 28-30, 34-36, 39, 47-49, 51, 52, 55, 61, 65, 68-74, 77, 78, 128, 129, Chapters 5, 6 *passim*, 159, 166, 167, 173, 179, 181, 182, 186, 198, 209, 212, 214, 216, 221, 223
Penicuik, 15, 23-25, 34, 41, 47, 48, 51, 52, 75, 82, 92, 112, 129, 154, 156, 195, 196, 200, 201, 206, 223
Rae, James, 82
Rae, William, 100
Railway Inspectorate, 49-52, 59, 60, 66, 67, 80, 93, 112, 116, 125, 180, 182, 186, App1
Reid, John, 72
Romanno Bridge, 22, 24-26, 57, 91, 99, 111, 112
Simpson, Andrew & family, 105, 122, 123, 202, 204, 205
Small, Peter, 105, 121, 122, 164, 181
Somerville, Jane & family, 90, 91, 100, 122, 123
Speirs, Robert, 100
Spiers, Neil, 121
Splash, The, 2, 66, 110, 127, 129, 208
Stobie, Robert & family, 121-123, 130, 202, 203
Symington, 11, 12, 18, 214
Symington, Biggar and Broughton Railway, 18, 19
Talla Waterworks, 81, 82, 89, 92-94, 99, 111, 112, 118, 134, 181, App 2.
Territorials Camp July 1910, 147-149
Thankerton, 11, 12, 192
Thomson, William, 120, 122-124
Thorburn, Walter, 17, 30, 35
Waddell, John, 40-43, 53, 56, 185, 186
Watson, Robert, 26, 212
West Linton (Linton), 4, 9, 10, 12, 13, 15-26, 28-30, 34, 35, 38, 41, 42, 49, 50, 53, 56-61, Chapters 4, 5 and 6 *passim*, 190, 192, 194-197, 200, 201, 205, 206, 208, 212, 219, 220, 223, App1.
West Linton Agricultural Show, 149-152
White, John, 9, 35, 38, 61, 64
Wilson, James, 70, 72
Wilson, Robert, 117, 120, 121
Woddrop, William, 9, 31, 35, 37, 38, 58, 64, 212